SAFE PASSAGE QUESTIONED

Contributors

Kathryn S. Andersen
Carolyn Annerud
Claude Bachelard
Sheldon Bart
Carmen Becker
Robert N. Becker
Robert Burton
Davis G. Durham
Lennart Fagraeus
Ruth Ann Ger
Kenneth R. Haslam
Robert K. Headland
Norman C. Headley
John A. Heap
Jack D. Lange
Carolyn S. Langer
Desmond J. Lugg
Harry Mahar
Alan H. Milne
Richard N. Moersch
David M. Rootes
Brian H. Shoemaker
E. Newbold Smith
John Splettstoesser
Bernard Stonehouse
Theodore B. Strange
Peter G. Sullivan
A. Diederik Van Galen
Robert E. Wheeler

SAFE PASSAGE QUESTIONED

Medical Care and Safety for the Polar Tourist

John M. Levinson, M.D., Editor
Errol Ger, M.D., Medical Editor

Cornell Maritime Press
Centreville, Maryland

Photographs, unless otherwise credited, are by John Levinson.

Library of Congress Cataloging-in-Publication Data

Safe passage questioned : medical care and safety for the polar tourist / John M. Levinson, editor ; Errol Ger, medical editor.
p. cm.
Based on a conference held at the Scott Polar Research Institute in Cambridge, U.K. on Oct. 29–31, 1995.
Includes bibliographical references and index.
ISBN 0-87033-504-9 (pbk.)
1. Circumpolar medicine—Congresses. 2. Tourist trade—Polar regions—Health aspects—Congresses. I. Levinson, John M., 1927–

[DNLM: 1. Naval Medicine—congresses. 2. Safety—congresses. 3. Cold Climate—Arctic Regions—congresses. 4.Cold Climate—Antarctic Regions—congresses. 5. Travel—congresses. VG 103 S129 1997]
RC955.2.S24 1997
616.9′881—dc21
DNLM/DLC
for Library of Congress 97-41984
CIP

Manufactured in the United States of America
First edition

To Jack D. Lange, M.D.

Honorary Editor
Chairman, Advisory Board of Directors
Aid for International Medicine, Inc.
Friend and Physician
Author and Publisher
Worldwide Medical Consultant and Philanthropist,
who has given over one-half million medical textbooks to developing countries.
Royalties from this book will go to AIM, Inc., to further this work.

Contents

Foreword

Three years ago John Levinson and I, both widely experienced in polar shipborne travel, found ourselves together on an Antarctic cruise. In the evenings we discussed many matters; one topic that kept recurring was medical services aboard polar cruise ships.

He as a medical officer and I as a potential patient with a lay but legitimate interest concluded that on most of the ships in which we had traveled medical services were less efficient than they could and should be. Between us we knew many other medical officers and lay folk with polar shipboard experience and responsibilities. Clearly it was time for a conference to pool experience, define problems, and seek solutions.

The outcome was a conference on medical aspects of polar tourism held at the Scott Polar Research Institute, Cambridge, United Kingdom, on October 29–31, 1995. From that conference emerged this volume—a report to the community in general, and perhaps to cruise operators in particular—on three days of excellent and profitable discussions.

We discussed the potential *patients*. Many of us started with the concept that cruise ship patients are mainly passengers, drawn from a relatively narrow social stratum, sedentary, often post–middle-aged to elderly, staying aboard for short periods, and presenting a limited range of disabilities. Several speakers reminded us that the ten thousand or so passengers due to visit Antarctica in the coming season would be served by six thousand to seven thousand crew, of different nationalities, most of them younger, many leading more active and hazardous lives in engine rooms, galleys, dining rooms, and on deck, working hard and continuously, often under stress, and staying aboard for very much longer spells.

We discussed *operational safety*. Ships, inflatable boats, and helicopters can be dangerous platforms, particularly for those unfamiliar with their ways, and especially in rough weather. Operations that are often repeated tend to gather dangers, and dangers make work for ship's doctors. Shipboard and medical officers (MOs) acquire many duties concerned with health, safety, and accident prevention. They cannot tell seamen how to run operations; they can and must use their skills in avoiding trouble and speak up when they perceive unnecessary risks. Are passengers and crew properly briefed on safety? Are safety helmets and life jackets worn? Are first-aid kits in place and properly maintained in engine rooms, galleys, inflatables, and lifeboats? How do we bring stretcher cases aboard and into the hospital? Do any of the crew have useful nursing or paramedical skills?

We discussed *responsibility*. To whom are temporary MOs responsible? To themselves? To the cruise leader? To the captain? It matters little when all goes well, and everyone is enjoying a polar vacation. But suppose passengers feel neglected or ill-served, and writs start to fly like storm petrels? Then responsibility will be established very quickly, and probably by those with the smartest lawyers. Does standard insurance cover the medical officer who is working, perhaps unpaid and without formal contract, aboard a cruise ship? If a contract exists, does the company take responsibility?

We discussed *appropriate treatment*. Temporary MOs who are cardiologists; orthopedic surgeons; ear, nose, and throat specialists; or gynecologists may deal easily with general medical problems (nausea, sleeplessness, cuts and bruises) aboard ship, but feel at a loss with the occasional cases (for example, severe dislocations, damaged hands, and shattered legs) that lie far from their everyday experience. What is the appropriate treatment? It may be appropriate to do very little for a patient who will be in a specialist's hands within a week. But again we were reminded of the crew, who may not have the option of leaving the ship for a well-equipped U.S. hospital.

We discussed *medical facilities aboard*. We heard hair-raising tales from temporary MOs who had come aboard with little equipment and found even less waiting for them. We heard of X-ray machines that did not work, outmoded defibrillators with instructions in foreign languages, medical kits that were surplus from World War II, looted drug cupboards, out-of-date medicines, and stretchers hidden by the bosun to keep them out of the hands of the painters. We argued the possibilities of devising a "standard medical kit for ships," and differed fundamentally on what such a kit should contain, whether much or little, and at what level of sophistication.

"Facilities aboard" includes of course the medical staff themselves. I have served with misgiving on cruise ships with only Russian and Russian-speaking doctors, not because the doctor might be incompetent (that is the case whatever the doctor's nationality) but because of the difficulties of consultation between a doctor and a patient with no language in common.

We discussed *networks of advice and support* available to doctors at sea through international radio channels and networks of polar stations and other ships, also available by radio. We wondered how many temporary MOs would know how to approach them? We wondered how many knew the mechanisms for laying on medical evacuation facilities from Ushuaia or Punta Arenas, and whose responsibility—theirs or their nominal employers—it would be to set this wonderful, but very expensive, operation in motion? Whose business is it to see that every temporary MO has all this information and help at his fingertips?

Finally we discussed *outcome*. What should come out of these discussions? Did we need a textbook for temporary shipboard MOs? A set of guidelines? A newsletter? A recommended form of prayer? After much thought it was decided that we needed this book, to embody the substance of the conference, plus more that has emerged since and could usefully be added.

The story told here should interest every potential recruit to the role of ship's medical officer, every doctor who has served, and all cruise operators who take seriously their responsibilities for the health and safety of their passengers. For potential polar tourists, I'd advise: Don't leave home before you read it!

Bernard Stonehouse, D.Phil.
Swaffham Bulbeck, Cambridge, United Kingdom

Preface

My first recollection of medicine at sea was told to me by my grandmother when I was a very little boy. In 1935, my grandparents were on the USS *President Hoover* proceeding from Los Angeles to Honolulu when the high drama occurred. The ship was stopped in the middle of the Pacific Ocean in order to provide a more stable platform for the surgeon to perform an appendectomy on an ill passenger. The surgery was performed by a U.S. Navy surgeon, a passenger on the voyage. Evidently the ship's surgeon had not performed an appendectomy in years and was very pleased to have such a capable passenger do the surgery. In the days before air evacuation, before antibiotics, and long before the era of modern anesthesiology, this operation was tricky at best. (Little did I know when I first heard the story, how important medical assistance could be for tourists on board a ship.)

For many years, ship's surgeons traveling to the Arctic and Antarctic have had increasing concerns about the quality of shipboard medical care. This has not been an isolated observation. Many physicians who have served on a variety of ships run by different tour companies have experienced identical feelings.

When I served as medical director for a polar tour company, I was repeatedly confronted with doctors who, although they thoroughly enjoyed the trip and the experience, expressed dissatisfaction with the entire medical system on board the ship and some vowed "never again." Many expedition leaders as well as scientific lecturers have voiced similar concern. All were deeply critical of safety on board ships, as well as the safety issues related to inflatable watercraft and helicopters. I personally regarded safety as the foundation of preventive medicine at sea, and finally realized that all the safety and medical issues on these ships had to be rethought and profound changes made to prevent a mass disaster. Finally, I realized that to try to make meaningful changes, I must resign as a medical director and ship's surgeon. This I did in March 1995.

Immediately plans were initiated for a world conference entitled "A Medical Standard for Expedition Travel and Tourism in the Polar Environment." Physicians experienced in polar medicine from around the world were invited, as well as polar explorers, polar scientists, and various travel companies and representative organizations with special interest in the Arctic and Antarctic. I knew we were on the right track when Dr. Desmond Lugg, head of polar medicine of the Australian Antarctic Division, phoned me from Tasmania and said, "Where the hell have you been? You should have called this meeting thirty years ago. Of course I'll be there! You know, the medical care with these tourist groups is a disaster waiting to happen."

The response from the medical profession was remarkable, and attendance was expanded with polar explorers and scientists as well as graduate students from the Scott Polar Research Institute in Cambridge, England, where we met October 29–31, 1995. It was a serious group, and among the observers attending were Capt. Lawson W. Bigham, United States Coast Guard (Ret.), who captained the *Polar Sea,* the first U.S. icebreaker to reach the North Pole; Michelle E. Raney, M.D., who was the winter-over physician at the Amundsen-Scott South Polar Station in 1979 and has the distinction of being the first woman to winter over deep on the Antarctic continent; and Dr. Charles Swithinbank, a distinguished glaciologist who has been engaged in polar research for almost fifty years.

From the strong consensus of concern that developed for improving safety and medical care, we planned to publish the proceedings of the meeting. But something more was needed. The proceedings were dissected and redissected and the best portions retained. Additional authorship was obtained, enabling us to compile a coherent presentation on these special problems in the high latitudes of our world. To all of these contributors, I am indebted.

This book presents a brief history of exploration and tourism in the polar regions and the story of medical care there from the earliest days until the present. In a straightforward manner, we have addressed the weaknesses and the safety nets, and the often inadequate medical care that exists in these regions today. We want tourists to know what they can realistically expect and how they can prepare for this experience in the most exciting part of the world. Hopefully, not only the first-time traveler, but also those who in large numbers return again and again, will find this of value.

Equally importantly, we hope that each tour company involved in polar travel, as well as all expedition leaders and their staffs, will find this book helpful.

Similarly, we feel that seasoned as well as new ship's surgeons should gain further insight into what their responsibilities are with particular emphasis on the polar experience.

With the major concerns on the issues of safe polar travel also being expressed by travel experts, the American Medical Association, the American College of Emergency Physicians, and other professional organizations, the time is ripe to make the necessary changes. We hope we are helping lead the way to make the passage safer.

Without some very special people, this book would have never evolved. The late Lars-Eric Lindblad, who revolutionized travel with the little red ship, the *Lindblad Explorer,* gave me my first chance to practice medicine at sea over twenty-seven years ago, and Mike McDowell, who also worked many years with Lars-Eric, gave me the opportunity to be his ship's surgeon and the first medical director for his company, Quark Expeditions, Inc., which is preeminent in polar travel. For both these experiences I am grateful.

The Delaware Congressional Delegation led by then-Congressman Thomas R. Carper (now the governor of the state of Delaware), Senator Joseph R. Biden, Jr., and Senator William V. Roth, Jr., felt my concerns about travel in the Antarctic were valid and arranged for me to meet with the principals at the National Science Foundation who deal with these topics to state my case.

The directors of many national polar programs, the heads of their polar medicine divisions, and many members of the staffs of these organizations have provided important information. On a number of occasions, not only information but also assistance in medical emergencies has been graciously provided by the Australian Antarctic Division, the British Antarctic Survey, the French Antarctic Service, the National Science Foundation of the United States, and the New Zealand Antarctic Program. Without the help of these organizations, often given under very trying conditions, lives might have been lost, and I would not have gained the experience so necessary to edit and help author this book.

On these polar cruises I obtained help and knowledge from many, many people. Several are very special. Peter Golikov, captain of the Russian icebreaker *Kapitan Khlebnikov,* handled the ship superbly, at times under extremely difficult ice conditions, and maintained a great sensitivity to medical needs. John Splettstoesser, an experienced geologist, polar explorer, and expedition leader, had a special concern for safety at sea and taught me much in that area. Keith Shackleton, one of the world's great naturalists, who is considered by many to be the dean of polar artists, is one of the members of the original *Lindblad*'s Southern Ocean Drivers Society (SODS). Always the perfect English gentleman, he was above all an extremely competent and safety-conscious Zodiac driver who was also very helpful to me in the learning process.

I am particularly indebted to Dr. John Heap, director at Scott Polar Research Institute (SPRI) for providing their outstanding facility for the conference that led to this book. Dr. Bernard Stonehouse, senior scientist at SPRI and a well-known polar explorer, was also of invaluable help in the field as well as at the conference table. Wally Herbert, the renowned British explorer, also taught me much along the way.

Suggestions also came from passengers, many of whom received medical care on ships in polar waters, and they gave important insight on how things might be improved.

I am deeply appreciative to the many physicians who worked with me on the Arctic and Antarctic cruises for sharing with me their problems and frustrations. This solid background of material has proved vital in writing a responsible book.

Many members of The Explorers Club have assisted me and urged me to write this book. Among them is a dear friend of many decades, Jack D. Lange, M.D. As founder and president of Lange Medical Publications, he has raised the level of medical education and knowledge throughout the world. In early 1970, the *Lindblad Explorer* had no medical library. When informed of this, Jack made certain that a small library of Lange books was on board, after which he could honestly say that he had books going to all seven continents! Because of his deep interest in medical education, his promotion of medical improvement wherever he traveled, and his great assistance and counsel to all of us who attended the conference, we are pleased to dedicate this book to him.

A special debt of thanks is due to my wife, Carlie. Knowing of my love of both medicine and the sea, she has urged me to travel these many times in the polar regions. When possible, she joined me, but always she has encouraged me and been most supportive.

Lastly, the time and effort given by my good friend and colleague, Errol Ger, M.D., as medical editor, must be mentioned. His crisp and critical analysis of information and his reliability have been so important and helpful.

I might mention many, many others who have helped in this effort, but neither space nor time allows me to thank them all. However, without the broad assistance of the type I have mentioned, along with the expertise and assistance of our diverse authorship, this book could not have become a reality.

John M. Levinson, M.D.
Editor

Early polar explorers used piles of rocks called cairns to store food for emergencies or to leave messages.

SAFE PASSAGE QUESTIONED

CHAPTER 1

Brief History and Description of the Polar Regions

> The polar regions are similar—cold, remote from civilization, difficult for people to live in, and beautiful or dreary, exciting or boring, according to taste. But they are different, too, as though a Creator had set out to design two ends for the Earth, fundamentally the same but different in as many curious and interesting ways as possible.
>
> —Dr. Bernard Stonehouse, 1990

Polar tourism now includes both the North Pole and the South Pole. There are virtually no areas at the uttermost ends of our world that cannot be visited. Returning tourists report being overwhelmed by the vastness and beauty of the ice and snow, excited by the wildlife and the oneness with nature they have experienced. Further discussions usually bring forth the vast distances that they have traveled and the dangers of storm and sea in this hostile environment. These perceptions are very real. To the medical profession, they present profound challenges.

As a prerequisite for going to the polar world, the expeditioner and tourist is well advised to know some of the history and geography, as well as the similarities and differences between these two ends of the world. It is hoped that the information in this chapter will "whet the appetite"; further knowledge can be obtained by reading books of the type listed in the references section of this book.

THE ARCTIC

In 330 B.C. Pytheas of Massilia was a great Greek navigator and sailor. He sailed to the far north looking for the lands that must lie under the constellation of the Great Bear (Arktos). He reached England, and after staying for many months, continued farther north, along the coast of Scotland, and past the northern tip of the Orkneys. He described a sea of a strange substance—neither of land or sea or air on which one could not walk—obviously some form of fragmented sea ice. It is said he was trying to reach the land known as Thule, where the night did not exist during the summer and the daylight was gone all during the winter months. Regrettably, he left no journal about this six-year voyage.

About 500 A.D. St. Brendan, an Irish abbot, is reputed to have made voyages looking for the promised land of the saints. He sailed in a curragh, a boat made of a wooden frame over which animal skins were stretched.

Between 700 and 1000 A.D. the Vikings (Norsemen) sailed to the British Isles, then to the Faeroe Islands, and on to Iceland. Probably some monks had previously visited Iceland. Erik the Red discovered Greenland in 983. Leif Eriksson, his son, brought Christianity to Greenland, and in the year 1000 crossed the Atlantic and probably was the discoverer of Newfoundland.

Over the next five hundred years there are scattered reports of expeditions by the British, Portuguese, Dutch, Russians, and others, as Europeans probed into the distant lands of the North. The British Northeast Passage Expedition in 1553 was the next most significant expedition. The list on pages 8–9 details the explorations toward the North Pole in chronological order, their method of attainment (by air, over the surface, or by sea), and the first crossing of the regions. This list, prepared by R. K. Headland, is only a synopsis. A list of books covering the subject in depth is included in the references section of this book.

THE ANTARCTIC

About 530 B.C. Pythagoras postulated that the Earth was spherical, and some seventy years later Parmenides divided the Earth's sphere into five zones which included two frigid zones at the poles. Seleukos about 140 B.C. supposedly postulated the existence of a Southern Continent. The early Greek philosophers and geographers believed in balance, and they

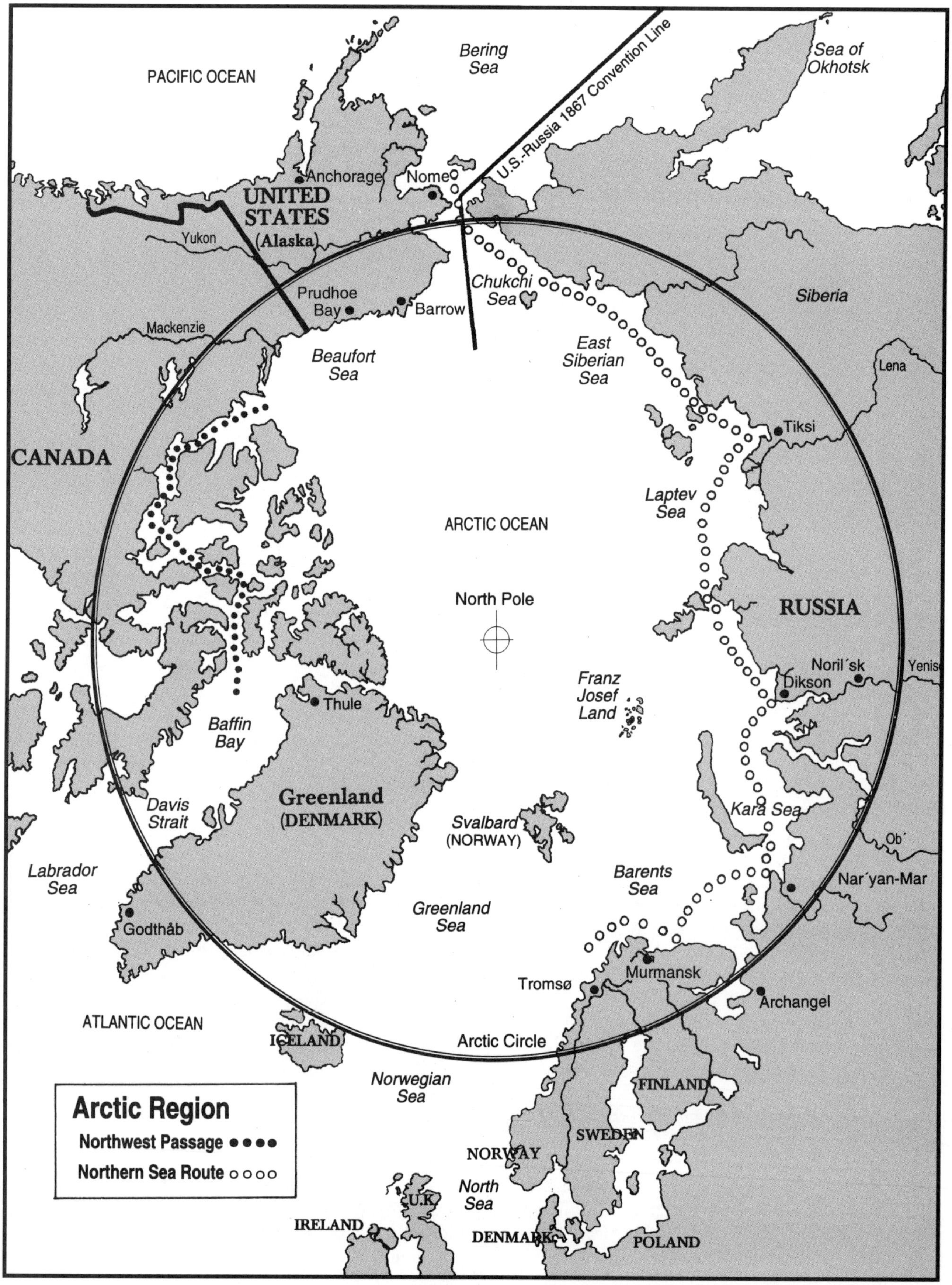

PACIFIC OCEAN
Bering Sea
U.S.-Russia 1867 Convention Line
Sea of Okhotsk
Anchorage
Nome
UNITED STATES (Alaska)
Yukon
Prudhoe Bay
Barrow
Chukchi Sea
Siberia
Mackenzie
Beaufort Sea
East Siberian Sea
Lena
Tiksi
CANADA
Laptev Sea
ARCTIC OCEAN
North Pole
RUSSIA
Noril´sk
Dikson
Franz Josef Land
Thule
Baffin Bay
Greenland (DENMARK)
Davis Strait
Svalbard (NORWAY)
Kara Sea
Ob´
Labrador Sea
Barents Sea
Nar´yan-Mar
Godthåb
Greenland Sea
Murmansk
Tromsø
Archangel
ATLANTIC OCEAN
ICELAND
Arctic Circle
Norwegian Sea
FINLAND
Arctic Region
Northwest Passage ●●●●
Northern Sea Route ○○○○
SWEDEN
NORWAY
North Sea
U.K.
IRELAND
DENMARK
POLAND

The Arctic.

Borchgrevink Hut at Cape Adare erected in 1899 (interior).

named this yet-undiscovered landmass Terra Australis Incognita, that is, the Unknown Southern Continent. Being at the other end of the world from that lying under the constellation of the Great Bear (Arktos), this area became known as the Antarctica (from the Greek Antarktikos), or opposite the Arctic. For many of those early years, nautical charts showed a detailed outline of a continent that had yet to be proven to exist. Flat-earth orthodoxy persisted until voyages of exploration in the fifteenth century. Strangely, many centuries ago the Maori, natives of New Zealand, formed legends about a white land in the far South. Early explorers pushed the imaginary boundaries of this continent farther south, but probably the Great Southern Ocean was not penetrated until Gabriel de Castilla of Spain sailed south of Drake Passage in 1603.

In 1774, the famed British navigator, James Cook, circumnavigated the world's fifth-largest continent, Antarctica, but never knew it was there! In 1820, the Russian Bellingshausen was credited with being first to view this unknown continent. With the intense competition for sealing and whaling, many ships sought their quarry farther and farther south. Possibly they, too, saw this strange new land, but because of the secrecy necessary for their economic success, they rarely recorded new lands in this area. In 1895, Borchgrevink, on the whaler *Antarctic,* claimed to be the first to land on the continent—possibly he was the first outside the Antarctic Peninsula. Four years later, in February 1899, Borchgrevink and members of the Southern Cross expedition landed at Cape Adare in Victoria Land, over 450 miles (724 kilometers) north of Mt. Erebus, and erected a prefabricated hut, thereby becoming the first men to spend the winter on this new continent. The years between 1895 and 1922 are known as "the age of heroes" in polar exploration and those between 1923 and 1990 have been termed "the mechanized age." Explorers from many countries came to establish territorial claims, to see and try to understand this new land, and above all to conquer the South Pole. Interestingly enough, this was achieved some fifteen years after the first human being set foot on the continent, which is in

Borchgrevink Hut at Cape Adare (exterior).

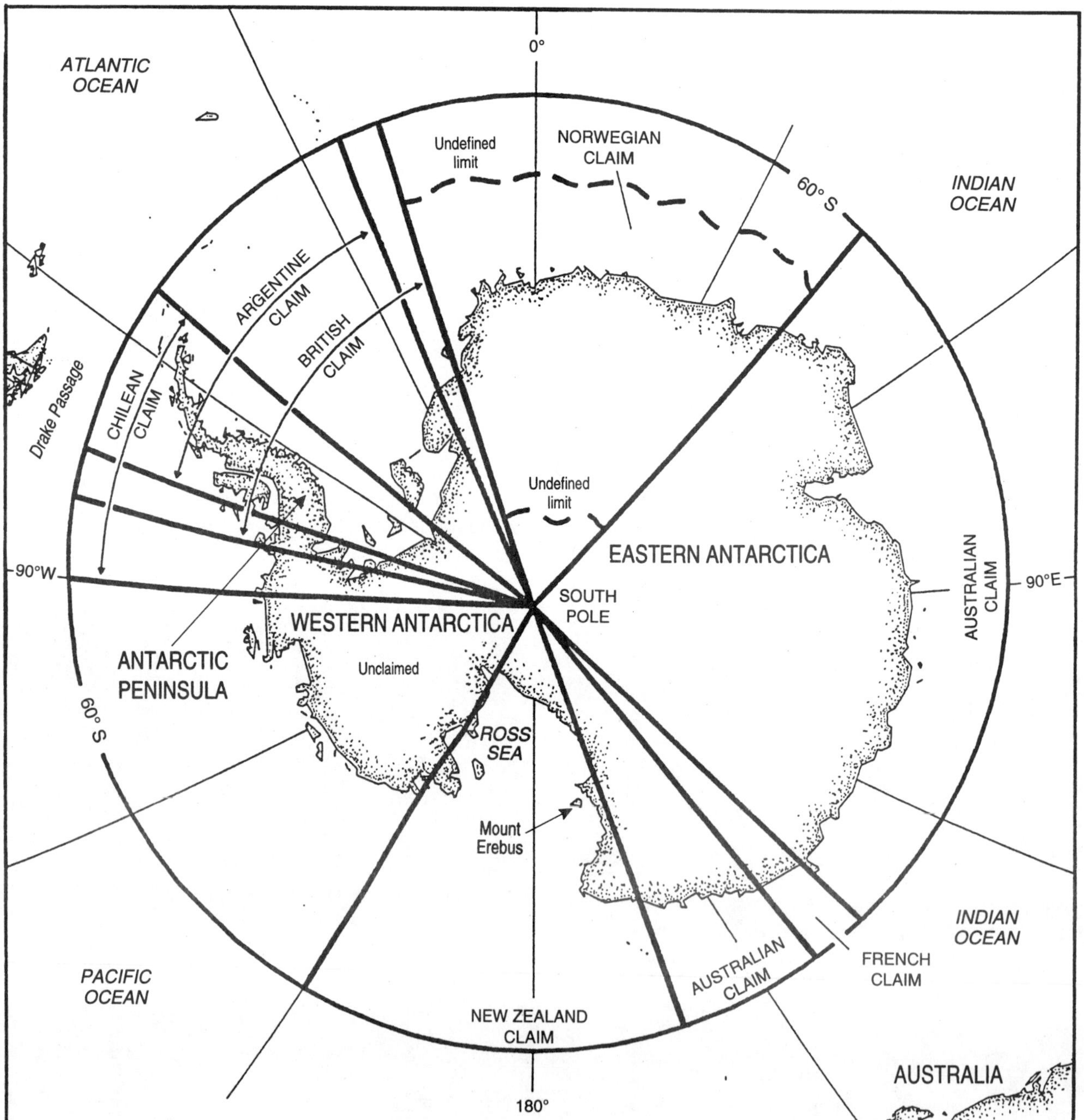

Antarctica territorial claims.

stark contrast to the hundreds and hundreds of years it took man to conquer the North Pole.

In the wake of the explorers from many nations territorial claims were made that radiate out from the South Pole to the periphery of Antarctica. Although Australia, France, New Zealand, Norway, and the United Kingdom recognize each other's claims, Argentina and Chile have disputed not only the United Kingdom's claims, but also one another's. Interestingly, neither the former Soviet Union nor the United States has made any formal claims, but each reserved the right to do so.

Under the sponsorship of the International Council of Scientific Unions, the International Geophysical Year (IGY) was held from July 1, 1957, to December 31, 1958. The aims of the IGY were to explore Antarctica as well as outer space utilizing Earth satellites and the new rocket and balloon technology. The IGY, which was enormously successful, involved scientists from sixty-seven countries. One of the many scientific projects spawned from these efforts was the Scientific Committee for Antarctic Research (SCAR), a nongovernmental organization that continues actively today. Scientists from more than twenty countries participate, functioning through ten permanent working groups.

As the IGY was drawing to a close, representatives of twelve countries met from June 1958 until early 1959 at the National Science Foundation in Washington, D.C. The Antarctic Treaty, which was the culmination of these meetings, became effective June 23, 1961. Article IV of this treaty is crucial in that it recognizes the insolvability of the various territorial claims. Essentially this has stabilized the conflicting political ambitions on this international continent. A fundamental understanding of the treaty is recommended for all tourists to the area (see appendix A).

The Antarctic list on page 12 was also prepared by R. K. Headland; it details explorations toward the South Pole in chronological order, their attainment by air and surface, and the first crossing of these regions. The names, dates, and places mentioned are not necessarily the most important, but are representative of this new exploration.

In the past decade, there have been a plethora of individuals and organizations traveling to and from the polar regions—many looking for a way to achieve another "first." They walk, they ski, they ski using parachutes as sails, they use motorized transport; but the use of the dog and the sledge is over. Dogs have been banned because of concern for the environment as dictated by the Antarctic Treaty. Resupply by aircraft is not uncommon, and many of these new "explorers" are ferried out by aircraft once they have reached the pole. Tourists may now enjoy a cup of coffee at the South Pole or a full barbecue at the North Pole and return home comfortably! While most of these people should be considered "adventurers," some have faced many of the same challenges as the early

Iceberg in East Antarctica—height measured 288 feet above sea level by altimeter of helicopter.

CONCISE ARCTIC CHRONOLOGY

1553 Sir Hugh Willoughby (England), with companies aboard *Bona Esperanza* and *Bona Confidentia,* reached 72°N on the Novaya Zemlya coast, 14 August.

1587 John Davis (England), with companies aboard *Elizabeth, Ellen,* and *Sunshine,* reached 72.20°N off Greenland, July.

1594 Willem Barentsz (Netherlands), with a ship's company, reached 77°N rounding Novaya Zemlya, July.

1596 Jacob van Heemskerck (Netherlands), with companies aboard two vessels, reached 80.18°N off Svalbard, 17 June.

1607 Henry Hudson (Britain), with company aboard *Hopewell,* reached 80.38°N off Svalbard, 16 July.

1766 Vasiliy Chichagov (Russia), with companies aboard *Chichagov, Panov,* and *Babayev,* reached 80.47°N off Svalbard, 16 July.

1773 Constantine Phipps (Britain), with companies aboard *Racehorse* and *Carcass,* reached 80.80°N off Svalbard, 27 July.

Subsequently many whaling vessels reached high latitudes.

1806 William Scoresby (Britain), with company aboard *Resolution,* reached 80.50°N off Svalbard.

1827 William Parry (Britain) and party, with two sledge boats from *Hecla,* reached 82.75°N off Svalbard, 25 July.

1876 Albert Markham (Britain) and two sledge parties reached 83.34°N off Ellesmere Island, 12 May.

1882 James Lockwood (United States) and two others dog-sledged to 83.40°N off Greenland from Fort Conger, 13 May.

1895 Fridjof Nansen and Hjalmar Johanssen (Norway) dog-sledged to 86.22°N from *Fram* in the Barents Sea, 8 April.

1900 Umberto Cagni (Italy) and three others dog-sledged to 86.57°N from Zemlya Frantsa-Iosefa (Franz Josef Land), 24 April.

1908 Frederick Cook (United States), with a sledge party, claimed to have reached 90°N, 21 April.

1909 Robert Peary (United States), with an expeditionary party, dog-sledged to 87.78°N from Ellesmere Island, 31 March. Peary and five others continued north and possibly passed 88°N.

1909 Robert Peary (United States), with a sledge party, claimed to have reached 90°N, 6 April.

1925 Roald Amundsen (Norway), Lincoln Ellsworth (United States) and four others flew north from Svalbard in two aircraft, crash-landed, and drifted to 87.83°N, 21 May.

1926 Richard Byrd (United States), with an aircraft crew, claimed to have reached 90°N by air from Svalbard, 9 May.

1926 Roald Amundsen (Norway), Lincoln Ellsworth (United States), Umberto Nobile (Italy) and eleven others crossed 90°N by airship *Norge* (flying Svalbard to Alaska), 13 May.

Subsequently one dirigible balloon and many other aircraft have flown over the North Pole.

1937 Ivan Papanin (Soviet Union) and party landed at 89.43°N by aircraft from Zemlya Frantsa-Iosefa and established the first Arctic Ocean drift station, 21 May.
1948 Pavel Gordiyenko (Soviet Union) and five others landed at 90°N from an aircraft, 23 April.
Subsequently many aircraft have landed at the North Pole.
1958 William R. Anderson (United States), with crew aboard the nuclear-powered submarine USS *Nautilus,* reached the North Pole while submerged, 3 August, on voyage from the Pacific Ocean to the Atlantic Ocean.
1959 James Calvert (United States), with crew aboard the nuclear-powered submarine USS *Skate,* surfaced at the North Pole, 17 March.
Subsequently many submarines reached the North Pole and some surfaced there.
1968 Ralph Plaisted (United States) and three others reached 90°N by surface (snow scooter) from Canada, with aircraft assistance, and returned by air, 19 April.
1969 Wally Herbert (Britain) and three others dog-sledged to 90°N, while crossing the Arctic Ocean (Alaska to Svalbard), 6 April.
Subsequently several expeditions have crossed the Arctic on the pack ice through the North Pole and many have made one-way surface journeys leaving by air.
1977 Yuriy Kuchiyev (Soviet Union), with crew aboard the nuclear-powered icebreaker *Arktika,* reached 90°N by sea from near the Novosibirskiye Ostrova, 17 August.
1991 Anatoly Gorshkovskiy (Soviet Union), with crew and passengers aboard the nuclear-powered icebreaker *Sovetskiy Soyuz,* reached the North Pole by sea while crossing the Arctic Ocean (Murmansk to Provideniya), 4 August.
Subsequently each summer has seen trips by icebreakers carrying tourists to the North Pole.

explorers. Indeed, being adventuresome is worthy for its own sake, and many of these people conduct a real inner search as well as a physical exploration.

A COMPARISON OF THE POLAR REGIONS

Much is different about these two polar regions, and it is best to consider them separately and then appreciate the differences.

Antarctica is the fifth-largest continent. It embraces one-tenth of the Earth's surface and has an area of roughly 5.3 million square miles (13.7 million square kilometers). It is larger than the United States and Mexico together, or approximately two times the size of Australia. Most of the area, however, is made up of a vast permanent ice sheet averaging 6,600 feet (2,012 meters) in thickness. The actual landmass of Antarctica is only about 2.7 million square miles (7 million square kilometers) in area, and includes a large archipelago of mountainous islands. Only about two percent of the land is not completely covered by ice and snow.

Antarctica is the coldest continent. During the coldest months of the year in Antarctica, the August temperature ranges from –40° to –94°F (–40° to –70°C), and in the warmest month, February, it ranges from 5° to –49°F (–15° to –45°C). The lowest temperature ever recorded in the world was –129.3°F (–86.6°C), noted at the Russian base Vostok, the base closest to the Amundsen-Scott base at the South Pole but still over 700 miles away (1,126 kilometers).

Antarctica is also the windiest continent. Cold winds essentially slide down from the vast ice fields of the center portion of the continent toward the lower coastal areas. At the edge of the ice plateau, the winds accelerate, thereby lifting and blowing great clouds of snow into the air. The strongest winds are usually found along the coastal slopes of Greater Antarctica. Some coastal areas have almost constant strong winds, whereas other areas may be quite calm much of the time and then suddenly experience these hurricane force winds as the air rushes down through the glacial valleys. These downslope winds, sudden and unexpected, are called "katabatic winds." When Douglas Mawson, the Australian explorer, established a base at Cape Dennison in 1912, he recorded the speed of the wind for a two-year period. He found the average wind speed during that time was 45 MPH (27.9 KPH), but he noted gusts of over 150 MPH (93 KPH). In recent years, gale winds have been recorded at 200 MPH (124 KPH). Frequently, in walking, it takes almost a superhuman effort not to be blown away, and standing up straight may be virtually impossible.

Antarctica contains approximately 90 percent of the world's ice, which is 75 percent of the world's store of freshwater. The vast icebergs that one sees in the Southern Ocean either come from the calving or breaking off of glacial sheets of ice as they go to sea, or they can be ice formed by freezing of the salt water, so-called saltwater ice. Back in 1987, a massive piece of a glacier broke off, producing an iceberg the size of Long Island, New York. This was tracked by satellite over the next several years as it disintegrated into smaller pieces of ice, most of which have now completely disappeared. Through studies of this type a great deal is being learned about the currents of the Southern Ocean.

Curiously though, Antarctica is the driest continent. Most of the continent is truly a desert. There is little precipitation in the interior, and the vast amount of ice that makes up the polar cap has accumulated there over a period of millions of years. The annual accumulation for the entire continent amounts to less than 2 inches (5 centimeters) of water equivalent which is just slightly more than that which falls on the Sahara Desert. In some coastal areas, however, particularly on the west side of the Antarctic Peninsula, far more precipitation is received, and the tip of the peninsula receives approximately 35 inches (89 centimeters) of water equivalent per year.

The main body of the continent is called East Antarctica, and much of its border lies conveniently along the Antarctic Circle and the Atlantic, Indian, and western Pacific oceans sectors. The curved, or tail-like, projection from the continent is made up of an expanded landmass and is known as West Antarctica, the long narrow portion being called the Antarctic Peninsula. This extends approximately 744 miles (1,197 kilometers) toward the tip of South America and is located in the eastern Pacific Ocean sector.

East Antarctica is mainly covered with ice, but in some coastal areas jagged rocks project through. The Antarctic Peninsula, however, is a long chain of mountains topped by icy plateaus and sculptured by vast glaciers. Most of the coastline is actually cliffs of ice, but in some areas—particularly on the Pacific side—one encounters rocky exposed shorelines. The ice-free shorelines, such as those along the western side of the Antarctic Peninsula and its island chain and the Ross Sea area, are the places that are most accessible for landing.

Taking this tremendous amount of ice into consideration, Antarctica becomes also the highest continent. The highest point is the peak of the Vinson Massif, with an elevation of 16,960 feet (5,169 meters). There are many mountains over 9,900 feet (3,018 meters), most being covered with ice. The great ice dome covering most of East Antarctica reaches a height of 13,860 feet (4,225 meters), while the ice plateau of West Antarctica has an average height of approximately 6,600 feet (2,012 meters). The Transantarctic mountain range is exposed for about 1,240 miles (1,995 kilometers) along the coast of Victoria Land in East Antarctica, where it holds back the huge ice dome. The glaciers that worked through this range eventually merged and formed the great Ross Ice Shelf. The Transantarctic Mountains are covered over with ice near the South Pole, but are exposed at the other end of the range where they are known as the Pensacola Mountains in Coats Land on the opposite side of the continent. Another great range in East Antarctica is 800 miles (1,287 kilometers) long, and the peaks have reached 9,900 feet (3,018 meters), but it is completely obliterated by the ice dome. Other great ranges along the coastal areas in the Indian and Atlantic Oceans sectors appear only as isolated peaks or occasional rock outcroppings that are hardly noticed.

Between these mountain ranges are extensive low-lying plains and basins that are covered over by some of the thickest ice in the world. In fact, the South Pole itself is located 9,240 feet (2,816 meters) above sea level on top of a layer of ice. The weight of the ice on the continent has depressed the surface, so that one-third of the continent has been pushed below sea level. There are other areas of East Antarctica where some of the bedrock, even though it is well below sea level, has a covering of over 13,000 feet (3,962 meters) of ice.

East Antarctica is basically a giant shield of metamorphic rock, dating back over 500 million years. Studying the Antarctic is extremely exciting for the geologist, and the theories of plate tectonics, which appear largely to be proven by fossil deposits, have given us a whole new understanding of our world.

From a functional standpoint the most important topographical feature of the offshore region of the Southern Ocean is the Scotia Arc, that is, a ridge at a depth of about 6,562 feet (2,000 meters). Various islands project from this ridge, such as South Georgia, Deception, Elephant, South Sandwich group, South Shetlands, and South Orkneys. About 70 million years ago violent upheavals and volcanic activity began in the islands of the Scotia Arc; this activity subsided about 35 million years ago. Several islands in the South Shetlands and the South Sandwich Islands are volcanically active today, and much of West Antarctica still experiences earthquakes. East Antarctica is more stable, but there is still volcanic activity from Mount Erebus on Ross Island and Mount Melbourne in Victoria Land.

Arctic flowers are common above the tree line in summer.

Deception Island, one of the most exciting spots that tourists visit today, has a very large chinstrap penguin colony on the outside of the island at Bailey's Head. It may be very difficult to land there due to adverse weather conditions. Entering the vast collapsed caldera through Neptune's Bellows, visitors can view the remains of a large whaling station in Whaler's Bay and also the remnants of British and Chilean stations that were destroyed by volcanic eruptions in 1969. Many visitors have gone swimming in the thermally heated waters near the black lava beach at Pendulum Cove.

Conservation efforts have allowed penguins to return to their former numbers in Antarctica, and one might speculate that there are hundreds of millions of penguins there today. The giant sea elephants have returned and the seal population is following suit. There are no land animals on this great continent; the seals and the penguins only "visit" for short periods of time each year.

By contrast, krill, the largest biomass in the world today, are found in the rich Southern Ocean and nourish abundant life. These shrimplike animals of under two inches in length support hundreds of million of penguins, seals, and whales annually.

Antarctica is a continent that largely fills the Antarctic Circle. The Arctic, on the other hand, consists of a large ocean bordered by the northern parts of the mainlands of North America and Eurasia and their outlying islands. Some of these islands are vast, mountainous, and have large interior ice caps such as Greenland and the northern half of Novaya Zemlya. Others are low-lying islands that are not glaciated such as Wrangel, located about 100 miles (161 kilometers) off northeastern Siberia and the western islands of the Canadian Arctic. The total number of species and the biological productivity is far less here than in Antarctica. Strong surface winds often occur, causing drifting of snow and severe wind chill. Above the tree line is tundra vegetation including grasses, mosses, lichens, and little plants that exist on permafrost soils but are frozen solid for all but the short but intense summer growing time. Just as in the Antarctic, bird life abounds, but seals are sparser, and the great walrus are confined to certain areas due to the earlier practice of overhunting. The musk ox is returning; the polar bear, although still hunted some, still reigns supreme. The native populations still trap the arctic fox, but most foxes obtained commercially today have been raised in pens. The arctic hare is an animal that also struggles in this harsh environment.

The Arctic Ocean is approximately twice the size of the Mediterranean sea, and many areas are several miles deep. A wide and shallower shelf is found along the Siberian coast. The ocean is mostly covered by pack ice, frozen seawater averaging about 9 to 10 feet (2.7 to 3 meters) thick, and the ice drifts about the polar basin under the influence of currents and winds, and is changed by blizzards and refreezing. Between Svalbard (an island group that includes Spitsbergen and Bear Island) and Greenland is the largest body of water going south carrying ice and debris toward the temperate zones. In the Bering Strait, on the other side of the pole, the surface current is northward. In the summer, the ice pack in the Arctic is not as thick and its edge recedes about a 100 miles (161 kilometers) northward.

Because the waters of the Arctic are permanently covered with drifting pack ice, sunlight does not permeate deeply enough through the surface to nourish or encourage biological change. The result is that the true marine Arctic remains cold and relatively life-

CONCISE ANTARCTIC CHRONOLOGY

1603 Gabriel de Castilla (Spain), with a ship's company, probably penetrated the Southern Ocean south of Drake Passage.

Subsequently several merchant vessels reported being blown south of 60°S rounding Cabo de Hornos in severe weather.

1773 James Cook (Britain), with companies aboard HMS *Resolution* and HMS *Adventure,* crossed the Antarctic Circle (66.55°S off Enderby Land), 17 January 1773.

1774 James Cook (Britain) on the same expedition reached 71.17°S off Marie Byrd Land, 30 January.

1820 Fabian von Bellingshausen (Russia), with companies aboard *Vostok* and *Mirnyy,* sighted the Antarctic continent at about 60.35°S off Dronning Maud Land, 17 January.

1823 James Weddell (Britain), with company aboard *Jane,* reached 74.25°S in the Weddell Sea, 20 February.

1842 James Ross (Britain), with companies aboard HMS *Erebus* and HMS *Terror,* reached 78.17°S in the Ross Sea, 23 February.

1900 Hugh Evans (Britain) and three others sledged to 78.83°S on the Ross Ice Shelf, 23 February.

1902 Robert Scott (Britain) and two others sledged to 82.28°S on the Ross Ice Shelf, 30 December.

1909 Ernest Shackleton (Britain) and three others sledged to 88.38°S, 9 January.

1911 Roald Amundsen (Norway) and four others dog-sledged to 90°S, 14 December.

1912 Robert Scott (Britain) and four others sledged to 90°S, 17 January (all perished during the return journey).

1929 Richard Byrd (United States), with an aircraft crew, claimed to have flown over the South Pole from the Ross Ice Shelf, 29 November.

1947 Richard Byrd (United States), with crew aboard two aircraft, flew over the South Pole from the Ross Ice Shelf, 15 February.

1956 John Torbert (United States) and six others flew across Antarctica over the South Pole (Ross Island to Weddell Sea and returned without landing), 13 January.

1956 Conrad Shinn (United States), with crew of an aircraft, landed at the South Pole, 31 October. A permanent station was then established and sustained by aircraft.

Subsequently many aircraft have landed at the South Pole.

1958 Vivian Fuchs (British Commonwealth) and an expeditionary party reached the South Pole by motor vehicles, 20 January, and continued to cross Antarctica (Weddell Sea to Ross Sea).

Subsequently various expeditions have crossed the Antarctic through the South Pole by surface and many have made one-way surface journeys leaving by aircraft.

less. It is only near the land or in the subarctic, where the ice pack is seasonal, that the waters are warmer, calmer, and richer in nutrients. A proliferation of plant and animal life exists there.

In general, the Arctic is warmer than the Antarctic. However, even in the warm summer months, the temperature does not exceed 50°F.

The North Pole, just like the South Pole, is a mathematical point where the imaginary line of the Earth's axis passes through the Earth's surface. At that location the sun is seen to circle the horizon without setting for six months a year, and then there are six months of darkness. This alternating phenomenon explains why summer and winter alternate at the poles. Just as the North Pole is a mathematical point constantly moving, so is the South Pole. A traveler can locate the pole by celestial navigation or satellite computation, but today it has been made very simple with the use of global positioning systems. Both the North and the South also have magnetic poles, areas where the horizontal pull on a magnetic compass needle is almost nil, and the needle swings around trying to point northward. This exact position moves yearly, and in each case is hundreds of miles away from the geographic pole.

As one tries to compare these two ends of the Earth, what stands out the most is that the North Pole is located in an ice-covered ocean surrounded by land, while the South Pole is located on an ice-covered continent surrounded by water. In the Southern Hemisphere, between latitude 45°S and the Antarctic Circle, 90 percent of the Earth's surface is made up of ocean. Correspondingly, in the latitudes of the Northern Hemisphere, almost the exact opposite proportion exists.

Antarctica is essentially round, and the westerly winds constantly blowing around its perimeter give the area a climate with few variations, as compared to the Arctic. Elevation and distance from the sea cause some change in the Antarctic climate, but otherwise differences are really quite small and have their origin largely in changes of local landscape.

The arctic tundra is a far more bizarre terrain than most realize. The climate in the Arctic covers such extremes that there is a great diversity of plant and animal life thriving within its boundaries. The snow line, which is roughly coincidental with the frost line, rises to about 2,500 feet (762 meters) above sea level for three months of the year, and so the birds, animals, insects, and flowers can all survive on the snowfree tundra.

The Antarctic, on the other hand, is notable for the extreme severity of its climate, where even in the summer the frost line averages no higher than about 20 feet (6 meters) above sea level. In Antarctica, only two species of insects, several vascular plants, and scattered mosses and lichens exist.

Another curious comparison: In the Arctic, seals are terrified when they are out of the water and they encounter a polar bear, the great land predator of the north. They also are fearful of man, who in the north frequently hunts the seal. In the Antarctic, however, there are no land predators. Man has not hunted seals or penguins in the Antarctic for many decades. The various Antarctic seals can be approached without difficulty. Penguins do not even fear the vicious leopard seal on the ice, but in the water they are panicky when they sight this same animal.

While the implications of global warming and the ozone hole are beyond the province of this book, it is interesting to note that Antarctica contains 90 percent of the world's ice. If this ice melted, the sea level of the world would rise by several hundred feet. Not only is Antarctica one of the most unusual and beautiful places in our world, but the impact of the continent for all of us in our changing world is ominous.

CHAPTER 2

Polar Tourism: Past, Present, and Future

If you look like your passport photograph, you're not fit to be traveling.

—Sir Vivian Fuchs

A fortunate few have orbited our planet. These new explorers have been amazed at the kaleidoscope of colors on Earth and surprised by the dazzling whiteness of the polar ice caps. This reflected sunlight from our world's vast storehouse of ice and snow gives the orbiting astronaut the impression that the Arctic and the Antarctic are much the same. Only in the past century have explorers learned the vast differences in these areas. Inevitably, the tourist follows the explorer, and there is well-documented evidence of Arctic tourism by 1856 and Antarctic tourism by 1957.

ARCTIC TOURISM

Exploration of the Arctic began over two thousand years ago. Up until 1856, this part of the world was the exclusive province of the explorer. Then came whaling, fishing, and hunting, and later mining, trade, and the various maritime activities by navies of the great powers. In early June 1856 Lord Dufferin on his ship, *Foam,* organized a private British tourist voyage, with the objective of cruising for pleasure on his own yacht in northern seas. He went ashore at Engelskbukta, Spitsbergen, at 79°N, on August 6, 1856. This was probably the first voyage to Svalbard undertaken solely for pleasure.

That same June, Prince Napoleon sponsored a private tourist cruise on the *Reine-Hordenst.* On this French tourist expedition he managed to reach 62 miles (100 kilometers) south of Jan Mayen Island (about 300 miles or 483 kilometers east of Greenland). He then traveled to Iceland and on to Godthab, Greenland.

In July 1881, the Norwegian tourist expedition led by Captain Gran on the *Pallas* traveled to Svalbard waters. This was the first organized commercial tourist cruise in the Arctic. Wildlife observations were recorded, and many of the passengers hunted reindeer. During the next three decades, several vessels made routine summer cruises to Svalbard and a major tourist industry developed. In addition to the thriving Norwegian tourist industry, British and German expeditions traveled the same route.

In 1896, Harry DeWindt led a British tourist expedition from New York, a private venture with the objective of traveling from New York to Paris primarily by land through Alaska and Siberia. It was quite a "tourist expedition" as at one point they had to wait five weeks for the arrival of the U.S. revenue cutter *Bear* for a passage across the Bering Sea, and they spent some weeks awaiting suitable sledging conditions for their journey across Siberia. Toward the end of that time, the Chukchis convinced them that the journey would be impossible. Instead they returned on the whaler *Belvedere* south, and at Unalaska Island, they rejoined the *Bear* which brought them to San Francisco in November.

Svalbard, because of its location and accessibility over these years, had been a favorite attraction. A few scattered trips were taken for painting landscapes, and hunting expeditions were mounted from Russia, Britain, Norway, and the United States not only for Svalbard, but also for Greenland.

Before the turn of the century, railway services were becoming well developed in northern Sweden. The Lulea-Marvik Railway Line in Norrbotten County of northern Sweden reported that between 1935 and 1939 the annual average number of overnight visitors increased from ten thousand to fifteen thousand.

Little tourist traffic was seen in the northern Canadian Arctic in the 1930s other than the *Nascopie,* the Hudson Bay Company supply ship that regularly serviced the eastern subarctic and Arctic archipelago and usually carried a small contingent of tourists. According to the official passenger list in 1937, approximately 15 percent of the registered passengers were carried as "official tourists."

Since World War II, the explosion in automobile travel has been reflected in gradually increasing tourism in the Scandinavian north, and where roads are developed a similar phenomenon has occurred in Canada.

Lindblad Explorer.

In 1984, the *Lindblad Explorer* traveled across the Northwest Passage, and the following year the *World Discoverer* made the same voyage. During 1986 the passage was not crossed due to ice conditions west of Bellot Strait, but it was traveled again by the *Society Explorer* in 1988, and the *Polaris* traveled along the coast of Baffin Island, Iceland, and Greenland. In 1991, Quark Expeditions, chartering from the Murmansk Shipping Company, took the nuclear icebreaker *Sovetskiy Soyuz* to the North Pole and another historic voyage across the Northeast Passage, or the Northern Sea Route as it is termed by the Russians. In 1992, Quark increased their chartering from the Russians, and their Far Eastern Shipping Company began to supply diesel icebreakers and smaller research vessels for the tourist trade. Quark ran three nuclear icebreaker trips to the North Pole and across the Northern Sea Route. Blyth and Company ran a historical northern voyage, and Seaquest Cruises sent the *Frontier Spirit* through the Northwest Passage.

Sovetskiy Soyuz, *nuclear icebreaker.*

In 1993, an interesting event occurred. Blyth and Company Travel anticipated sending the *Akademik Ioffe,* on two cruises to the eastern Arctic and Davis Strait, two cruises to Greenland and the eastern Arctic, and one cruise to Davis Strait, Baffin Island, and Hudson Bay. These cruises were all canceled because the Canadian Coast Guard would not certify the ship as it did not meet Canadian safety standards. The Canadians also insisted that the Russian M-2 helicopters could not be used in Canadian waters, and the *Kapitan Khlebnikov* was required to have a Canadian helicopter aboard for the Northwest Passage. It has been said that the helicopter decision was based more on political considerations than on safety reasons.

Kapitan Khlebnikov, *diesel icebreaker.*

Various other cruise ships were used through the Northwest Passage, the Northeast Passage, and for trips to the North Pole, Greenland, Svalbard, and Franz Josef Land. A whole new world of adventure cruising had been born, but as already had been seen in Antarctic cruising, unpredictable ice conditions can play havoc with an itinerary.

Russian polar travel had been at a minimum for most of the twentieth century. Because few tourists ever wanted to go to the very far north of Russia, this industry never developed prior to the Russian Revolution in 1917. From then until the 1990s, Communism, World War II, and the cold war precluded tourism. The Kola Peninsula, except for the city of

Murmansk and the Archangel region, was closed to foreigners until 1990. For many years international tourism was discouraged by the Soviet regime, and there were many constraints on the foreign visitor. Northwest Russia, all the way across through Siberia, is primarily a huge wilderness consisting of forests, taiga, and tundra. No tourist infrastructure existed.

Things changed suddenly. The few cities and outposts across the top of northern Russia were largely involved in harvesting raw materials produced by the workers in the gulag system. With the cataclysmic changes that occurred in the Soviet Union, and then its eventual demise, the gulag system literally collapsed. This meant that fewer people had to depend on transportation in the far north. With the end of the cold war, Russian troop deployment across the far north also rapidly decreased. Russia, which owns the largest modern icebreaker fleet in the world—larger than that of the rest of the world put together—was faced with the problem of utilizing these ships. This, coupled with the opening up of polar Russia from west of the Barents Sea to east of the Chukchi Sea, meant that a previously clandestine half of the circumference of the Arctic Ocean was now available for tourism. These factors profoundly changed the complexion of Arctic polar travel.

The tourist industry in Greenland is not as yet well developed, and only about a thousand cruise passengers visit yearly. Several thousand tourists arrive by air, many of whom spend only hours there, but the number of campers, skiers, and expeditioners, although small in number, is increasing. Of the over 100,000 "tourists" who pass through Iceland, many are en route to and from Europe and North America and are literally there only for hours. Svalbard tourism is limited to about 30,000 people: a third probably never leave Longyearbyen, a third are trekkers, and the last third consists of those who arrive by air or coastal liner cruises, plus a small group using Zodiacs and similar inflatable watercraft to travel along the coast. Approximately 500,000 tourists travel to northern Scandinavia each year, mainly by overland transportation, but the number reaching the true Arctic is not known. Of the more than one million tourists to Alaska yearly, only 25,000, or 3 percent, venture into the Arctic. Lastly, the 200,000 plus tourists to the Northwest Territories and the Yukon are almost exclusively overland tourists, and the extent of their travel to the high Arctic is not well documented.

In May 1994, the first circumpolar flying expedition was organized. Eighty-eight passengers flew to fifteen Arctic cities in eight circumpolar countries. Cooperation in economic and humanitarian ways has been increasing between the Inuits of Alaska and the Chukchis of Siberia, and with the tremendous changes in Russia, it is apparent that circumpolar tourism in the Arctic will undergo many changes in the next few years.

ANTARCTIC TOURISM

The earliest recorded tourism in the Antarctic consisted of New Zealand government expeditions sent to inspect provision depots and to search for castaways on Campbell Island, Auckland Island, and Macquarie Island (known as subantarctic islands). These regularly scheduled voyages left annually from Bluff, New Zealand, starting in March 1882 and ending in 1927. Many carried passengers, but good records about these trips are difficult to find. In 1924, the Falkland Islands dependencies government mail service was inaugurated with *Fleurus* providing service for the government outposts and whaling communities at South Georgia in the South Atlantic. Similar contact was also made with some of the surrounding island groups. Various vessels replaced the *Fleurus* over the years, until the voyages were terminated in 1971, when the *Darwin* was withdrawn from service.

On November 4, 1910, a note appeared in the Christchurch, New Zealand, newspaper, *The Press,* announcing that a voyage to McMurdo Sound during the austral summer was planned. The efforts languished, and after Capt. Scott's ill-fated expedition to the South Pole, nothing further was mentioned about this planned voyage.

On July 8, 1930, *The New York Times* published an advertisement for an "Antarctic World Cruise, the Most Wonderful Voyage Ever Planned." Prices ranged from U.S.$6,500 to U.S.$25,000 for the world-circling trip on the *Volendam,* embarking from Southhampton. The Holland American Line was to operate this trip which would last from December 15, 1932, to April 15, 1932. The passengers would be limited to two hundred. Capt. John Stenhouse, formerly with Sir Ernest Shackleton's *Aurora* expedition of 1914 to 1917, and of the ship *Discovery* in 1925 to 1927, was to be master of the ship. The advertisement also disclosed that women traveling on this trip would be the first ever to look at the ice barrier. Unfortunately, for reasons unknown, the voyage never took place.

In 1940, the *Windward* was being readied for Antarctic tourist trade, but this trip also was canceled, this time because of the outbreak of the Second World War.

The next actual Antarctic tourist visit was probably on December 22, 1956, when a Douglas DC6B of the Linea Aérea Nacional (Chilean national airline) flew nonstop from Chacabuco in Argentina over the South Shetland Islands carrying sixty-six passengers. This was the first Antarctic tourist flight, and in the following year a Pan American Airways stratocruiser from Christchurch landed at McMurdo Sound on October 15, 1957. This was the first commercial flight landing in Antarctica with the first tourists to reach the continent. A decade later, in 1968, the Admiral Richard Evelyn Byrd Polar Center of Boston, Massachusetts, sponsored a round-the-world tourist flight over the North Pole and the South Pole in a chartered Convair 990A jet aircraft. The seventy passengers aboard also landed at McMurdo.

It was 1958 when an Argentine vessel, the *Les Eclaireurs,* made two cruises, each with about a hundred tourists aboard, that visited the South Shetland Islands and the west coast of the Antarctic Peninsula. Polar tourism by cruise ship to the Antarctic Peninsula was now well under way. Over the next few years the Chilean vessels made several similar voyages, and in 1966 Lars-Eric Lindblad, of Lindblad Travel, took fifty-eight passengers to the South Shetlands from Ushuaia, Argentina, on a voyage that was accompanied by the Argentine naval vessel *Comandante General Irigoyen.* Several more of these trips were made to the Antarctic Peninsula, and in 1968 the *Magga Dan* made two cruises to the Ross Sea. These too were organized by Lindblad, with the ship embarking from Bluff, New Zealand, and visiting various subantarctic islands near New Zealand and Australia. The passengers were among the first to visit the historic huts of Borchgrevink, Scott, and Shackleton.

These successes led to the commissioning of the *Lindblad Explorer* in 1969. This Norwegian-registered vessel carrying ninety-two passengers began a long series of visits to the subantarctic islands, the peninsula, and the continent of Antarctica. With several name changes—currently she is known as the *Explorer*—she has returned to the Antarctic each season.

In addition to the usual tourist ships, occasionally ships have been available from the Argentine and Chilean navies which, when relieving their stations in the Antarctic Peninsula and in the South Shetland Islands, have carried tourist passengers. Both Argentina and Chile have also used their airstrips on Seymour Island and King George Island off the Antarctic Peninsula to convey tourists to and from ships. The Chilean navy still continues these occasional voyages, but since the grounding and subsequent sinking of the *Bahia Paraiso,* in January 1989, 1.86 miles (3 kilometers) from the U.S. base in Palmer Station on the Antarctic Peninsula, Argentina has been out of this business. Occasionally, world-class vessels with large numbers of passengers include Antarctica on their itineraries, and they may or may not make landings by inflatable watercraft.

Following a few occasional flights to Antarctica in 1977, Australia and New Zealand began regular sightseeing tours. After approximately fifty flights, service was terminated when on November 28, 1979, a New Zealand DC-10 struck Mount Erebus on Ross Island. All 257 persons aboard were killed.

Over the past ten years, private aircraft landing on blue ice has increased tourist possibilities to Antarctica. Adventure Network International now maintains a base at Patriot Hills at the top of the Antarctic Peninsula, only some eight hundred miles (1,287 kilometers) from the South Pole. Tourists can now be ferried from Punta Arenas, a seaport city in southern Chile, by DC-4 to this base from which ski-equipped DAC-6 Twin Otter aircraft go to the South Pole. Also, trips are made to the Vinson Massif, the highest peak in Antarctica, which is a major attraction to mountaineers. Commercial aircraft sightseeing flights from New Zealand and Australia are also returning.

IMPLICATIONS FOR THE FUTURE

There is no way to accurately estimate the number of visitors to the Arctic. There are eight countries bordering the Arctic Circle, and with various definitions of the Arctic, this makes gathering statistics very difficult. However, most informed sources agree that over 100,000 tourists visit the true Arctic annually.

A statistical analysis of tourism to the Antarctic is also far from perfect but it is much easier. In just under forty years of record keeping, seaborne tourist numbers, listed in the table on page 20, added to the few thousand people who come by private yachts and aircraft to land on Antarctica, produce a total of approximately 85,000. Astonishingly, well over half of these tourists have come since 1990!

Antarctic yacht activity is increasing. Over 150 yacht visits have been made over the last 30 years, and, during the 1995–96 season, 17 yachts made 22 expeditions to Antarctica carrying 150 people, including 123 fare-paying passengers.

Since 1994, Qantas Antarctic day sightseeing overflights from Melbourne, Australia, utilizing Boeing 747 aircraft, have made flights of approximately twelve hours' duration including orbits over scenic sites and lectures on conservation, history, and the

Abandoned Russian station (1929–63) at Quiet Bay, Gukor Island, in Franz Josef Land.

local environment of Antarctica. During the 1995–96 season the 9 flights carried 2,958 flight-seeing passengers. Between December 1, 1996, and February 16, 1997, 3,448 passengers participated in 10 flights. Aerolineas Argentinas has operated commercially scheduled transpolar flights between Argentina and New Zealand for many years aboard its Boeing 747 aircraft.

Although there was a decrease in shipborne tourists this past season, IAATO projects 10,590 travelers on 15 visits for the 1997–98 season in the Antarctic. Much of the increase in numbers is due to the return of the *Marco Polo,* a tour vessel with a capacity of 800 passengers. IAATO's forecast for number of passengers participating in seaborne Antarctic tourism reaches 14,250 for the 2001–02 season.

When one considers that the first real cruising began in the Antarctic in 1970 and in the Canadian Arctic in 1984, both of these spearheaded by voyages on the *Lindblad Explorer,* it is apparent how recent this surge has been for the cruise industry. In 1971, half a million North Americans took a cruise vacation, and twenty years later that figure had increased dramatically to four million. The number of passengers embarking from North American ports will probably increase from over five million in 1994 to more than six million in 1997. With 250 cruise ships already traversing the oceans, nearly 10 percent of which visit polar waters, it is evident that there will be many new as well as old problems to be solved.

On August 17, 1977, the Soviet nuclear icebreaker *Arktika* reached the North Pole. Through the summer of 1997, a total of twenty-seven trips had been made to the North Pole by Russian nuclear or diesel icebreakers, including one trip each by icebreakers from Canada, Germany, Sweden, and the United

Sovetskiy Soyuz *at North Pole, July 13, 1992.*

The nuclear icebreaker Russia *crashing through polar ice.*

States. Eighteen of these twenty-two cruises have carried passengers to this increasingly sought-after destination. One tour company has been considering taking passengers not only by nuclear icebreaker, but also by Russian nuclear submarine to the North Pole and then exchanging passengers for the homeward voyage!

The mix of the passengers on these voyages is most interesting. Probably the majority are from the United States. In the Arctic, however, many Canadians are seen, and in the Antarctic many from Australia. Frequently passengers are making return trips to these areas which have captivated them. The Antarctic tourists on most ships tend to be in their sixties, but in the past several years younger people have joined the ranks of those making the trips. Viewing wildlife, gaining an education about the polar regions, and taking photographs are some of the leading reasons for making the voyage, but many tourists are also interested in conservation and in history. On Arctic trips, many want to visit the native peoples, and in the Antarctic, some have a very special interest in polar bases. Travel on a Russian icebreaker and having the wonderful experience of watching a powerful ship crush through vast fields of ice is an experience that no tourist will ever forget.

The potential growth for tourism in the Arctic and subarctic areas is tremendous. New sites and new routes are being developed, and tourists' interest in the indigenous peoples is increasing. It has previously been mentioned that the use of the Russian chartered ships in the Arctic season complements their austral summer use in Antarctica. Vast areas of Russia have not yet been seen except by a few tourists.

In the Antarctic and subantarctic islands many more tourists can be expected. The Ross Sea area is becoming increasing popular with tourists from Australia and New Zealand and among those who are interested in the history of Antarctica. The resurgence

The editor at North Pole, July 13, 1992.

Sovetskiy Soyuz *in high Arctic, July 10, 1992.*

of airborne tourism from Australia and New Zealand will attract many.

The Antarctic Treaty Organization, the National Science Foundation from the United States, IAATO, and many other concerned organizations have put in place many excellent regulations for visits to the Antarctic (see appendices A and B). These serious and sound efforts are helping maintain a pristine Antarctica in spite of mounting tourist pressures. Similar efforts should be sought for the Arctic, where the problems are not too dissimilar.

Roger Tory Peterson, world-renowned ornithologist, frequently traveled on tourist ships to study penguins.

ANTARCTIC TOURISM
(ESTIMATES)

Year	*Number by ship*	*Number by air*
1957–58	194	
1958–59	344	
1965–66	58	
1966–67	94	
1967–68	147	
1968–69	1,312	
1969–70	972	
1970–71	943	
1971–72	984	
1972–73	1,175	
1973–74	1,876	
1974–75	3,644	
1975–76	1,890	
1976–77	1,068	
1977–78	845	
1978–79	1,048	
1979–80	855	
1980–81	855	
1981–82	1,441*	?*
1982–83	719	2
1983–84	834	265
1984–85	544	92
1985–86	631	151
1986–87	1,797	30
1987–88	2,782	244
1988–89	3,146	370
1989–90	2,460	121
1990–91	4,698	144
1991–92	6,317	178
1992–93	7,037	185
1993–94	8,016	59
1994–95	8,210	112
1995–96	9,212	155
1996–97	7,322	104
TOTAL	83,470	2,212

This table is a composite of information from sources listed in the references to this book. Visits by some private yachts, private aircraft, and overflights are not included in the above totals.

**During 1981–82 some passengers came by both air and sea.*

CHAPTER 3

Polar Medicine: A Historical Perspective

> The scurvy flew through the schooner's crew as they sailed the Arctic sea; they were far from land and their food was canned so they got no vitamin C.
>
> —C.H.A. in St. Bartholomew's Hospital Journal, 1928

Polar medicine embraces all the fields of medicine and surgery, with emphasis on problems relating to the extreme cold and isolation. Geographically, the polar regions might be considered to be above latitude 66°32′ north of the equator and 66°32′ south of the equator, that is, the areas where the sun neither rises nor sets on one day per year. In considering the history of polar medicine, one should include the medical care of the seafaring explorers and traders, sealers and whalers who sailed, literally, to the utter ends of the world. Often they were away for years at a time. Some were attempting to find the North Pole, while others were searching for the great southern continent. Many, however, were looking for the sea route that would eliminate the arduous overland route between Europe and the Far East for the trade of silk and spices.

EARLY POLAR MEDICINE

Particularly in the earliest days, there were few medical privations, as the state of medical art in the so-called civilized world was also very primitive. Before the eighteenth century, the impact of the medical profession was truly negligible. Few could afford to pay the physician for his often expensive services, and his attendance in matters of life or death frequently made little difference. It was not really until after 1850 that the practice of medicine and the organization of medical services began to make large-scale differences in human survival rates. Indeed, this was true also at sea, but fortunately there were some notable exceptions.

About the earliest days of the great explorations by sea, little is known. However, it is well documented that Ferdinand Magellan left Spain looking for a western sea route to the Indies and was killed in the Philippines. One of his ships, however, did complete this first circumnavigation of the world in 1519. Medical care for these early sailor-explorers, if any, is not documented.

From 1553, when Sir Hugh Willoughby sailed on the British Northeast Passage Expedition, until Admiral Robert E. Peary returned from the North in 1909, there are 757 recorded deaths in Arctic exploration. Starvation, scurvy, cold, and drowning were the major causes. Accidents were rare. (See appendix C for details on causes of death.)

Captain James Cook sailed in 1771 with a surgeon and two surgeon's mates, and he carried antiscorbutics in various forms. On Cook's three around-the-world voyages, it is said that daily lemon juice was taken by each crew member and none got scurvy. This is pure myth! Cook did prevent scurvy in most of his crew, but he used such a variety of measures that he himself did not know what was really effective.

In 1773, Constantine John Phipps led the British naval north polar expeditions from London. He wrote about taking extra clothing and extra spirits, and he went into great detail on the importance of properly distilling seawater to provide fresh water for the crew.

POLAR MEDICINE IN THE NINETEENTH CENTURY

Probably the first in-depth explanation of medical care at sea, however, is provided by William Parry, R.N., commander of the Northwest Passage Expedition in 1819. He wrote of having a small supply of mustard and cress which he put in shallow boxes filled with mold and placed near the stovepipe, and by these means, even in the severity of winter, he could have a crop in six or seven days after sowing the seed. By ingesting one ounce of this "salad" per day, dramatic results were seen in those suffering from scurvy. Parry accurately described "snow-blindness" and found that a "cooling" wash made of a small quantity of acetate of lead mixed with cold water often relieved the irritation in several days. As a preventive, he put black crepe in the frame of eyeglasses, effectively providing the men with "snow glasses." On this same voyage, Parry, in the appendix to his writings, has a nine-page section entitled "Remarks on the State of Health and Disease Onboard the *Hecla* and *Gripper*." This is a classic early description of diseases and injuries at sea and how they were treated. Case reports are given, conclusions are drawn, and preventive medicine is stressed. One case of "an attack of inflammation of the lungs" is followed by the clinical course of the disease and the demise of the patient. The report of a well-done autopsy then follows. Certainly this type of medical study was far above average for its day.

When Sir John Franklin sailed in May of 1845, all of England believed that conquering the Northwest Passage was within his grasp. However, much of the food for the trip was stored in the new tin containers. The tin container had been patented in England in 1811 and was used immediately by the Royal Navy in most parts of the world. Modern anthropological and forensic medicine has disclosed that the faulty soldering of these tin cans produced lead poisoning in those who ate the contents, and along with scurvy, starvation, and cold, led to the death of all 135 of these sailor-explorers.

By 1859, over fifty expeditions had been mounted searching for the missing Franklin, his men, and his ships. Emerging into prominence during that time as America's first Arctic explorer was Dr. Elisha Kent Kane, who served as surgeon on the first Grinnell Expedition and, several years later, led his own expedition to the Arctic. He himself was not a well man, but he noticed that the absence of "cold germs" kept his rheumatic fever at bay. Although he was deeply concerned about warm clothing, his men's boots and moccasins were inadequate, and frostbite, even more than scurvy, crippled them. Several of his party died of gangrene following frostbitten feet. On his second expedition, he was deeply troubled with the ship's rat population. Extermination by igniting brimstone, leather, and arsenic belowdecks was ineffectual, and eventually the explorers simply learned to live with the rodents. In fact, when rations became short during the second winter, rats were put on the menu as "Arctic deer," and Kane ate them, considering them quite palatable. Probably, this fresh meat saved him from scurvy.

Ships beset for the long Arctic winter presented the Royal Navy with other problems. "Cabin fever" was expected, but they also found real risks of "madness and disease." The sailors developed pale complexions and lassitude, and in their damp and cold quarters tempers flared and disease was not uncommon. In the hope of preventing some of these disorders, rigorous routines were developed. The entire ship's company would be made to trot around the snow-packed deck while the captain and the surgeon inspected the vacant mess deck below. Later, all hands went over the side, circumnavigating the ship for several hours. The men in hammocks fared better than the officers, as the midships often was warmer. The officers' bunks were against the frozen hull, and ice in their bunks was common. Ships were inspected daily for correctable sources of dampness. Fumigation was carried out weekly in a vain attempt to rid the hull of infection and dampness. Stovepipes were ingeniously run through various areas in the ship in an attempt to warm the quarters. The sailors/explorers spent the long evenings preparing for musical theatricals. Instruments, costumes, material for sets, etc., were provided on board the ships. The leaders claimed that the elaborate preparations were preferable to boredom and improved the sailors' mental and physical health.

Gray whale carcass at New Cheblina, Siberia.

Life on whale ships was extremely unpleasant. Seamen who were afflicted with pleurisy, severe fevers of whatever origin, and bodily injuries were often driven aloft to work on sails. Failure to go meant the whip, which was administered freely. There was literally no medical care for these poor individuals. The whalers and sealers, as they traveled through the South Pacific, had problems not encountered in the polar areas. On some islands, the natives were found to be clean, intelligent, and hospitable. The sailors were treated with great respect, gifts were exchanged, and food was provided. They then left unharmed. On the next island, however, following similar or even more lavish treatment, they were sometimes provided with native women for the evening, and early the following morning, being so disarmed, they were taken prisoner and prepared for the cooking pot. Stories of grotesque torture are far from uncommon. A great anxiety developed among the crews of the whale ships, and every effort was made to avoid the "black islands."

Fortunately for humans, the farther north or south one travels heading for the polar areas, the fewer bacterial and parasitic diseases are found. However, cholera, malaria, and dozens of other disorders were not uncommon in the sailors who had visited tropical islands on their way to the polar region. One particularly vicious infection was caused by the Chinese cockroach. These dangerous insects would attack humans, eating holes in their limbs to the bone. Death was not uncommon.

By any standards, working conditions in the whale fishery industry were very poor. After a whale had succumbed and was brought to the ship, and the "try-pots" were set to boiling, the slabs of blubber were thrown in and rendered to oil. The men flensing the whales often did so in bare feet, and severe injuries of the extremities were common, as was the danger of being burned by the try-pots. The medical care for these ailments was bleak.

Vermin in the hold were all too common, and the remedy was to "smoke ship," as has been mentioned earlier. At this time, if possible, the crew went ashore for "recreation," subjecting them to the dangers that also have been mentioned.

The philosophy of the sailor regarding accidents was interesting. Little sympathy or congratulations were offered for narrow escapes. These men regarded accidents as blunders, and a narrow escape from death generally was a subject to be joked about.

Many whaler captains felt that the hurricanes in the Pacific were more dangerous than rounding Cape Horn or navigating the icebergs of the Arctic. The possibility of dying or being maimed when a small whaleboat was struck or overturned by a whale was all too real and many men suffered one fate or the other.

There was often a real disparity in the food dispensed to the officers as compared to the crew. One captain is quoted as saying, "Any man that cannot eat anything, cooked in any way, at any time, out of anything, and this, too, under the sight of any dirt, the effect of any smell, the sound of any noise, and the feeling of any motion should never go to sea."

In the subantarctic islands, as well as some areas in the north, bird eggs were actively sought and ingeniously taken by the sailors. Lean whale meat was a welcome substitute for salt pork and beef that had been on board for many months. When the seas were too rough for cooking, men subsisted for days on end on bread and water. In both the American and the British whale fleets, scurvy and frostbite were common. The loss of fingers and other gross changes resulting from frostbite were sometimes confused with leprosy. Hence the whalers returning from Greenland with these deformed and missing digits were avoided by the Shetlanders and Orchadians. Influenza and rheumatism were also prevalent during the winter.

It is interesting to note that English whale ships always carried a doctor. Dr. Nathaniel W. Taylor wrote in 1853 that if the American ships had done the same, many lives might have been saved.

The warm clothing that is essential to prevent frostbite and death in the severe polar climate was often missing on polar expeditions. Traditionally, fur clothing was used, but it had severe limitations. Running behind a dogsled, or as Grinnell explorer Kane put it, "sweating along at eight miles [13 kilometers] per hour," is uncomfortable at best. The moisture was retained, and sealskins and furs became very hard. The Eskimos got around this by sleeping naked under animal skins while their furs and skins worn during the day dried in the heat of the blubber lamp. The permeable nature of wool, on the other hand, allowed the moisture to be wicked away from the body and to the outside. The explorer, who usually slept in a small tent without a blubber lamp, slept in his clothes and thus found wool a favorite. Following the turn of the century, Thomas Burberry perfected a lightweight closely woven fabric that repelled dampness while admitting air. Burberry christened his invention "gabardine" after the Jewish cloak of the same name. The great explorers, Amundsen, Nansen, Scott, and Shackleton all preferred this material to fur. Amundsen even had tents made of gabardine.

Food became a great preoccupation with many desperate explorers. In 1853, Greely describes how, in their desperation for food, the explorers boiled their sealskin clothing, yielding a nourishing broth. Tea leaves were used several times and then eaten, and lichen scraped from rocks and a few small shrimp that were netted saved explorers' lives for many months. In that desperate last year, one member of the party, Private Henry, was executed by firing squad for repeatedly stealing food—much of it sealskin that he hoped to chew for nutrition.

After the famed rescue of the six survivors of Greely's group from Camp Clay, the twenty dead were removed from their shallow graves and taken back to New York. Autopsies showed large areas where muscle tissue had been removed and the skin oversewn with surgical precision. Just as the last of Franklin's expedition had succumbed to cannibalism, Greely's men did the same for survival. Similar charges have been levied against some Uruguayans recently forced down in a plane crash in the Andes. These survivors had made some very complex decisions.

Polar bear liver is known to be extremely rich in vitamin A, to a level that can be toxic to humans. Salomon Andrée, aboard the *Eagle* in 1897, knew this and took precautions. But he didn't know about trichinosis, so the polar bear got him another way. Mawson and his party in Antarctica learned the hard way that dog liver is also extremely rich in vitamin A. They lost the soles of their feet and exfoliated other areas, but sustained no permanent damage.

POLAR MEDICINE IN THE TWENTIETH CENTURY

At the start of the twentieth century medicine in polar regions had still not advanced to any significant degree. Drygalski's German south polar expedition of 1901–1903 had a separate scientific party under Emil Werth that spent sixteen months on the Kerguelen Islands in the South Indian Ocean. An outbreak of beri-beri, a thiamin deficiency, caused several deaths in the party.

Robert K. Headland, the archivist and curator at the Scott Polar Research Institute, provides some interesting insight into early polar medicine. In bygone days (the late eighteenth and early nineteenth centuries), he states, the ship's captains' medical handbook provided treatment for a great variety of conditions using numbered groups of medicines with great emphasis on venereal disease and scabies. At the end of this "very practical book" was the recommendation that, if all else failed, "committal to the deep" should be employed. He makes a further point apparent to all scholars of polar history: Many of the early ship's surgeons were also natural historians. This was to be expected because medicine, in those days particularly, was merely biology applied to one mammalian species! Also doctors could do little for the sick and injured, and their biological background was used in a very suitable way when they served as the historian for the scientific discoveries being made on these voyages.

The major scourge of polar exploration, however, had always been scurvy. In 1901, Edward Wilson, Scott's surgeon on board the *Discovery,* examined the crew for scurvy and then wrote: "There is no sign of it in any one, as far as I can see. The gums of many are red and swollen, but it is the redness and swelling of slight inflammation, rather than scurvy congestion, and to my mind is to be attributed to clay pipes, strong tobacco, coarse feeding, neglect of the tooth brush and the constant use of foul language."

SCURVY

Scurvy had been observed, without any knowledge of its origin, by the earliest explorers. From 1440 onward, Portugal was a great sea power and sent ships exploring the west coast of Africa. Vasco da-Gama rounded the Cape of Good Hope in 1498 and noted, in his diary, that "many of our men fell ill there. Their hands, feet and gums growing over their teeth so that they could not eat." The expedition sailed up the east coast of Africa and bought oranges from the Moorish traders. Dramatically, all the sick sailors recovered their health. There were many other expeditions documented with a description of scurvy and reports of the crews obtaining fresh fruits and vegetables and recovering their health.

In 1743, four Russian sailors were stranded on the more remote eastern coast of Spitsbergen for six years. One of them had previously wintered there, and he instructed the others to eat scurvy grass *(Cochlearia officinalis).* They also lived on frozen meat and drank the warm blood of reindeer. Three of these sailors survived the six years.

Journals from British expeditions to the polar regions indicated that they usually expected their men to remain healthy for up to two years before they began to show signs of scurvy. A typical diet in an 1877 expedition consisted of preserved vegetables, one ounce of pickles, one ounce of meat, and one ounce of lime juice per day. Lime juice and lemon juice were used interchangeably.

By the second half of the nineteenth century, the British Navy was confident that lime juice was the answer to the problem of scurvy. In 1876, a naval expedition returned from one year in the Arctic. Of 120 men, 60 had suffered from scurvy and 4 died from it. The lime juice theory began to be disputed. It was later learned that the lime juice taken on the expeditions had been run through copper pipes as part of the preservation process before it was placed into casks.

In 1900, the British Medical Association had a discussion on scurvy in its general meeting. The opening paper was read by a retired naval surgeon, who said, "From intensive researches in the literature, I am forced to the conclusion that the presence of some toxic material in the food is the cause of scurvy and also that lemon juice has been erroneously accepted as a certain preventative and that fresh or pure provisions are the true antiscorbutics." Later studies have shown the destructive effect on vitamin C when foods come into contact with small amounts of copper or copper salts.

An expedition of thirty-eight people under Commander Robert Falcon Scott sailed from New Zealand on December 21, 1901. They had brought their ship into McMurdo Sound on the Antarctic landmass by February 8 and remained there for the winter. By September 1902, two men had developed definite signs of scurvy, and medical examination of the rest of the crew members revealed widespread signs of the disease in the early stage. During the winter, they had all lived largely on meat. Dr. Koettlitz, second in command, ordered the killing of seals for meat, began to grow mustard and cress for consumption, and placed lime juice on the mess tables at dinner. Despite this, some expedition members still developed signs of scurvy, and even Shackleton was noted to be breathless and coughing up blood.

Scott's second and last expedition sailed from New Zealand in November 1910. The explorers built a hut on the shore of McMurdo Sound. The diet of these men was more varied than on the first expedition and lime juice was available. As part of the entertainment, during the winter, there were regular lectures and debates. Atkinson, one of the two naval surgeons, lectured on scurvy and spoke about the relative values of fresh meat and vegetables, adding that fresh vegetables are the best curatives and lime juice is useful only if taken regularly. Scott reached the pole on January 16 only to find the Norwegian flag there. By then, Petty Officer Evans had a wound on his hand from a cut received some two weeks earlier that was showing no signs of healing. Evans continued to deteriorate and died on February 18, after two weeks of acting stupid and confused. It has been suggested that this behavior was due to a fall, and he might have had a brain hemorrhage because his scurvy made him more likely to bleed.

From 1875 to 1905, there was growing confusion over the cause of scurvy. The medical writings of the time indicated that it seemed probable that insufficient vegetables played a part in the production of the disease, yet this did not afford a complete explanation of the occurrence of all the symptoms. In 1905, experiments were done on guinea pigs that were denied a full diet. They were fed just a single grain, which was baked into bread. All these animals died, on average after thirty days, from the effects of scurvy. Subsequent experiments were done on guinea pigs on a scorbutic diet to see the effect of various supplements and showed the extremely low value of preserved lime juice. Fresh lemon juice is a far better supplement than lime juice. In fact, lime juice had less than 10 percent of the activity of fresh lemon juice.

In adults, scurvy remains latent for three to twelve months following severe vitamin C deficiency. Symptoms are preceded by lassitude, weakness, irritability, weight loss, and vague muscle and joint pains. Splinter hemorrhages may form near the ends of the nails. The gums become swollen, purple, and spongy, and they bleed easily. Secondary infection, gangrene, and loosening of the teeth occur. Old scars break down and new wounds fail to heal. Spontaneous hemorrhages may occur in any part of the body. The bleeding is particularly noticeable in the legs. The legs become swollen and can become very painful from bleeding into the muscles.

Vitamin C is essential to collagen formation, which is the basic building block of bone and soft tissues, and it is essential for wound healing. It was not until 1932 that Hungarian-born scientist Albert Szent-Gyorgyi was able to isolate vitamin C. By this time, it was well known that lemon juice was a potent source of vitamin C and would prevent the onset of scurvy.

Certainly, the work of chemists in discovering the structure of vitamin C and in developing inexpensive ways of synthesizing has been a great blessing. Scurvy is now an extremely rare disease. There are infrequent reports in the literature of cases in areas where there is famine or inadequate access to fresh produce.

MEDICAL EQUIPMENT AND SUPPLIES

The level of medical equipment and supplies carried on expeditions throughout the history of polar exploration was not very impressive by any standards. Sir William Edward Parry, who sailed on the *Hecla* in 1818, was the first sea captain known to have carried some real medical equipment on board ship and he kept very good records. Virtually nothing, however, is known about medical kits used by explorers between Parry's voyages and the ill-fated Greely expedition of 1881. Greely carried the very latest in *scientific* equipment, but he was sadly lacking in adequate *medical* equipment and supplies. In view of the tragic fate of his expedition, it is ironic to note that shortly prior to his leaving, the firm of Burroughs Wellcome & Co. issued "Tabloid Medical Equipments" especially designed for and prepared to meet the needs of explorers. The explorers who first reached both the north and south poles carried the Tabloid system.

The sole medical equipment carried on the *Nimrod* by Ernest Shackleton, as on his subsequent expeditions, was a "Tabloid" outfit, on which he reported: "The British Antarctic Expedition 1907–09 was equipped with a very complete medical equipment contracted for solely by Messrs. Burroughs Wellcome & Co., and consisting of 'Soloid' and 'Tabloid' preparations which are the only forms that can be conveniently carried and preserved under such conditions. . . . All the tabloid products that remain are now in as good condition as when first handed over to my care two years ago."

The Tabloid kits were of either leather or metal and carried the medications and equipment common in those days: laxatives, bandages, tourniquets, iodine for antisepsis, boric acid, ointments, smelling salts, scissors, and several other small instruments.

On Douglas Mawson's 1911 expedition to establish a hut at Commonwealth Bay in Antarctica, he carried one of the renowned kits. It was considered "elaborate," but it was not any bigger than a family doctor's bag of the early part of this century. The most used of all the pills in the kit were the laxatives.

Mawson's kit, 1929. Photo by R. Reeves of the Australian Antarctic Division.

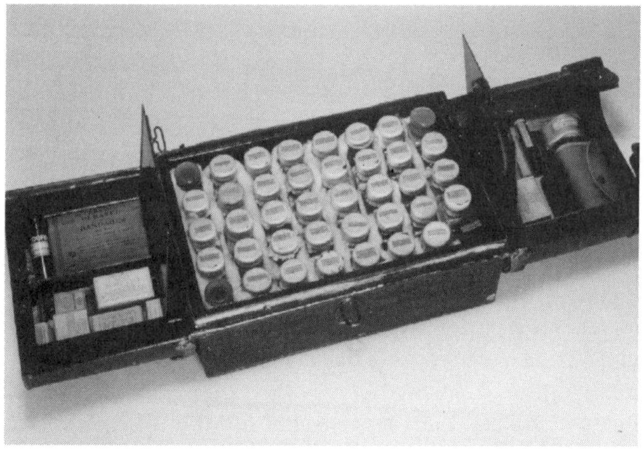

Mawson's kit, 1929. Photo by R. Reeves of the Australian Antarctic Division.

MODERN MEDICINE IN THE ARCTIC

In stark contrast to Antarctica, today approximately two million people live above the Arctic Circle. These year-round residents are found in Iceland, Svalbard, northern Finland, northern Sweden, northern Norway, the northern portions of Russia and much of Siberia, along with Arctic Alaska, the Yukon, the Northwest Territories, and the high Arctic of Canada and Greenland. The vast majority of these people are Caucasians who have moved north. Their medical needs are met in diverse ways. Also in contrast with Antarctica, private doctors, clinics, and hospitals are found all the way around the Arctic Circle, and large hospitals are seen in some of the major cities.

The native peoples are Eskimos, that is, the Chukchis from Siberia as well as the Inuits from Alaska and on across Canada into Greenland. These populations present special problems. Their only occupations are hunting for food and making their own clothing. Formerly, there were tens of thousands of Eskimos, often living in isolated groups of twenty-five people, many miles away from anyone and anything. These nomadic people had little in the way of what one might consider health care for many generations. The shamans ministered to their needs and probably until the middle of the last century were able to offer their patients about the same degree of help as doctors could in the western world.

One of the most fascinating papers ever delivered before the New York Obstetrical Society was given on January 16, 1894. Frederick D. Cook, M.D., related his observations as the ethnologist on the first Peary North Greenland Expedition. This is the same Cook who claimed to have reached the North Pole in 1908, the year before Peary made the same claim.

A walrus "haul-out," which consists of a large number of animals assembled on a beach, is observed by tourists from a Zodiac.

He told how the Esquimaux lived on a complete meat diet, which was raw and frozen two-thirds of the time. They melted snow for drinking water and literally never bathed. Young mothers-to-be were placed in a shelter with frozen meat to last two weeks when birth was imminent. If the mother survived the ordeal and the baby cried then others went to assist her. In times of famine the childless women and the old women were turned out to starve, and their bodies were eagerly devoured by other members of the tribe. Cook felt this was not cannibalism, but a matter of self-preservation. Usually, the Esquimaux were not polygamous or polyandrous but their custom condemned neither, and men as well as women occasionally had multiple mates at the same time. Children belonged to the mother. Among the northern tribes there was little illness except rheumatism and occasionally tonsillitis and mild forms of "la grippe." In the southern tribes over 50 percent suffered with tuberculosis. Every year there was an epidemic of "la grippe" that caused the death of thousands in southern Greenland and Labrador. Cook found no system of medical treatment for their diseases.

With the almost complete dismantling of the nomadic life of the Eskimo people, they have been coalesced into small towns and cities where they are largely supported by the Russian, American, Canadian, and Greenland governments. Clinics have been established and medical care is freely provided. Although many medical and social problems have developed, the basic medical care available to these peoples has certainly improved. One must remember that infant mortality in the Canadian arctic was above 10 percent for many years. Life expectancy was only 60 percent of the national average in 1970 and the outbreak of influenza at Cambridge Bay in the Northwest Passage was catastrophic in 1948. Tuberculosis, alcoholism, and heavy abuse of tobacco are common problems today. In Greenland today, nearly half of the births are to unwed mothers, and approximately one-third of the population of almost sixty thousand people have suffered from various venereal diseases. Occupational health studies show disturbing findings as these nomadic people try to cope with an industrialized society.

The Northwest Territories (NWT) of Canada cover a vast area of 1,304,903 square miles (3,379,699 square kilometers). The almost sixty thousand residents live in over sixty widely dispersed communities, many of which have less than six hundred inhabitants. Yellowknife, on the Great Slave Lake, with a population approaching fifteen thousand, is the capital and the largest community, and has the main referral hospital in the Northwest Territories.

Well over a thousand miles to the east lies Baffin Island, the largest landmass separated by water from the main Northwest Territories. It lies above Hudson Strait and between Fox Basin and Davis Strait. Most of the island is above the Arctic Circle. The Baffin Regional Health Board operates their main installation, the Baffin Regional Hospital in Iqaluit. Iqaluit is very much a frontier town—low buildings, caribou legs in the alleyways, and a view of the snow-capped hills on the other side of Frobisher Bay. The twenty-four-bed acute care facility is open twenty-four hours a day. An emergency room and outpatient department treat approximately four thousand people each month, and they average about sixty surgical cases each month. This is the main health care facility for this island, which is almost 2,000 miles (3,218 kilometers) long, and stretches north to Lancaster Sound.

The laboratory at the regional hospital can do a good range of basic tests, and X-ray and ultrasound equipment is available. There is a small physiotherapy department and all other support services that go with a hospital of this size. A six-person dedicated medevac nursing team handles air transport evacuation and intensive care and special care services for patients admitted to the hospital.

In addition to the Baffin Regional Hospital, the Baffin Regional Health Board operates twelve nursing stations, also known as community health centers. There are no doctors at these facilities; the nurses function on a primary care basis, and also cover public health, audiology, mental health, and home care.

The Health Board contracts with McGill University in Montreal some 1,250 miles (2,011 kilometers) to the south to supply Baffin Regional Hospital with all needed specialists on a rotating basis. Montreal is the first southern evacuation point for patients treated at the Baffin Regional Hospital.

In Montreal, the Baffin Regional Health Board also operates a twenty-two-bed boarding home known as the Baffin House, which is used exclusively for native people. Native food is served, and the staff consists of two nurses and native clerk-interpreters.

There are six physicians on the Baffin Hospital staff, and at any given time one will be a surgeon. Two are always anesthesiologists, and there will be one other person with specialty training. McGill provides a pediatric resident who serves for six weeks and is replaced on a rotating basis.

The six staff physicians are assigned a number of Baffin communities. If the nurse at one of the nursing stations has a patient who is not responding, she has a phone conversation with a staff physician in Iqaluit. Physicians also visit the communities on a rotating basis every four to six weeks. Normally staff physicians at the Baffin hospital are transients. Unfortunately, the health board has difficulty finding physicians who will stay there on a long-term basis. There are no roads out of Iqaluit; consequently, air medevacs perform the role of ambulances. The hospital charters aircraft out of Iqaluit. A nurse, sometimes accompanied by a doctor, flies out to the community to stabilize the patient. "Load and go" is the parlance of the team. In this area nurses are close to becoming nurse-practitioners.

Search and rescue is carried out by Iqaluit-based Emergency Measures Organization (EMO). If the hospital receives a call that someone is lost on the land, this information is turned over to the EMO. The EMO personnel retrieve the missing person and bring them to the nearest nursing station. The medevac team then flies to the nursing station and escorts the victims to the Baffin Hospital.

Some three hundred medevacs occur each year. In winter, exposure is the leading cause. Other problems include children developing severe chest infections; people getting lost on the frozen land; snowmobiles breaking down with an operator who does not have survival gear. In spring and summer, when travelers from the South swell the population, there are more patients with cardiac disorders and accident victims to care for. Often, Inuit elders wander out on the land when they are quite ill, frequently forgetting to take needed medication with them, and medevac teams retrieve these individuals. Not infrequently, overseas flights are redirected to Iqaluit when passengers become ill.

The Baffin Regional Hospital is experimenting with telemedicine and teleconferencing to link Iqaluit and the Baffin communities with Montreal. Through this exciting technique, patients can be "seen" by physicians in the south without traveling the great distances.

There is a high suicide rate on Baffin Island, particularly among the Inuit, because native culture is in transition. Traditional skills are disappearing and modern education has not yet become a high priority to the people. Currently there are no Inuit nurses or physicians in practice anywhere. The Iqaluit-based Numavut Arctic College is developing, and, in cooperation with the Baffin Regional Hospital, a culturally sensitive degree program for nurses is in progress. Health education is very much in need on Baffin Island, but innovative methods will be necessary to bring health concepts to the people in a way that will be culturally acceptable to a sensitive native people. Unfortunately, most health care at the Baffin Regional Hospital is given through interpreters—this fact itself causes difficulties and imposes limitations.

This spare but well-structured health system on Baffin Island offers the indigenous population the best health care they have ever had. Farther north toward the Pole, there are fewer and fewer indigenous people in the many islands in the Northwest Territories. Not too dissimilar health care efforts exist in Greenland, Iceland, the Scandinavian areas, and Alaska. Russia and Siberia stretching around the other half of the Arctic Circle cannot offer the indigenous people or the traveler the same quality of health care as seen in the West.

The relationship of the tourist to medical care in the Arctic is a difficult one. Near the great cities—Murmansk, Russia, and Fairbanks, Alaska, for example—modern care is available. To obtain any degree of sophisticated medical care, however, often means transfer by aircraft to a major medical center—a luxury only some can afford. On icebreakers traversing the Northern Sea Route or even through the Northwest Passage, and on those ships that are traveling about Greenland or to the North Pole, the same problems with communication and distance occur. Transportation to more sophisticated medical care can be extremely difficult, if not impossible. The similarities to conditions in the Antarctic are apparent.

MODERN MEDICINE IN THE ANTARCTIC

Unlike the situation in the Arctic, there are no indigenous people on the seventh continent. In 1903, W. S. Bruce built a meteorological station on Laurie Island in the South Orkneys. When his expedition left the following year, the British had no interest in continuing the station, so it was handed over to an Argentinian party. Since that time it has been maintained by the Argentinian government and renamed the Orcadas Scientific Station.

By the late 1940s, permanent bases had been established on subantarctic islands and a number of summer stations built on the continent, but it was only in 1954 that the first large permanently maintained base was established on the continent when Australia built its Mawson Base. The great interest in the International Geophysical Year of 1957–58 led to a marked increase in exploration, so that by the end of 1958 there were fifty bases belonging to twelve countries operating in Antarctica. Today there are well over fifty bases, and they may be classified as all-year-round, summer only, or occasional usage. Numbers vary yearly, but certainly over two thousand people inhabit bases in the summer, and approximately eight hundred in the winter months. All the bases are maintained for scientific purposes, but Argentina does have one base which is being run as a colonial settlement. Medical care is available at all of the bases. The physicians tend to be extremely well-trained, and at many bases they are well prepared for major surgery and have an extensive drug inventory as well as a good medical library. For many months each winter it is a virtual impossibility to bring in aid from the outside world or to return patients to their native countries, so this preparedness is a vital necessity.

On January 7, 1978, Emilio Marcos Palma was born at Argentina's Esperanza Base at Hope Bay. He was announced as the "first Argentine Antarctic citizen." His mother had been flown in to the station when she was seven months pregnant and prepared for the event. Other arranged births have occurred there, with a claim of citizenship in Antarctica to underscore Argentina's claim to a large slice of Antarctic territory.

Back on October 8, 1913, Solveig Gunbjörg Jacobsen was born at Grytviken Harbour on South Georgia in the Falkland Islands. Subsequently about ten more children have been born there. These subantarctic births were not "arranged," but occurred as a consequence of the established sealing and whaling community there for many years.

Although historically the medical departments of many major Antarctic bases have been extremely helpful to tourists in distress, that is not their primary function. They are maintained for the scientific communities at the bases. The staffs at the bases have done excellent medical research on problems of altitude, cold, the ozone hole, trauma, submarine medicine, and other pertinent topics. They are prepared to care for healthy young men and women, but not for the elderly with chronic disabilities. They have neither the time nor the supplies to be counted on to care for tourists or expeditioners in distress. This point of view has been openly expressed by various governments, including the United Kingdom and the United States. See chapter 4 for details on the medical departments and experiences of various countries that maintain Antarctic bases.

CHAPTER 4

Medical Capabilities at Antarctic Bases and Their Relationship to Tourism

> Throughout the whole period of the expedition—from December 2, 1911, to February 26, 1914—the health of the expedition was remarkably good. Undoubtedly Antarctica has a salubrious climate, and it is simply because one returns in a measure to the primitive that such an ideal result is obtained.
>
> The first thing to resist is the cold, and additional clothing is the first and adequate means to such an end. No one needs to be specially inured to a rigorous climate. If he has a normal circulation he immediately reacts to a new set of temperature conditions, and in a few weeks may be acclimatized. Most of the members of the expedition were Australians, so that the change of latitudes was rather abrupt but none the less stimulating and healthful.
>
> Appetite for food had suddenly a new piquancy, hard manual work was a pleasure, in a novel and wonderful environment, the intellect and imagination were quickened and the whole man embodied the *mens sana corpore sano.* That is why illness was practically unknown for more than two years: and, further, it may be said with partial truth that in the high sense of physical and mental fitness he possessed for a time, lies the explanation of the proverbial desire of an explorer to return to the ice-lands.
>
> —Dr. A. L. McLean, Chief Medical Officer, Australasian Antarctic Expedition (AAE), 1911–14

The medical staff and facilities of Antarctic bases range from minimal to large and rather sophisticated. Much can be learned by examining what countries with long Antarctic experience have done to staff and equip their polar stations and polar ships. In emergencies, they have assisted visitors to the Antarctic, but their ability to do so is severely limited.

For a fuller understanding of the mission and the capabilities of the medical support in the Antarctic, information supplied by the medical directors of four of the Antarctic programs—Australian, British, French, and American—is presented in the following section.

THE AUSTRALIAN EXPERIENCE

by Desmond J. Lugg, M.D., FAFOM, Head of Polar Medicine, Australian Antarctic Division, and Chairman, Scientific Committee on Antarctic Research (SCAR) Working Group on Human Biology and Medicine

Australian polar medical logistics

Since 1947 Australia has continuously occupied stations in the Antarctic regions. The development of health care on Australian National Antarctic Research Expeditions (ANARE) has led to a very professional remote medical service, which has lessons for Antarctic tourism.

In summer 1994–95 around 450 personnel were on Australian ships, at stations, or participating in summer field operations, and during austral winter 1995, 80 persons wintered at Casey, Davis, Mawson, and Macquarie Island. The 1994–95 season closed in April 1995 and the following season commenced in July 1995 with a winter marine science cruise studying sea ice.

As Australian stations do not have all-weather airfields, there are no permanently based aircraft capable of flying to the outside world from these stations, and no direct intercontinental flights are possible during the year from Australia. With the stations inaccessible for most of the year, a doctor accompanies each ship, station, and summer field group. The doctor must deal with any medical, surgical, or dental emergency.

Until 1963 there was no head office medical support, and medical consultants, most not conversant with ANARE equipment, personnel, and operations, were called on for advice. Since 1963 health care organization both at head office and on the expeditions has undergone progressive development, and today a very experienced polar medicine group is charged with providing a total health care service to the remote ANARE as well as conducting a program of research aimed at increasing the knowledge of human interaction with the Antarctic environment. Particular emphasis is placed on studies facilitating safe and efficient living and working in Antarctica.

The increasing standard of health care is in part a reflection of community attitudes and the expectations of the groups in Antarctica and their families at home, who consider that ANARE personnel should receive medical care equal to Australian standards. Today it is unrealistic to expect a doctor to have all the specialist skills available to most of the mainland Australian community. However, no longer can ANARE medical services be regarded as basic expedition medicine, and, despite the limitation of one doctor, there is a continuous effort to provide better health care.

Three full-time doctors are based at the head office in Hobart, although they also spend considerable time providing health care in Antarctica on summer voyages and field programs. The total complement of doctors in the program varies between seven and fourteen depending upon the time of the year. There is one branch administrator who also performs the quarantine functions.

Since the establishment of ANARE around 150 doctors have been recruited to staff both summer and winter operations. Difficulties in recruiting have occurred for many years necessitating reviews of recruiting profiles and processes. The reasons for poor recruiting are many including the availability of doctors with skills to cope with the breadth and remoteness of practice as well as isolation from families, colleagues, and continuing medical education.

Despite a policy that requires a doctor to accompany each polar group, no cancellation of a wintering has yet occurred because of the unavailability of a practitioner. The problem of recruiting has been helped by doctors doing repeat years and by women entering the Antarctic workforce. One doctor has wintered on six occasions and several others have wintered five times. In 1976 the first female doctor wintered and over thirty percent of the wintering doctors since then have been women.

Medical staff training

All expedition staff spend at least several months on general expedition as well as in specific training. As part of their orientation, personnel attend basic first-aid courses; additional medical courses are arranged for key personnel such as those going on winter tractor traverses. Manuals such as the *ANARE First Aid Manual* are designed to assist the remote populations. Four members of each winter group attend the Royal Hobart Hospital for courses in anesthetics and sterile operating theater techniques. These lay staff would be called on to assist the sole doctor should an operation be necessary.

Training is provided where appropriate for all doctors in environmental and occupational health, anesthetics, surgery, laboratory techniques, radiography and radiology, physiotherapy, medical communication, or any field that the individual feels is needed. In recent years increasing use has been made of computers, and courses are now given to assist the remote doctor to make better use of the facilities available. A station doctor can now communicate directly with the head office by satellite links and central computers.

As dentistry is a major problem despite predeparture dental checks, a two-week course at the Royal Dental Hospital of Melbourne trains doctors to carry out restorations using both low-and high-speed drills and the latest dental materials. Reviews such as that by L. D. Fletcher in 1983 and visits by a senior dentist from the Royal Dental Hospital have been particularly important in ensuring that the correct training, equipment, and dental materials are provided to deal with the problems being experienced. A report from a recent dentist's visit stated: "It is reassuring to see that the medical practitioners at Casey have at least the standard of facilities available as the Royal Dental Hospital of Melbourne where they receive their training."

It is most desirable for the maintenance of health at stations that personnel chosen are physically fit and free of disease. ANARE medical screening standards are high and everyone must pass these before they can sail. The guidelines are under constant review in order to guarantee that the latest medical advice is taken into account in framing the guidelines. Investigations include blood donor screening, chest X ray, and ECG (stress ECG for those over fifty-five years of age).

Considerable time and effort is put into screening, and the reports of examinations by doctors from the Australian Government Health Service (AGHS) are reviewed by the senior medical officer of the Antarctic Division. In general, conditions where good health depends upon medications are not acceptable. Specific conditions that are not acceptable include asthma, hypertension requiring medication, coronary artery disease, diabetes, and peptic ulcers. The guidelines and procedures have been the subject of a review by an ombudsman who found them satisfactory. Adaptability tests of personnel are performed by the Department of Defense Army Psychology Unit. In spite of all these guidelines screening can fail, as illustrated by a VIP on a summer round-trip voyage. He told the examining doctor that he had considerable experience landing from small boats onto islands off the Australian coast; in Antarctica he could not climb onto the ship and had to be lifted on board in the ship's boat.

Supplies, equipment, and communications

Once healthy staff are selected, suitable facilities in Antarctica must be provided. Opportunity was taken during the recent rebuilding of the three continental stations to upgrade the medical suites. Each suite contains a consulting room, dental and examination room, operating theater, laboratory, two-bed ward and bathroom, storeroom, and an area with a bath for treatment of hypothermia. The foyer is large and can be used for triage. The surgery is well equipped with instruments and a comprehensive inventory of pharmaceuticals and supplies. Equipment includes an X-ray machine, ECG monitor and defibrillator, anesthetic machine, pulse oximeter, electrosurgical unit, dry chemistry laboratory analyzers, dental supplies, an autoclave and gas sterilizer, and therapeutic ultrasound machine. In early 1993 the old Macquarie Island surgery was renovated and enlarged so that a dental unit and new equipment could be accommodated.

Medical kits are prepared in Hobart for the ships' surgeries and at the stations for each summer field operation. Disposable sterile equipment is a boon in Antarctica, and much can be resterilized with gas if the packaging deteriorates or if the shelf life is exceeded.

A wide range of pharmaceuticals is available and as with equipment, the selection is continually reviewed and upgraded; for example, for management of spontaneous fissures or splitting of the skin of the hands in the polar environment, also called polar

Australian physician at the well-equipped Casey station, Antarctica.

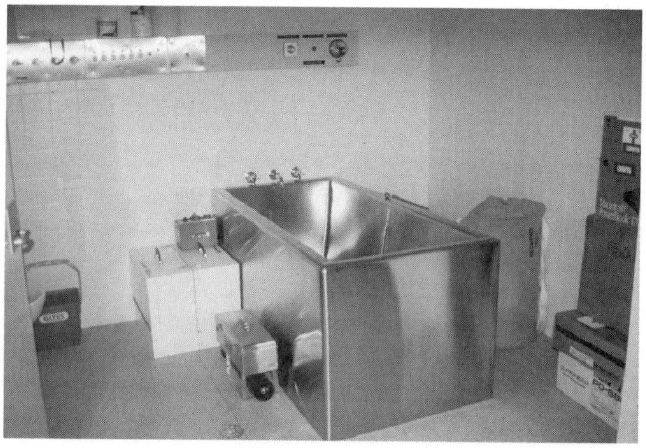

Hypothermia tank at Australian Davis station, Antarctica.

hands. A new computerized ordering system is reducing costs and creating efficiencies. However, the short shelf life of drugs continues to cause problems. Many pharmaceuticals purchased in Australia that come from overseas have little shelf life left before they are sent to Antarctica, and resupply will be at least a year away.

An excellent library is available, and each year new volumes are added to keep the references as current as possible. Through ANARESAT (the ANARE satellite communications system), doctors can access medical data banks and the World Wide Web. Determining the most efficient use of this is a continuing project.

Medical communications have always been of utmost importance. Twenty years ago radiotelephone, telex, voice radio, and facsimile were available but all were subject to the blackouts of polar cap absorption (PCA). Today, using ANARESAT allows a three-digit direct dial telephone service from the head office to any extension on any of the stations, telex, facsimile, electronic mail message, and data transfer facilities, as well as an image transfer system for sending photographs either taken on a digital camera or video camera, or scanned from a photograph taken by a conventional camera. The latter system transmits excellent images of diagnostic quality, including X rays.

By using a mobile paging system the head office doctors are always on call for their colleagues down South. The collective expertise and experience of the staff doctors is backed up by over fifty consultants in all medical specialties around Australia, many of whom have wintered in Antarctica. The Antarctic Division employs specialists as ship's doctors, who, as well as providing the health care, report on the practice of their specialty in Antarctica.

Telemedicine has been used successfully from Antarctica to Australia for decades. Treatments have been prescribed for patients thousands of kilometers away by this method. To date no malpractice suits have occurred. Such experience should prove invaluable to those using telemedicine in space. Reports of a U.S.-Soviet Telemedicine Conference in the United States in 1991 and 1992 comment on discussions on whether "physicians could be sued by patients thousands of miles away whose treatment was prescribed by satellite." It was stated that the group was told, "We'll know telemedicine 'has arrived' when we have our first malpractice suit—and we'll know telemedicine works when the first suit goes into arbitration."

Epidemiology of polar medicine

H. King has shown the value of epidemiology to polar medicine. A number of epidemiological reviews of ANARE by D. J. Lugg, P. J. Gormly, and H. King have confirmed that trauma and accidents are the most common conditions, although most of these are of a minor nature. Injuries range from abrasions, lacerations, sprains, and fractured bones to burns and multiple injuries causing death. Deaths have also resulted from drowning, hypothermia, appendicitis, cerebral hemorrhage, myocardial infarction, carbon monoxide poisoning, and perforated gastric ulcer. Cold injury is not a common occurrence. Not all the emergencies are simple as illustrated by the following serious cases: a poliomyelitis illness described by Budd in 1962, a ruptured intracranial aneurysm by Pardoe in 1965, myocardial infarction, intestinal hemorrhage by Podkolinski and Semmens in 1979, and an acute abdomen by Priddy in 1985. Other difficult cases have included carcinoma of the breast and testis, squamous cell carcinoma, ovarian cyst, fever of unknown origin, malaria, detached retina, and even a case of sarcoidosis, a rare multisystem disorder of uncertain etiology.

Psychiatric problems have not been a common feature. As a percentage of total morbidity, mental health disorders (according to the World Health Organization's International Classification of Diseases, ICD-9, 1977) are around four to five percent. With insomnia, regarded by some as endemic, and other conditions being included in the classification, it is obvious that significant psychotic and neurotic illness occurs at a frequency much lower than four percent.

In recent years doctors with ANARE have provided assistance to tourist vessels in the diagnosis and management of a number of medical conditions including acute dental problems; fractured ankle, leg, and ribs; dislocated shoulder; and cervical spine injury. In the last case the station X-ray unit was dismantled and flown to a tourist ship to aid in the diagnosis.

Although evacuations have been effected, inevitably in the summer months, the ANARE system works on the principle that the station must deal with any emergency and that evacuation is not possible. A wintering doctor must be prepared to deal with a variety of cases.

In order to quantify the occurrence of ill health in Antarctic personnel, to compare incidence rates with those of the domestic population, to assess temporal, seasonal, and occupational trends, and to identify high-risk groups, a computerized ANARE Health Register was established in 1986. As the doctor records the case in the medical log, details are coded and sent via the ANARESAT to the division's main computer.

The data from three years of operation of this register were published in 1991. In five years of operation 952 person-years from 1,800 personnel have given a total number of consultations of over 7,236 (initial consultations 4,831). Modifications have been made to the register with procedures now being recorded along with prescription of pharmaceuticals to gain a more accurate picture of case management.

It has been mandatory since the repatriation of a doctor from ANARE in 1950 for all doctors to have undergone appendectomy before leaving for Antarctica. Among staff members a case of appendicitis occurs about every second year. A study of appendicitis among staff members in polar regions by Lugg has shown that most national Antarctic groups have had a higher rate of appendicitis than is found in the countries of origin of the expeditions.

Research

From the outset many of the Australian doctors have performed research. There is a very close nexus between health care and research in the applied areas such as health and behavioral studies, nutrition, epidemiology, cardiovascular studies, thermal comfort, photobiology, and diving medicine. Research into the capacity of expeditions to resist infection has indicated that living for long periods in Antarctic isolation causes reduced skin immune responses. These studies continued in 1996 with a flow cytometer being used at the Mawson base.

Both health care and human factors research in Antarctica gains greatly from international collaboration especially within the framework of the Scientific Committee on Antarctic Research (SCAR) and between the Antarctic Division and many centers of research both in Australia and in other countries.

The use of Antarctica as an analogue for space should benefit not only people involved in polar operations but also the future explorer of space. In 1993 NASA Life Sciences Division signed a collaborative agreement with the Polar Medicine Branch of the Antarctic Division and studies on viral reactivation and behavioral adaptation are currently being performed in Antarctica.

In managing health in Antarctica the doctors must be past masters of improvisation. One scientist lost both glasses and contact lenses so new ones had to be ground out of Perspex in the station workshop, to a prescription provided by an ophthalmologist in Australia. The records show ingenuity with descriptions of teeth being manufactured out of a seal's tooth, intricate parts of equipment being fabricated, and toothpaste being manufactured. Although husky teams have been phased out, veterinary care was once an integral part of the doctor's duties.

Probably the ultimate in improvisation occurred in 1961 when the surgeon at the remote Russian base of Mirny on the remote eastern coast of the Greater Antarctic Peninsula diagnosed himself as having acute appendicitis. The doctor was the only medical practitioner for miles and miles around, so he enlisted the aid of two of his colleagues who held retractors and a mirror while he performed what is best called an autoappendectomy. The operation was a complete success. When one views the tiny operating table and the ancient instruments used under such harrowing conditions, one cannot help but have the greatest admiration for the Russian surgeon's ability and courage. Obviously, it is a plus to have had an appendectomy before wintering over in the Antarctic, and many stations now try to have two physicians on staff at all times to avoid the problem that faced the Soviet physician at Mirny.

Two Russian physicians in room where Russian physician performed autoappendectomy in 1961.

Another interesting incident occurred at the Mirny station on June 14, 1996, when the U.S. icebreaker *Nathanial B. Palmer,* anchored at the edge of the pack ice just 12 miles (19.3 kilometers) from the base and brought four tons of food and supplies. The thirty-six Russian scientists and other personnel stranded at the base were desperately short of food and supplies. Following the collapse of the Soviet Union in 1991, the support to distant Russian polar bases became a low priority. That, coupled with the great distances and the vicissitudes of weather, have made survival in the Antarctic a challenge in self-sufficiency.

Interestingly enough, between 1898 and 1922, 489 men wintered over in Antarctica and there were only 17 deaths. Accidents accounted for most of these. Today accidents are still a leading problem, but fortunately, most are minor and medical care is better.

Safety

The safety record of ANARE has been satisfactory, but the aim is to further reduce morbidity. An occupational health and safety coordinator is currently upgrading this area and assisting in bringing to ANARE the numerous new legislative changes to occupational health and safety. Continuing reviews of near-miss situations will provide further useful information to change work and recreational practices. Two such cases illustrate problems for doctors on both tourist and nontourist ships. The first, a young scout, fell into the water after disregarding advice on how to move from ship to amphibious vehicle in moderate swell, narrowly avoiding being crushed against the ship. The second jumped 7 feet (2 meters) off a vehicle to the ground, sustaining a fractured leg which necessitated round-the-clock nursing for the remainder of the voyage.

Recommendations for improvement

After thirty-three years of involvement in ANARE, I can see a number of possible changes. One is the appointment of two-doctor teams, a concept already enjoyed by a number of nations. This will improve ability to provide remote health care and will occur as a result of legal and compensation reasons. In view of the costs involved, it will be a political and not a medical decision. One only has to look at the difficult but possible scenario of an obstructed labor, with the sole medical practitioner anesthetizing, performing a lower segment Caesarean section, resuscitating the baby, and dealing with the expectations of the spouse and the confined isolated group, to see how precarious our remote health care really is.

Despite such forebodings ANARE's medical group continues to build on its tradition and provide the best health care service it can within current staffing and funding in the remote environment in which the scientists and support staff work.

From the ANARE experience there are lessons for the medical management of Antarctic tourism. Although the ANARE population (selected, screened, highly motivated, age range twenty to sixty-five, mean age thirty to forty, predominantly male, in excellent health) is no more representative of an average population than a tourist group is, and since the length of stay in Antarctica is much longer than that of tourists, virtually any medical condition can arise. No polar-specific disease has been found in Antarctica, but accidents can occur at any time.

First and foremost a basic standard for tourist medical services should be drawn up by IAATO. This should be based on epidemiological data, experiences of operators and support given by agencies such as ANARE, populations traveling, and length of time and ability to evacuate seriously ill patients. The basic standard should define surgery, equipment, pharmaceuticals, and support for the doctor. The desired skills and experience of the doctor are of great importance, including the fact he or she must be a "super generalist." Each tourist group should be lectured on safety and survival issues both before and during the trip.

A medical infrastructure, such as that described, is most important for the isolated doctor, as this gives excellent backup for a telemedicine capability; the only other necessity is a satellite phone link. There is no need for video links as X ray and medical pictures can be transmitted relatively cheaply on a basic phone link.

Another important consideration is to decide what level of predeparture screening is necessary. This should be somewhere between the current practice of *doing nothing* and *requiring a stress ECG for those over forty years old,* as recommended by one operator. The ethical considerations of a nonmedical tourist leader having medical reports on his charges must be questioned. Medical defense and potential litigation are also areas needing clarification. Included in this issue is the question of blood transfusion, the feasibility of using a *walking* donor blood bank, the safety issues of transmission of viruses, and the laboratory matching requirements. Medical evacuation is possible from some geographical areas but is very expensive and this concern must be considered.

Based on the long experience of polar medicine, tourist operators can take heart from the sentiments of the doctors of the heroic era. Jones in 1915 started his report of Mawson's Western Base Group by saying: "There was a very marked absence of serious illness during the whole period of our stay," and McLean in the same year at the Main Base opens his account with "Throughout the whole period of the expedition, the health of the expeditioners was remarkably good." Tourist operators, however, should be mindful of the emphasis by Macklin in 1922 that selection of healthy people for expeditions in polar regions was most desirable. Macklin suggested that the chief work of the doctor was done before the ship left England.

THE BRITISH EXPERIENCE

by Dr. Alan H. Milne, Senior Medical Advisor, British Antarctic Survey Medical Unit

Apsley Cherry-Garrard, who accompanied Captain Robert Falcon Scott of the Royal Navy on his 1910–13 expedition, observed, "Polar exploration is at once the cleanest and most isolated way of having a bad time which has been devised."

Antarctica is the ice-covered landmass lying over the South Pole. Of the seven continents, the Antarctic is the coldest, windiest, highest, driest, and least accessible. Ice covers more than 99 percent of Antarctica's 5,405,400 miles (14,000,000 square kilometers) with an average thickness of .93 miles (1½ kilometers). There is no indigenous population.

For over forty years, Britain has conducted a scientific research program in Antarctica. The program is based on long-term studies of earth, atmospheric, and life sciences. The survey's purpose is scientific endeavor (with minimum environmental impact) based on a multidisciplinary research strategy to take its program into the next century. Studies include those having vital global significance, for example, continuing and developing research on atmospheric ozone depletion.

For this work, the survey maintains five stations, at coastal sites, throughout the year, from one of which extensive field parties are mounted. Usually, there are sixty to seventy wintering personnel. This number is increased to over two hundred during the summer months. The operation is supported by the survey vessels, the royal research ships *Bransfield* and *James Clark Ross,* four twin-engined Otter and one Dash 7 aircraft, snow tractors, and snowmobiles.

Home is the place of work, and that place is a ship, base, or field camp, all remote, and frequently subjected to inclement conditions. The work can be stressful and tiring. It can be monotonous. There can be emergencies. Physically and mentally demanding responses may be required. There is isolation from family. There is lack of privacy. Manual work includes moving cargo, travel over rough country, and heavy physical work in the field. Agility is important, for example, getting in and out of inflatables and small boats in lively conditions alongside the ship and shore, or climbing free-hanging rope ladders. Work includes periods of intense activity, for example, annual base relief on a twenty-four-hour shift basis.

Year-round work on base includes general husbandry, scientific work, and diving. There is an appropriate balance of scientific and support staff. Each year, approximately half the station complement is replaced. The vital continuity of experience and expertise is promoted through those who remain for a second year to complete their Antarctic tour.

Field work, sometimes lasting for many weeks, requires a self-contained unit of snowmobile, sledge and tent, food and clothing, scientific and personal gear, radio for communication, and medical equipment. Travel may be across sea ice and glaciers. Field parties may meet with very wild climatic conditions.

Specific hazards that may be encountered include trauma, local and general cold injury, snow blindness, carbon monoxide poisoning, and disorders caused by altitude and diving. The risk from environmental dangers is minimized by thorough preventative measures.

British Antarctic Survey personnel are on a tour of duty for up to two and a half years, with periods of inaccessibility to hospitals of twelve months or more. Both survey ships and the four larger bases have a doctor on complement, with medical backup advice available from the United Kingdom.

The prevailing conditions are such that medical evacuation may be precluded either by air or sea for several months, and even from the time of evacuation there may be considerable time before specialist medical care is available. The exacerbation of a medical disorder, or the sustaining of an injury in addition to a current medical condition, might have serious consequences.

The approach to care is broadly defined as embracing, in an integrated system, these nine essential elements: pre-Antarctic service medical screening, recruitment of doctors, doctors' medical and research preparation, medical training for nonmedical personnel, twenty-four-hour emergency and less urgent cover for advice as well as routine communications, medical supplies, environmental and occupational health, research, and overall coordination.

Consideration of each follows:

Pre-Antarctic service medical screening

Robust physical and mental health is needed for the prolonged, isolated Antarctic tour. The screening prior to departure for the South seeks to establish a view on medical fitness with a particular focus on

1. The health and safety of the individual and of his or her companions.
2. Ability to perform the appointed tasks.
3. The impact on individual and operations if, for example, medical evacuation is required for a possible foreseeable condition.
4. The risk of adverse effects on the efficiency and well-being of the small remote community.
5. Minimizing the difficulty for the survey in exercising its responsibility for the overall care of its employees.

The medical examination comprises

1. Current and past medical history by discussion with the examining doctor with reference to the examinee's completed questionnaire.
2. Physical examination.
3. The following laboratory tests:
   - dipstick urinalysis
   - blood grouping with tests for hepatitis B and C, syphilis, and HIV, conducted with the examinee's informed consent following modified pre-HIV testing counseling. All who journey South may be required to either donate or receive blood.
   - testing for tuberculosis for those scheduled to over-winter.
   - audiometry for specific occupational groups.
   - resting electrocardiogram if aged 35 or over.
   - further tests at the discretion of the examining doctor.
   - additional tests to comply with the U.K. statutory requirements relating to examinations of seafarers, pilots, and divers.

Every effort is made to permit the time and opportunity for clarification of any doubt regarding medical fitness, for example, a report from family doctor, a specialist referral for assessment, or a correction of a disorder.

The survey practices the "philosophy" of consideration on medical fitness advice being based on individual circumstances. Certain disorders, listed as part of the BAS policy on medical screening, are viewed as incompatible with Antarctic service. However, there is seldom automatic rejection based on diagnostic categories (for example, diabetes or asthma) or foreseeable medical problems from past or current medical history. Such rejection would be easy, and it would give strong protection against potential occasional major distress and upheaval, but it would be at the price of denying good service to BAS.

Asthma is a not-uncommon example of each case being assessed on its own merits. The individual with severe asthma, possibly with cold-induced exacerbation, possibly with a history of urgent hospitalizations, or whose approach to asthma control was considered irresponsible, would be viewed unequivocally as medically unfit for Antarctic service. The individual who has a mild allergy and infrequent episodes of asthma restricted to times of high pollen levels, and who would readily and certainly be self-treated and not require emergency care, has been considered fit for service. Similarly, personnel with foreseeable, but carefully assessed, medical conditions have served in the Antarctic successfully and uneventfully.

The fallibilities in the "individual circumstances" approach are twofold. First, medicine is not an exact science, and there is at least an element of lack of precision and certainty in forecasting the course of illness—even with careful, experienced deliberation by a specialist. Second, and limited to certain conditions (diabetes, for example), is the impact that an intercurrent illness or injury might have on that condition. These points notwithstanding, BAS continues not to drop a portcullis of preclusion against diagnostic headings in its approach to medical advice and executive decision on fitness.

4. Dental examination and correction as necessary

5. Immunizations

6. Advice concerning, for example, current prescription for spectacles and provision of spare pairs

Recruitment of doctors

Successful recruitment (of all personnel) has been, and remains, fundamental to the achievements of BAS and to the fulfillment of those who serve with the survey.

The essential elements in BAS selection are

- the advertising of posts and provision of information to prospective candidates.
- a detailed and searching application form.
- professional and character references.
- an interview, which is the most important component. This consists of a one-hour meeting of each individual candidate with a board, including the chairman, and which can draw on general and specific expertise appropriate to the occasion. The interview has three aims. First, to enable a confident decision to be made on a candidate's professional and personal suitability; second, to ensure that the candidate has the necessary understanding on which to base a decision should he or she be offered appointment; and third, to ensure that the candidate has had a good and fair hearing.
- medical screening (as discussed earlier).
- postselection evaluation.

Shackleton rationalized his approach to recruitment as follows: "The qualities . . . necessary to the explorer are . . . in . . . order of importance: first, optimism; second, patience; third, physical endurance; fourth, idealism; fifth and last, courage. . . . Few men are wanting in courage, but optimism nullifies disappointment and makes one more ready than ever to go on. . . . Impatience means disaster. . . . Physical endurance . . . will not compensate for the first two moral or temperamental qualities."

Though Shackleton's list of qualities still holds for those who undertake the Antarctic journey, the emphasis of present-day BAS recruitment relates more to the member of a research station than to the explorer.

To the desirable qualities identified already, we would add those of motivation, self-reliance, and leadership without ostentation. Supreme motivation could be presumed of everyone who responded, however tentatively, to Shackleton's supposed newspaper advertisement:

"Men wanted for Hazardous Journey. Small wages, bitter cold, long months of complete darkness, constant danger, safe return doubtful. Honor and recognition in case of success." The terms and conditions offered by BAS are arguably less stark!

The BAS selection process is directed predominantly at evaluating skill for the appointed job, and, of equal importance, suitability of personality to be a convivial living companion for a long period on a remote isolated Antarctic station.

Determining that a doctor is suitably skilled is relatively straightforward. Examination of his or her qualifications, consideration of individual work experience, and the opportunity to explore further at an interview give means of accurate assessment.

The professional background of doctors appointed with the survey ranges widely from those who have just begun to practice to those who have well-established practices in several disciplines, for example, surgery and anesthesia. Perhaps the "ideal" of experience for the Antarctic is that afforded by completion of vocational training for general practice, with its several hospital posts—including the very valuable term in accident and emergency—and the knowledge gained over a year from the day-to-day practice of a family doctor.

Assessing suitability of personality is less straightforward: By their natures and activities, the ships and Antarctic stations do not lend themselves to solitary individual existence. The prolonged, inevitable, near-constant contact with one's companions, initially strangers with differing backgrounds, experience, interests, and age, is one of the most rewarding aspects of an Antarctic tour, yet also one of the most exacting. Tolerance and good opinion of oneself and others, linked with sensitivity and humor, will overcome potential difficulties. Carrying out one's share of tasks and an uncomplaining willingness to do more at times, acceptance of others' foibles and a recognition of one's own, responsible observance of discipline and good manners all contribute substantially to strong morale.

The average age of wintering personnel is in the mid-twenties—a lengthy absence from home is more readily undertaken, personally and professionally, by the young. In addition, the scientific studies involved permit postgraduate opportunities more appropriate to the earlier career days. Recruitment of those over thirty-five should be approached with great caution, if only because of the possible relative social isolation occasioned by the distancing from age-related commonalties. Caution is also warranted regarding over-wintering of married personnel. Experience has shown that prolonged Antarctic absence can break the marital bond.

The doctor, because of the time required to gain qualification and experience, is usually one of the older base members. By nature of professional position and an extra few years possibly gaining some wisdom, the doctor can be placed to unobtrusively but effectively be a considerable force in husbanding well the sometimes-threatened goodwill within the group.

Complementary to survey policy is the wish that the individual will find the Antarctic tour fulfilling and carrying enduringly happy memories: "We were all of us awed by what we saw and heard beyond common experience of man." The Antarctic is an inspiring, though unforgiving, land. Ultimately, though, the success of a venture and the enjoyment and fulfillment comes from individuals and what they are and what they take South with them.

The recruitment policy strives, therefore, to appoint those who have a strong personal quality as well as job capability.

Doctors' medical preparation

There are five major components of the medical program:

1. Preparation for an effective role in what are usually specialist fields: general anesthesia, radiography and processing, dentistry, blood transfusion, physiotherapy, surgery, obstetrics and gynecology, and diving medicine
2. Emphasis on emergency care by attending advanced trauma and cardiac life support courses and briefing in the major accident plan for the ships and bases
3. Confirmation of first-aid knowledge and training to hold classes in it and other medical topics for colleagues on ships and bases
4. Familiarization with duties, procedures, and documentation, for example, routine and emergency communications
5. Opportunity, with reference to individual professional background, to gain experience in other specialties such as accident and emergency; ear, nose, and throat; and dermatology, principally by attending outpatient departments and tutorials

All training of doctors and nonmedical staff is linked with the medical equipment available in the Antarctic.

Research

Medicine and research are complementary. The research is designed largely to identify ways to improve health and safety in the Antarctic. The results have practical significance not only for BAS personnel but also for those who live and work in other remote locations.

The current main research programs undertaken by the station doctors are the following:

1. Medical: All consultations on bases and ships are entered into a computerized database. Subsequent analysis determines the nature of medical events and how they are dealt with. This information is used in the development of medical training programs, in determining any requirement for changes in the standards of fitness for Antarctic service, and in guiding judgments on the nature and quantities of equipment and drugs that need to be provided. The effects of environmental factors and diet on general health are also examined using the database, and measurements of individual exposures to UV light are correlated to ozone levels in the atmosphere.

   A good example of research strengthening the health care system is the medical assessment questionnaire (MAQ). The questionnaire was developed by the BAS Medical Unit in the early nineties during two years of trials in Antarctica, the North Sea, and the United

Kingdom. It was designed to communicate concise and accurate information on the features of illness from a nonmedical person to a doctor. It has now been incorporated into the field medical box to be used if there is illness within a group in the field, possibly located some hundreds of miles from the base.

2. Physiological: Our environment contains rigid time signals or zeitgebers. For biochemical synchronization, man needs a periodically changing environment that provides sufficiently powerful zeitgebers to keep circadian rhythms optimal.

The zeitgebers of environmental light and dark influence the extent of secretion of the pineal hormone melatonin (light suppressor), which affects performance, mood, and sleep. In the Antarctic there is prolonged darkness in the winter and prolonged light in the summer. The studies examine performance, mood, and sleep in relation to melatonin secretion and the influence of light and dark, including exposure to artificial light. This work has considerable significance in relation to circadian rhythms and to the understanding and management of seasonal affective disorder.

3. Bacteriological: The availability of small groups of healthy subjects in a "closed community" for long periods on Antarctic bases presents a unique opportunity for the detailed study of the normal human bacteriological flora and associated immune responses.

On return from the Antarctic, a period of up to nine months is made available to the doctor for analysis and preparation for publication of the research work undertaken in the South. Satisfactory completion by the doctor of the medical component of service and a research dissertation affords the opportunity of gaining the Master of Science in remote health care (polar option) conferred by the Robert Gordon University in Aberdeen.

Medical training for nonmedical personnel

A medical preparation course is held in the United Kingdom for all expeditioners as part of their general preparation for Antarctic service. The three main themes of the course are

- first-aid knowledge and skills, with a marked emphasis on practical sessions including scenarios
- topics of particular relevance to the Antarctic, for example, general and local cold injury and carbon monoxide poisoning
- lifestyle issues as part of a wider health promotion program to prepare new appointees for a social environment of which they have little or no experience

Similar courses, in modular form, are held by the medical officers for the crews onboard the two survey ships during Antarctic deployment. Every effort is made for all personnel serving overseas with the survey to receive this training and to follow it with regular refresher courses to the same standard either during the Antarctic tour or in the United Kingdom.

More advanced or specialized training, with the prerequisite of having attended the basic course, is arranged for the following individuals and groups:

- Those at a location distant from qualified medical help or involved in potentially hazardous work, for example, construction. This training entails aspects of taking medical history and clinical examination, and invasive skills: use of airway devices, establishing and maintaining an intravenous infusion. This "paramedic" form of training is undertaken in the United Kingdom before the Antarctic tour, and involves classroom theory and practical sessions and attendance at the accident and emergency department of a major hospital and with a city ambulance service.
- Members of field parties must be thoroughly familiar with the contents of their field medical box. For example, they need to know the indications, dosages, and administration of medicines carried, basic dentistry, suturing, and use of the M.A.Q. These aspects are addressed in training by the base doctor.
- The diving community receives guidance in diving medicine, considered essential to the knowledge and skill available to the year-round diving program in the Antarctic. Appropriate training is also given those who undertake the relatively rare excursions to altitudes at which the mountain sickness disorders may occur. These training programs are held in the United Kingdom and in the Antarctic.
- Two or three members of both ships' crews and each base are trained in the South to be assistant to the doctor in procedures such as operations (use of autoclave, scrubbing-up, opening sterile packs) and prolonged nursing. These individuals deputize medically in the doctor's absence and are available if the doctor is the patient.

The above programs all use the BAS medical handbook written specifically for survey personnel.

Further documentation, course programs, slides, videos, resuscitation mannequins, and other training aids are held on the ships and bases.

Cover for advice

There are satellite communications between the ships and bases and BAS headquarters in Cambridge and the medical unit in Aberdeen. Facsimile and telephone contact between an Antarctic location and the United Kingdom are used.

Routine medical (when queries may be raised from the Antarctic) and research messages are exchanged monthly, and an end-of-year report is prepared.

Twenty-four-hour cover for advice for emergency events is available from the medical unit through primary and back-up routes. The medical unit has access to specialists in all disciplines.

Medical supplies

The ships and bases have well-equipped surgeries. The facilities include resuscitation trolleys; X-ray, anesthetic, surgical, and dental equipment; electrocardiograph; and defibrillator. An emergency "grab bag" is stocked from the annually revised and replenished medical supplies.

One of the ships has a more comprehensive dental capability used by the survey's dental surgeon who is aboard for the duration of deployment.

To allow for the surgery being overcome by catastrophe such as a fire, a comprehensive medical case and burns box are stored well away from the main base complex.

Sets of equipment are provided for a major accident with several casualties. They are designed principally to care for those sustaining high-velocity impact trauma and burns. Emphasis is placed, therefore, on initial triage and capability to look after airway and cervical spine, breathing and ventilation with oxygenation, correction of hypovolemia (loss of body fluids), and analgesia.

The field medical box (FMB) is designed for two people for three months. Two "immediate aid packs" (IAP) are part of this box. The IAP, of which the key components are dressings and morphine for injections, is carried by all individuals in the field at all times. The aircraft and refuge huts and ship's galley hold emergency medical stores similar to those composing the FMB. The medical supplies are related to the training programs, an example of the value of an integrated approach to care.

On-site practice by simulating a major accident, for example, is crucial to effective responses should they ever be required.

Environmental and occupational health

The survey has a health and safety officer who is engaged in ensuring good practices under the U.K. regulations for "Control of Substances Hazardous to Health." The medical unit liaises with the health and safety officer, and is involved in areas such as clothing, rations, food hygiene, water supplies, heating, lighting, and ventilation of accommodation wings, audiometric programs, and sewage and waste disposal.

Overall coordination

This element of the medical care program includes policy, procedures, and development. Examples include

- annual review of medical supplies
- development of health promotion
- assessment of items of equipment

Cautionary note

It is certainly good to wish to experience the grandeur of the Antarctic, however, there must be provision to venture safely to and operate safely in this extreme, remote, savage, and unforgiving land. There are no alert, rescue, or health services in the Antarctic. A disaster there must be handled with no expectation of direct help from another party. This imposes a most heavy responsibility on national Antarctic operators (who, of necessity, provision only for their own endeavors), and, in the private sector, on shipowners, tourist organizations, and individuals.

It could be suggested that medical provision be along lines similar to those that are operational within the BAS. Obligations, though, are far from being limited to medical considerations. In all areas of Antarctic undertakings, the duty of care embraces the need for skilled and experienced personnel working with safe and high-quality equipment. For shipboard activities, for example, everything from accurate hydrographic charts to meticulously maintained and provisioned enclosed lifeboats should be available.

It would be woefully negligent for a private venture to assume that it could rely on the support of a national operator. Even if the vast distances of the Antarctic permitted help from the latter, instinctive humanitarian compulsion could very forseeably result in great risk, for example, venturing beyond the defined limits of safe travel in boats inadequate for the purpose.

It behooves all who travel to the Antarctic to be well prepared, and preparation in this case includes the availability of support contingencies in the event of emergencies.

THE FRENCH EXPERIENCE

by Dr. Claude Bachelard,
Chief Medical Officer of T.A.A.F. Health Department

Expeditions and travel toward the polar regions are increasing significantly. Tourism is the main contributor to this phenomenon. As the tourist population is potentially more exposed to sickness and injury than others because of their age and lack of fitness, it is necessary to improve the medical care in a way adapted to this specific situation. The following questions could be raised: Which physician and what medical equipment are needed on board vessels traveling or touring in the polar environment?

The following sections detail some very pragmatic and practical answers recently given to this question when designing, building, and preparing to run a new polar ship, the *Marion Dufresne II;* this new ship carries up to thirty-six tourists.

French polar agencies and ships

Terres Australes et Antarctiques Françaises (T.A.A.F.) and Institut Français pour la Recherche et Technologie Polaires (I.F.R.T.P.), the French polar agencies, have been consistently running logistical and scientific activities in four stations for more than forty years.

These stations are science oriented. Three of them are located in the southern Indian Ocean (Kerguelen, Amsterdam, Crozet); the fourth one, Dumont d'Urville, is on the coast of the Antarctic continent facing Tasmania (Australia). All the logistics of these stations rely on sea transportation using two ships. The first, a small icebreaker, the *Astrolabe,* sails between Tasmania and Dumont d'Urville during the Austral summer time (three months). This ship transports expeditioners, equipment, and supplies in about six days. There are up to sixty-five people on board.

The other ship, the *Marion Dufresne,* is used to link La Réunion island with the French subantarctic islands of, Kerguelen, Saint Paul and Amsterdam, and Crozet. This trip is about three weeks long. *Marion Dufresne* is a multipurpose ship transporting cargo, motor-fuel, expeditioners, and now tourists to these attractive regions. She is also used as a powerful oceanographic ship, mainly exploring the southern Indian Ocean. Up to 150 persons can live and work on board. The *Marion Dufresne II* replaced the old *Marion Dufresne I* in 1995.

Epidemiology on board French polar ships

Both of these ships are medically equipped. The *Astrolabe* has an infirmary. As she only sails short periods and transports few personnel, the medical staff is not permanent (the captain is in charge of medicine when there is no doctor on board). On board the *Marion Dufresne* sailing on longer voyages and with more people, there is consistently at least one doctor running a small "hospital."

The medical activity on board these two ships can be summarized as follows: As a mean, 2.4 consultations have been performed each day for a hundred persons exposed (300 days a year).

Most of the consultations were resolved by the nurse as they were without really serious medical problems. Major illness and serious injury (inducing hospitalization) is rare (0.6%); 0.05% cases required ship rerouting to a fully equipped medical center. One medical case (0.01%) justified surgery on board under general anesthesia. Illnesses, diseases, and injuries that occurred from 1980 to 1994 are presented in the following tables. The first table on page 42 shows the percentage for each medical category. Trauma (21%) is the most frequent. Skin (12%), respiratory (12%), and gastrointestinal (10%) problems are next. Cardiovascular manifestations are rare.

The second table shows that the frequency of medical (34) and surgical (31) problems is not significantly different. Acute sciatica (10) and urinary calculi (8) have been frequent medical major disorders; hand trauma (11) and appendicitis (5) have been the main surgical difficulties. One person disappeared and has been considered as "lost at sea."

The experience gained with these two ships allows us to establish some general guidelines on how to organize medicine on board vessels sailing in polar regions. These guidelines were used in the conception of the *Marion Dufresne II* medical organization.

Physicians and hospital on board the *Marion Dufresne II*

French law defines how the different types of vessels registrated in France have to be medically organized by describing the infirmary, specifying the type and number of medical personnel, and listing the medical equipment needed. However, these requirements had to be complemented according to experience related to the specific risks in polar regions: remoteness, polar climate, and activities.

The general target has been to reach a medical self-sufficiency allowing the facility to handle a usual general practice, effectively treat most major illness and trauma, and preserve the life of any patient long enough to reach a fully equipped medical center (about ten days).

The "hospital" was equipped so that the care limiting factor would be more related to medical personnel capability than to available medical equipment (as the physician's professional skill can vary greatly).

As tourists (often old people) were going to be involved in the travel an increase of cardiovascular and chronic illness was anticipated.

EPIDEMIOLOGY ON BOARD VESSELS (ILLNESSES, DISEASES, AND INJURIES, 1980–94)

Category	*Percent of Total*
Infectious	8
Psychoneurosis	4
Nervous and sense organs	8
Cardiovascular	1
Gastrointestinal	10
Skin	12
Respiratory	12
Dental	4
Musculoskeletal	9
Genitourinary	7
Trauma	21
Ill-defined conditions	4

MAJOR PATHOLOGY (INDUCING HOSPITALIZATION)

Medical (34)	*Surgical (31)*
Acute sciatica (10)	Hand trauma (11)
Urinary calculus (8)	Appendicitis (5)* × 2
Peptic ulcer (4)	Polytrauma (3)
Coronary disease (3)*	Broken ankle (2)
Epilepsy (2)	Chest trauma (2)
Pneumonia (2)	Skull trauma (2)*
Malaria attack (2)	Burn (2)
Diabetes melitus (1)	Ocular foreign body (2)
Tuberculosis (1)	Rectal foreign body (1)*
Asthma (1)	Strangulated hernia (1)

** Four surgical problems and one medical problem, considered critical, caused the rerouting of the ships as the conditions were hardly manageable on board.*

The *Marion Dufresne II* is fully staffed medically except on transit travels where only crew is on board. As this ship is permanently chartered by T.A.A.F., French law permits the use of T.A.A.F. medical mission doctors. They can be the expedition doctors traveling to or from the French stations or specially recruited physicians. The required level of medical skill is that of general practitioners specially trained (surgery, anesthesia, dental practice, remote medicine) or surgeons or emergency medicine specialists. On board the physicians are required to train the ship's officers to be potential medical assistants.

The "hospital" was designed with an emphasis on several issues. The location where it would be built had to have easy access for use of stretchers, it had to be quiet, and it could not be too sensitive to the movement of the vessel. The space allocated had to allow diverse care in a multipurpose room, hospitalization (three rooms), a doctor's cabin, and a great deal of storage space. In addition, the facility had to allow for easy maintenance.

Medical Equipment

Medical equipment acquired for the hospital had to be easy to use, safe, reliable, robust, easy to maintain and manage, and easy to store and trim.

In the first stage this mini "hospital" was equipped with all that is needed to perform general practice in a remote environment:

1. First aid
   - first-aid kits
   - splints
   - stretchers
2. Diagnosis
   - all clinical examination and diagnosis equipment
   - ECG machine
   - simple biological sets (mini hematocrit, paper reagent strips for performing blood and urine chemistry, pregnancy test, and microscope); blood group tests
   - small medical library
   - X-ray machine with processing equipment
3. Care
   - large pharmacy (disinfectants, drugs)
   - bandages and dressings
   - minor surgery instruments and sutures
   - temporary conservative dental care instruments
4. Hygiene
   - washing
   - sterilization
5. Administration and management
   - desk
   - computer
   - medical registers

Remote medical equipment

Remote practice requires an adequate self-sufficiency in surgery, anesthesia, resuscitation, monitoring, hospitalization capacity, and medical communications to cope with various critical problems. The following list includes some vital equipment.

1. Surgery
   - operating table
   - light

- surgical instruments
- suction unit
- full range of surgical instruments
- pneumatical tourniquet

2. Anesthesia, resuscitation, monitoring
   - local and general anesthetic equipments
   - respirator
   - medical gas (O_2, N_2O)
   - monitoring unit: cardioscope, defibrillator, SO_2, core temperature
3. Hospitalization
   - beds
   - bath
   - accessories
4. Medical communications
   - radio communication (voice and fax) with medical advisory nets using INMARSAT

In the interest of preparing tourists for the possible risks of Antarctic travel, the following information and a medical examination form are given to all tourists going to Antarctica with French tour companies.

TOURISM AND HEALTH

A trip in Terres Australes et Antarctiques Françaises Territory does not necessarily face you with a dangerous, hostile environment producing taking of excessive risk.

However, you are requested to consider health and medicine in this context with careful reflection. All visitors to Terres Australes et Antarctiques Françaises must be in good physical condition and free from any disability which could impede their health or restrict their activities when faced with rough transportation and disembarking conditions, as with harsh weather (low temperatures and strong wind).

It should be noted that T.A.A.F. medical facilities are necessarily limited (one physician running the infirmary) and evacuations are not easy to perform and often cannot be accomplished rapidly. Therefore, it is important that all visitors to T.A.A.F. be screened medically to prevent exacerbation of pre-existing conditions.

In consequence, would you be so kind as to undergo the required medical examinations and send the forms back to:

Service Medical T.A.A.F.
34, rue des Renaudes
75017 Paris (France)

Please keep a copy with you to be given to the doctor on board the ship.

Persons currently under medical treatment must bring enough medicine for the duration of the trip.

THE UNITED STATES EXPERIENCE

by Harry Mahar, Ph.D., Safety and Health Officer, Office of Polar Programs, National Science Foundation

The National Science Foundation (NSF) as overall manager of U.S. activities in Antarctica oversees the operation of three year-round research stations, numerous seasonal field camps, and two ice-strengthened research vessels in the Antarctic. Each year, approximately twenty-five hundred persons work in Antarctica under the auspices of the NSF's United States Antarctic Program (USAP), the majority spending up to five months there during the austral summer season (October to February), while a few (approximately three hundred) spend the entire year there. Although there are geopolitical reasons for maintaining a U.S. presence in Antarctica, the primary reason is to conduct research on worldwide and regional problems of scientific and social importance and to expand fundamental knowledge of the region, a research commitment that grew from the success of the 1957–1958 International Geophysical Year (IGY) exploration of Antarctica.

Since Antarctica has no indigenous human population and is physically remote from other inhabited areas of the world, all life-support functions must be provided to the seasonal and year-round (that is, "winter-over") staff. All personnel, equipment, materiel, and supplies are transported via ship or aircraft to the primary continental logistics base, McMurdo Station, or via ship to Palmer Station on the Antarctic Peninsula. Because of the harsh environment, access to these stations is limited and may involve complete physical isolation from the rest of the world for up to eight months of the year.

While in Antarctica, all USAP personnel in need of routine or emergent medical care have access to medical clinics at each of the three year-round stations. The size and capabilities of each of these clinics have evolved over the approximately forty-year history of the program to meet the needs of the USAP research activities in the region in a cost-effective manner. The medical care system is one component of an integrated approach to ensuring the health and safety of USAP participants while in Antarctica; other components include an aggressive prevention program geared to minimizing accidents and injuries, a public health component focusing on preventive care and sanitation issues, and a training and educational component.

The lessons learned by USAP in providing for the health and well-being of USAP participants in such a challenging and isolated environment may have utility for commercial tour operators and leaders of private expeditions in the planning and execution of trips to polar regions where commercial medical care is unavailable. In such instances, it is imperative that sponsors of such tours or expeditions develop a self-sufficient approach to their activities.

Provision for medical care

The capabilities of the USAP medical system are designed around the demographics of the population served and based on the historical trends in care. The population served tends to be relatively young adults: 85 percent of the staff is between the ages of twenty and forty-five and 30 percent are female. Since all USAP participants must meet certain medical and dental screening criteria before deploying, the population is healthy to begin with. As a result, the demands on the medical care system are relatively modest, when compared to other similar size, but unscreened, groups, and the capabilities of the clinics are toward emergent care rather than treatment of chronic disease conditions.

Diagnostic and treatment capabilities at each of the clinics are limited because of the absence of sophisticated support services typically found in a hospital environment (for example, full-range clinical laboratory services, intensive-care units), but on-site diagnostic capabilities are augmented with advanced telecommunications/telemedicine to tertiary care providers located in the United States. None of the clinics currently have major surgical capabilities. In those situations where the medical care needs of the patient exceed the on-site capabilities of the clinic, the patient is stabilized and transported to a tertiary care facility in New Zealand, South America, or the United States.

The medical clinics at each of the three year-round stations are staffed by physicians, with additional health care providers at McMurdo Station, the largest of the three stations and the logistics hub of the program. The physician selection process focuses on internal medicine and emergency care specialties. Prior to deployment to Antarctica, physicians are provided with additional training in areas where they may not be experienced but would be expected to provide a needed service (for example, emergency dental procedures).

Clinic caseload summaries over the past five years indicate that approximately two-thirds of patient visits have been for routine illnesses or infections (upper respiratory tract infections, gastroenteritis, dermatitis), and the remaining one-third for accidental injuries (fractures, soft-tissue trauma, sprains/strains). On average, one or two emergency medical evacuations have been required per year, while a larger number of non-time-critical evacuations (about eighteen per year) have been provided where situations warranted (for example, for, diagnostic consults and orthopedic evaluations). These data are consistent with the experiences of other groups or analog populations, where small parties of medically screened individuals operate in isolated environments (oceanographic research vessels, military submarines). It is not expected that these trends would be representative of an unscreened population of similar demographics.

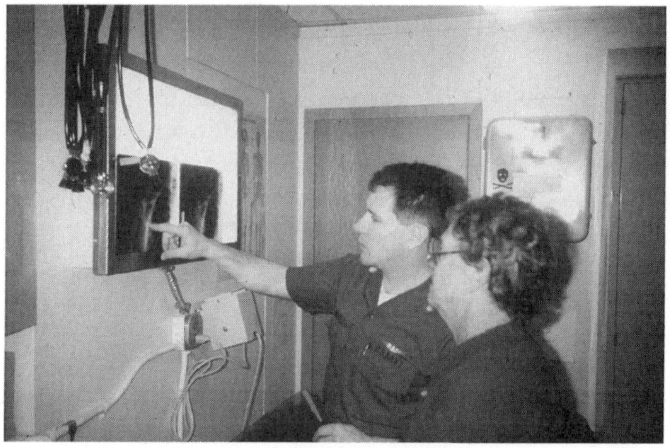

U.S. Navy physician at McMurdo station giving emergency consultation to tourist.

Complementary health and safety programs

The USAP relies on a number of prevention strategies to minimize the need for medical interventions in Antarctica. As indicated previously, approximately one-third of the medical clinic workload results from accidents or injuries which no amount of predeployment medical screening can eliminate. Training and inspection programs focusing on occupational hazards have reduced the number of job-related injuries requiring medical attention in the clinic. Since approximately 20 to 25 percent of injuries are associated with recreational pursuits (sprained ankles, fractures, etc.), awareness programs have been developed to inform sports enthusiasts of those risks. All USAP participants are briefed on proper cold weather precautions and are issued cold weather clothing appropriate for their work site. The effectiveness of this program can be demonstrated in the clinic statistics—less than a half dozen cold-related injuries are reported each year (typically minor frostbite injuries).

There are several preventive health programs intended to reduce the frequency or severity of respiratory or gastroenterologic illnesses, which represent approximately 60 percent of the current non–injury-related clinic workload. Monitoring programs for potable water systems and food-handling facilities (at the permanent station and seasonal field camps) ensure that those systems meet appropriate health and sanitation standards. Immunization and intervention programs for common respiratory illnesses (for example, influenza) have been attempted, but with limited success to date.

USAP participants are briefed on proper safety procedures around aircraft or boats, and those groups venturing into remote field locations must be properly trained in mountaineering/survival techniques before they depart from the station; once deployed, their status is monitored during the daily radio check. Flight following of all USAP aviation activities ensures that any overdue aircraft are promptly reported and search-and-rescue initiated in a timely manner.

Points to consider for Antarctic tour operators and expedition leaders

As tour operators and expedition leaders plan trips to the Antarctic region, there are lessons to be learned from the experience of various national programs maintaining ongoing research activities in Antarctica. To the extent the experiences of the USAP may be helpful, the following points are offered for consideration:

Self-sufficiency—Each tour or expedition should be self-sufficient, since no commercial infrastructure providing medical and search-and-rescue (SAR) currently exists in the area. National Antarctic research programs (including the USAP) do not have the resources or infrastructure to offer those services to commercial enterprises or private expeditions, and may be precluded by mission or policy directives from providing those services, even if requested to do so. Diversion of program assets for humanitarian rescue efforts can have a drastic impact on the research plan for the particular season.

Medical care capabilities—Groups operating in remote areas should have appropriate medical care available to meet the anticipated needs of the group. The harsh environment and logistics constraints may make any evacuation attempt problematic, so the tour operator/expedition leader should maintain a medical care capability commensurate with the demographics and health care status of the group served. Reliance on outside help, in the event of an exigency, is inappropriate.

Informed consent—Tour operators and expedition leaders should apprise cruise/expedition members of the risks associated with travel in the Antarctic and the capabilities within the tour/expedition to mitigate those risks.

EDITOR'S NOTE

It is apparent from the foregoing discussions that the medical directors of the Antarctic programs from Australia, Britain, France, and the United States have thought out their mission and their needs extremely carefully. Preventive medicine, safety, and preparedness have been stressed, and this is exactly how it should be. The directors have all stated clearly that their primary concern is to care for those working at their polar stations. It cannot be sufficiently emphasized that, although they have offered in the past, and certainly will offer in the future, emergency aid when necessary and when they are capable of doing so, all expeditions and tour groups must be prepared to care for their own problems.

Several of the other countries with bases in Antarctica have extensive and well thought out medical facilities. However, the facilities for some appear to be at a small dispensary level, and do not exude much confidence. Some of this may be cultural, that is, in the West health care has been greatly upgraded in recent years and the physician is an important decision maker. Conversely, in some countries the physician is considered more of a technician and hence has far less to do with planning and preparation.

In 1997, Antarctic Support Associates (ASA) became the National Science Foundation's primary support

U.K. Army physician for small Gurka detachment at South Georgia Island in the Southern Ocean.

contractor for the United States Antarctic program. Naval personnel are being replaced with civilian physicians, nurses, and technicians with broad medical experience and special experience in trauma. The United States has the largest number of personnel of any nation in the Antarctic; therefore, the changes in deployment at McMurdo Station, Palmer Station, and Amundsen-Scott South Pole Station are most significant. What responsibilities they will have in medical research in the future is unclear.

On May 1, 1997, an American research scientist died of heart failure, two days before planned evacuation from the largest base in Antarctica, the U.S. base at McMurdo Station. He was the forty-eighth American staffer to die in Antarctica since 1955. Nearly all the other deaths were due to accidents.

CHAPTER 5

Concerns about Medical Care for the Polar Tourist

Cruise lines are frequently practicing second-world medicine on people who have first-world expectations.
—Carter Hill, M.D., F.A.C.E.P., Chairman, Cruise Ship and Maritime Medicine Section, 1995

It may seem shocking, but no international maritime regulation requires that there be medical personnel aboard cruise ships, although Norway, Britain, and Italy do have rules in this area. The U.S. Government Accounting Office reports that 80 percent of cruise passengers come from the United States, but hastens to add that in 1995, 137 of the 139 deepwater vessels calling at U.S. ports flew flags of other nations, mainly those of the Bahamas, Liberia, Panama, Norway, and Italy. The Centers for Disease Control (CDC) in the United States inspects sanitary conditions aboard all ships calling at U.S. ports, and takes, in the words of the U.S. Public Health Service Act, "measures necessary to prevent the introduction, transmission, or spread of communicable diseases from a foreign country." Unfortunately, this "inspection" has nothing to do with examining the ship's physician's and/or nurse's qualifications. When one realizes that well under 1 percent of polar cruises originate from U.S. ports, it is clear that these regulations are of little importance from the U.S. tourist's point of view.

For many years, anecdotal evidence of the lack of top medical care available in the cruise ship industry has been increasing. With the explosion of medical knowledge and technology in the past three decades, it has become virtually impossible for any ship to be equipped to handle every medical emergency as it would be handled at a shoreside hospital. Some have done a commendable job; others have not kept up with changing times, changing needs, and changing demands. For reasons that will become more apparent throughout this book, preparing for emergencies in the polar environment is probably the most difficult challenge in shipboard medicine today.

IAATO

The International Association of Antarctic Tour Operators (IAATO) was founded in 1991 "to advocate, promote, and practice safe and environmentally responsible private sector travel to the Antarctic." The organization's bylaws, their guidance for those organizing and conducting tourism and nongovernmental activities in the Antarctic and guidance for visitors to the Antarctic are laudable (see appendix B). They meet with NSF and other polar organizations several times a year, both formally and informally, working on policy decisions. Unfortunately, until recently they have shown little interest in establishing standards for the medical welfare of the tourist or in their safety.

AIM BECOMES INVOLVED

Also in 1991, because of increasing concerns about problems regarding expeditioners and tourists in the Antarctic, Aid for International Medicine, Inc. (AIM) detailed these problems to senior people in the U.S. government. Governor Thomas R. Carper of Delaware and two U.S. senators from Delaware, Senator William V. Roth, Jr., and Senator Joseph R. Biden, Jr., advised the director of the National Science Foundation about the negative aspects of the relationship between NSF and explorers and tourists in the Antarctic.

In January 1992, the Director of Polar Programs at NSF asked AIM to form a committee to work with them on these issues. The AIM committee initiated study groups and held meetings with polar experts and the NSF. After three meetings, it became apparent that these efforts were not yielding results, and AIM disbanded the committee with the full agreement of all its members. The members felt that the issues could be addressed more properly through IAATO.

Regrettably, the issues of safety and medicine at sea did not appear to be a top priority at IAATO at that time, and no physicians came forth at IAATO meetings to discuss these major medical needs. In

1994, at the Scott Polar Research Institute, University of Cambridge, Cambridge, England, the director, Dr. John Heap, as well as another senior person, Dr. Bernard Stonehouse, expressed keen interest in convening a conference for medical and safety issues related to tourism and expeditionary travel in the polar environment.

They were certainly not the first to voice concerns about medical care and safety for the tourist and expeditioner in those distant lands. In February 1992, the noted polar explorer, Will Steger, in a letter to a colleague, expressed the concern that careful studies should be made of tourism, so as to be sure how many visitors the continent of Antarctica could support and where it could best support them. Steger went on to state that for the explorer, experience, support, provisions, insurance, rescue, and resupply should be carefully reviewed and evaluated before the journey begins. Furthermore, he stated that because the responsibility for safety in emergency situations invariably lands on the shoulders of those with bases on the continent, expeditioners journeying into the interior of the Antarctic should fully appreciate the risks being taken and be financially able to provide support for their own rescue in an emergency.

In February 1994, with the concurrence of the spokesperson for IAATO, AIM tried to address issues of safety in Antarctic tourism, including shipboard and onshore safety, the operation of inflatable watercraft and helicopters, and shipboard medical care. A questionnaire was issued to IAATO members along with a letter explaining that specific responses would be kept confidential and used only to develop a pool of information. No responses were to be attributed to any IAATO member or source. The information gathered was to be presented at a forthcoming IAATO meeting. In spite of a second letter and individual phone calls, the number of responses generated was small and the information shared was scanty. Some questionnaires were filled out by physicians and some by office help who were not well acquainted with the problems being studied. Some of the responses were far different from those given informally by physicians who had served recently for these same companies. One individual was really quite paranoid in explaining why she felt she could not send the answers to routine questions. The numbers of serious accidents acknowledged did not measure up to what was recounted informally by ship's surgeons on these same ships. Therefore, a statistical analysis of this data proved to be worthless. The impression gained, however, was that although a few ships may have been reasonably equipped, none were up to the American College of Emergency Physicians (ACEP) Guidelines and virtually none were prepared for a major disaster.

In the previous chapter, polar medical experts from some of the countries having the largest bases in Antarctica detailed their role in providing health care for the personnel and scientists at these scientific bases. The writers repeatedly stressed that their facilities were set up for this purpose, and they were not there primarily to offer help to expeditioners and tourists. In September 1995, the director of the Office of Polar Programs for NSF, commenting on a forthcoming conference sponsored by AIM, applauded AIM's efforts to establish minimum standards for medical care and self-sufficiency for private expeditions and tour operators traveling in polar regions.

Commencing on October 29, 1995, a three-day conference was convened by AIM at the Scott Polar Research Institute (SPRI) entitled, "A Medical Standard for Expedition Travel and Tourism in the Polar Environment." Twenty-two physicians from Australia, France, the United Kingdom, and the United States attended. The attendees represented in-depth experiences working at isolated polar bases, on ships in the Antarctic and Arctic, as well as in the practice of medicine in developed and underdeveloped countries, medical administration, medical publishing, research, and teaching. Polar explorers, graduate students at SPRI, and several guests with medical backgrounds brought the list to forty. Although many tour companies deeply involved in Arctic and Antarctic tourism, as well as IAATO, were invited, none attended the meetings. Presentations and discussions were held on safety, communications, disasters, physicians, medicines, and equipment. The special requirements for small tourist ships at extreme distances from medical center backup, as well as in the polar environment, with its own special problems, were addressed. Lectures and demonstrations were held on practical medicine in the polar environment; that is, attention was focused on what is medically best when time and distance make evacuation virtually impossible. The final day was spent reaching a consensus on establishing medical and safety guidelines for polar travel. Special concerns were also expressed for using the most advanced methods of communication and emergency evacuation.

CONTRIBUTIONS OF ACEP

To date, probably the greatest impetus to the improvement of medicine on board ship has come from ACEP.

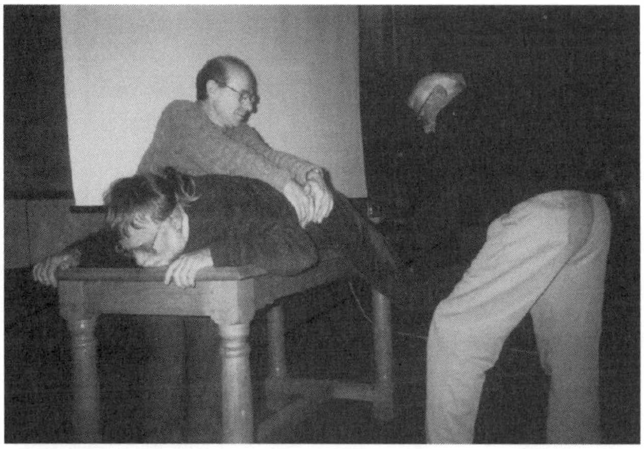

Errol Ger, M.D., demonstrating a method of relocating a dislocated hip at the AIM conference at SPRI, October 29, 1995.

In 1990, those physicians who were experienced in the practice of cruise ship medicine formed a section called Cruise Ship and Maritime Medicine. The physicians agreed that within the cruise ship line industry there were virtually no recognized guidelines or suggestions for companies to follow in the areas of medical staffing, facilities, procedures, and policies. They determined that millions of passengers, the majority from North America (approximately five million passengers in 1995) sail on cruise ships in a medical environment that most physicians would find inadequate. Virtually no help is available from the U.S. Coast Guard because rarely are ships carrying the U.S. flag, and most sailings are in international waters.

As a result of the formation of the Cruise Ship and Maritime Medicine section of ACEP, a small number of cruise lines have hired ACEP member physicians as medical directors, ship's surgeons, and consultants. A growing dialogue has developed, and guidelines to solve existing problems were published. Repeated revisions to these guidelines attempted to cover the ground as thoroughly as possible. The members of the section were aware that malpractice cases against both shipboard physicians and cruise lines were increasing rapidly due to alleged inadequate care, equipment, policies, and procedures. Change was needed. Passengers were demanding it, and cruise lines were being adversely impacted on public relations and financial levels. Obviously leadership was needed in this new medical quagmire.

The ACEP section currently has approximately three hundred members. Its stated objectives are to

> 1) serve as a resource to the cruise industry, their medical departments, and physicians interested in cruise ship medicine, 2) develop guidelines for quality and consistent medical care aboard cruise ships, 3) encourage research on cruise ship medicine, 4) provide educational opportunities for cruise ship medical and administrative staff members, 5) promote the importance and enhancement of onboard medical care, 6) educate the medical establishment about the content and complexity of cruise ship medicine.

Their mission statement also states the following:

> Several factors influence the specific requirements for medical staff and equipment on board a cruise ship. These include: 1) The size of the ship. 2) The total number of passengers and crew. 3) The average age of the passengers and their planned activities. An older age group will tend to have more chronic medical problems, such as heart and lung disease, that may act up while they are traveling. A younger age group

A medical lecture at the AIM conference, October 30, 1995.

Robert K. Headland, archivist and curator at SPRI, conducting a tour of the library.

> may have more injuries due to alcohol use and sports activities. 4) The destination and length of the cruise. Longer periods away from the home port, especially days at sea, necessitate stocking up on more frequently used supplies. Knowledge of the types and quality of medical facilities along the itinerary is important to determine if passengers or crew members can be sent shoreside for additional care or if they have to be air evacuated back to the home port. It's important to view a ship's medical facility as an infirmary and not a hospital. Although most of the medical conditions that arise aboard ship can be treated as they would at an ambulatory care center at home, more severe problems may require a fully staffed and equipped shoreside hospital after the patient is stabilized in the infirmary.
>
> Elderly passengers should be aware that Medicare does not cover medical expenses outside of the United States or its possessions. All people who travel outside of the US should check with their health care provider to determine what medical services will be covered. Supplemental travel medical and emergency evacuation insurance should be considered if their primary health care plan does not provide for these services.

The following is a summary of the section's "Guidelines of Care for Cruise Ship Medical Facilities" (see appendix E for complete set of guidelines). The guidelines are the recommendations of medical directors of six cruise lines and experienced ships' physicians from within the industry. These practitioners have credentials from U.S., British, Canadian, and Norwegian land-based facilities and are active members of ACEP. It is important to qualify these recommendations in the following manner: The specific medical needs of a cruise ship are dependent on variables such as patient mix (age, illness), number of patient visits, itinerary, etc. These factors will modify a ship's formulary, space, equipment, and staffing requirements.

Each ship engaged in cruising should have a ship medical center with medical staff (physicians and nurses), examination and treatment area, and an inpatient medical holding unit adequate for the size of the ship. The infirmary should supply 1.075 square feet (0.10 square meters) per passenger and crew unit, 1 ward bed for each five hundred passengers and crew (dimensions 9.8 × 13.1 feet [3 × 4 meters] for one-bedroom, 13.1 × 16.4 feet [4 × 5 meters] for two-bedroom), and one intensive care bed per ship (two recommended). An examination/stabilization room for contagious patients and a handicap restroom and shower access are recommended.

The medical staff should be experienced in the treatment of minor to severe medical and surgical problems including acute myocardial infarction, cardiac dysrhythmias, cardiac arrest, and respiratory failure. There should also be a formulary that provides medications and other supplies necessary to treat both the nonurgent and emergent types of illnesses and injuries that a practitioner would expect to see in an ambulatory care setting and temporary holding unit such as the infirmary. Staff should also exhibit competency or skill level in basic life support, advanced cardiac life support, intravenous line placement, and acute airway management. Current medical licensure in state, province, or country as appropriate should be available. Also important are discerning interpersonal skills and twenty-four-hour-call schedule and emergency availability. Board certification in emergency medicine, family practice, internal medicine, or general practice plus emergency/critical care experience; two to three years of clinical experience; minor surgical skills; and advanced trauma life support are all highly desirable in staff members.

When a majority of passengers are U.S. or Canadian citizens and the ship is sailing from U.S. or Canadian ports, a medical staff member should be fluent in English and familiar with U.S. or Canadian medical systems and medications. Fluency in the language spoken by the majority of passengers and crew is recommended. Well-organized and legible standardized documentation of all care in a medical record system similar to land-based facilities is required.

The following emergency medical equipment, medications, and procedures are recommended: cardiac monitor, defibrillator, electrocardiograph, airway management supplies, wheelchairs, portable stretchers, pediatric supplies (as dictated by passenger mix), refrigerator/freezer, extrication device, cervical neck collar, trauma cart supplies, suction devices, scheduled maintenance program for equipment, advanced cardiac life support drugs, orientation program for staff, trained cardiac arrest team, and regularly scheduled emergency drills. Also suggested are second/back-up monitor and defibrillator, infusion pumps, ventilator, pulse oximeter, oxygen concentrator, and external pacer capability.

Basic laboratory capabilities, including hemoglobin/hematocrit, urinalysis, pregnancy tests, and blood glucose, should be provided. Electrolyte test is optional. A lab quality control program should be in place. Consideration should be made of an X-ray unit on larger ships with more than a thousand passengers and crew or operating where transfers routinely are more than twelve hours away. The hospital aboard should be capable of performing X rays of the chest, extremities, neck, vertebrae, abdomen, and pelvis. A microscope and drug and alcohol test kits with protocols for testing should be available.

The medical staff should establish a passenger information program regarding onboard health and safety to prevent injury and illness (falls, seasickness, sunburn, shoreside food, and activity safety, etc.). They should make advanced assessments of passenger special needs and risks and provide a preventive vaccination/prophylaxis program (required/recommended) for specific ports of call. The staff should move to meet or exceed the Americans with Disabilities Act requirements.

A crew screening, health, hygiene, and safety program should be established that includes screening for tuberculosis, hepatitis-B, and syphilis. Also suggested are programs to initiate or update childhood vaccinations (DTP, MMR, HBV) and protocols to screen ill or high-risk crew members for communicable diseases (TB, HIV, HBV, syphilis).

The newsletter from the American College of Emergency Physicians, Cruise Ship and Maritime Medicine, March 1996, quoted the chairman of the section, Robert E. Wheeler, M.D., as stating that "The Guidelines of Care for Cruise Ship Medical Facilities," approved by the ACEP Board of Directors in September 1995, have sparked controversy within the cruise industry. Even though the guidelines were developed with input from several cruise line medical directors, risk managers within the industry have expressed concern that the guidelines will be viewed as "standards of care" for cruise ships and will be used against them in medical malpractice suits. Financial departments view the guidelines as promoting additional costs for the cruise industry by recommending specific equipment and staffing requirements.

The cruise industry took a giant step forward when they met on January 19, 1996, in Miami, Florida. The medical directors and risk managers representing twelve members of the International Council of Cruise Lines discussed the new guidelines prepared by Dr. Robert Wheeler's Cruise and Maritime Medical Section of the ACEP. Unfortunately, none of the cruise lines traveling to the Antarctic or the high Arctic were in attendance.

The experienced cruise ship physicians who helped to develop the guidelines did not intend these guidelines as "standards." The following passage from the document states this clearly:

> The Guidelines of Care for Cruise Ship Medical Facilities are comprised of liberal minimum recommendations for shipboard medical facility space, staff, equipment and health care delivery systems. A principal objective of the Guidelines is to provide assistance to the cruise industry in developing their own standards for medical services. Many of the major cruise lines are already meeting or exceeding the Guidelines' recommendations either by self design or as regulated by their ships' country of registry. The cost of following the Guidelines is far less than the expenditure associated with an injury or loss of life due to inadequate supplies and resuscitation equipment or an ill-qualified shipboard medical staff. Development of an industry-wide standard for shipboard medical services and adherence to this standard would actually help the cruise lines to decrease their liability for poor medical outcomes. A continuous quality improvement process for shipboard medical services utilizing the Guidelines would not only be cost-effective but it would also promote an enhanced image for the cruise industry and its medical departments.
>
> Access to acceptable medical services is a primary concern for many people who wish to travel outside of the United States including sailing on cruise ships. By the turn of the century 30 new ships will be added to world-wide fleets and a million new passengers will be added to the cruising public. It is our responsibility to promote the importance of quality shipboard medical services throughout the cruise industry and to assure both passengers and crew members that appropriate medical care will be available to them throughout their voyage away from home.
>
> There has been much favorable comment from physicians regarding these new guidelines, and Section members have been even asked to help with design of medical facilities in some of the newer ships.

OTHER VOICES FOR CHANGE

The Florida Medical Association is also concerned about the quality of medical care aboard cruise ships. An article in *The Wall Street Journal* of June 21, 1996, states, "A survey of medical facilities on cruise ships produced disturbing results. Two-thirds of ships surveyed have no laboratory-testing facility on board, and 10% don't have ECG equipment, which is essential to anybody with a heart condition. A full 27% of medical personnel (doctors and nurses) on board cruise ships aren't trained in Advanced Cardiac Life Support, procedures to follow when somebody's heart stops beating. 'It's a mixed bag in the cruise industry,' says John Curran, chairman of the Florida Medical Association's Council on Public Health. Passengers on cruises, he adds, should expect the same quality of care as they would get on land."

The American Medical Association has also expressed the hope that cruise ship facilities will be held to higher and more uniform standards. At the June 1996 House of Delegates meeting, the AMA adopted a resolution calling for federal legislation or an international treaty to establish standards for medical care for passengers aboard cruise ships entering or leaving United States ports. One must realize that since polar cruises rarely originate from or terminate in U.S. ports, that it means little unless the standards established apply to all ships leaving all ports.

Excellent as the ACEP guidelines might be for larger ships, there are some very special problems with small ships carrying relatively few passengers under the extreme conditions one has in the polar environment. There is no way the small ships can be equipped as fully as a 1,500-passenger cruise ship. While all tourist companies working in the polar regions should take heed of these new guidelines, modifications will no doubt be necessary to be acceptable for the polar travel industry. Since IAATO represents the companies doing the vast majority of the tourism in the Antarctic, as well as many of the companies conducting tourism in the most distant Arctic regions, a meeting of their own medical experts to study the "Guidelines" and to come up with the answers their special situation may require would be an excellent first step in meeting these special demands.

In December 1994, *Condé Nast Traveler,* one of the leading magazines in the travel business, published a special report entitled "Cruise Ships and Medical Care—Why It's Not Always Smooth Sailing at Sea." This article, read by over 850,000 prospective tourists, concludes that the quality of medical care varies considerably among various shipping lines. It is also true that it may vary considerably from ship to ship within the same line. The article also states that the majority of cruise lines put the medical department below most others in terms of financial support, which unfortunately is certainly true, and brings out the fact that the cruise line is liable for a physician's negligence in the treatment of a crew member, but not the treatment of a passenger unless there are very unusual circumstances involved. The reason is obviously that the ship's physician is carried as an independent contractor and hence falls outside of the cruise lines' insurance liability.

Similar concerns were voiced when TLC, Inc. held its tenth annual Non-Profits in Travel Conference in Arlington, Virginia, in February 1996. This conference claims to be a "cutting edge meeting in the travel industry." The large number of attendees and participants at the conference represented many hundreds of nonprofit institutions, travel suppliers, and government tourist offices from around the world. Several of the better attended meetings at the conference focused on screening medical risks, provisions for medical care that should or should not be made on a tour, as well as legal and medical professionals discussing when and how to comply with legal and ethical responsibilities involved with the Americans with Disabilities Act (ADA) and the Civil Rights Act. The questions asked of the physician/lawyer and the experienced cruise ship surgeon reflected growing anxieties in the travel industry.

THE CRUISE INDUSTRY SPEAKS

The glitzy color brochures on polar travel are frequently very misleading regarding medical care. Paradoxically, in a brochure for a trip aboard a nuclear icebreaker going to the North Pole, the only mention of medical care is that the ship has a "small infirmary," although it is one of the better equipped infirmaries in ships that ply the polar waters. Her normal complement includes a Russian surgeon, internist, and dentist, as well as a western-trained physician who has additional equipment and medicines for emergencies.

Mention should be made of safety on Russian nuclear icebreakers. The reactors are shielded by many feet of concrete and a number of nuclear physicists constantly monitor operations. Monitors verify that a person aboard receives *less* radiation outside the nuclear shield than in the sunshine on deck. Several years ago, an American radiologist carried an "X-ray badge" on him for the entire cruise to the North Pole. He found he received *less* radiation than he would have at home. The old joke from the Russians used to be that the safest place in case of nuclear war was behind the radiation shield on their ship. Without doubt there is no question about the nuclear safety on these ships, the world's most powerful icebreakers, and watching these great vessels cut their way to anywhere is terribly exciting.

Brochures for some of the cruises on the very large ships traveling to polar regions make absolutely no mention of the medical care available. One tour company that has been repeatedly advised about incorrect medical claims in their brochures states in a new brochure for a January 1998 cruise to the Antarctic that the ship has "a small shop, a hairdresser, and a *well-equipped hospital"* [emphasis added]. The "small shop" is far more adequate for its purpose than the "well-equipped hospital." Statements like this are totally misleading to the polar tourist. Several smaller vessels built for polar and oceanographic research carry a maximum of thirty-six passengers, and the brochure for these vessels boldly displays a "Hospital" designation. No mention is made, however, of what this facility really is or who staffs it.

Some of the brochures about larger vessels list phrases such as "world-class experience," but no mention is made about medical facilities. One cruise line had the audacity to show in their ship's diagram a "Medical Center." Another stated that the ship had a "fully equipped hospital." Ask any westerners what they perceive when you say the ship has a "Hospital" or "Medical Center"; it is bound to have no relation to what is on board these vessels. In the past two years, various brochures for the *same* diesel icebreaker showed in their deck plans a "hospital," an "infirmary," or no notation at all of a place for medical care.

One new company doing polar travel is advertising twelve Arctic and Antarctic cruises between June 1998 and February 1999. Their brochure makes no mention of any medical facility and several phone calls to the company revealed that "someone is our medical director, but not a doctor," and "we'll have a room for medical care, but we don't know anything more." A request for more information was not answered.

One very prestigious college alumni travel group in their eight-page brochure states, "Participants should be in active good health, ready to tolerate what could be substantial ship motion and nimble enough to negotiate gangways and somewhat wet landings." No medical facilities are mentioned.

Another company offering a "deluxe expedition" to senior physicians of the American Medical Association in January and February 1998 not only fails to mention anything about medical care or facilities, but its brochure is introduced by a physician titled "Chair, Senior Physician Editorial Advisory Board." The reader is advised to call an 800 number to promptly ensure receiving a substantial discount and to have any questions answered. The person answering that 800 line seemed bewildered when asked about medical matters and asked the caller to wait while she checked the computer. The best information she could provide was that there would be a physician and a little medical room!

This is either sloppy preparation of brochures, blatant dishonesty, or false advertising. Whatever the cause, the situation should be remedied.

THE CURRENT STATE OF AFFAIRS

Assessing the current state of medical care available to the polar tourists on board these ships is extremely difficult. As mentioned earlier, the questionnaires sent out to tour and shipping companies were incompletely answered, incorrectly answered in many cases, and in some cases never returned. Additional ships have been put on the polar routes for which complete information is not available. Certainly on a few vessels there has been an upgrade and hopefully more will occur in the very near future. Therefore, what follows is at best an estimate.

For the 1996–1997 Antarctic tourism season IAATO and NSF state that 13 ships made 104 voyages and carried 7,322 passengers. Nine of the thirteen vessels involved in that season were of Russian registry. All have a small infirmary, but usually it is not clean or orderly. All have a very limited ability to sterilize instruments, but only some have autoclaves. Although surgical instruments may be available, they are seldom ready in emergency packs. Sterile linen or disposable surgical drapes and gowns and surgical masks are almost completely unavailable. Medicines are often stacked in large paper containers, which are difficult to access and may be completely foreign to the western physician. Many medicines western physicians consider vital are lacking. Disposable sutures may or may not be available. Needles may be resterilized to be reused, with the possibility of spreading HIV or hepatitis virus. Although most all ships carry disposable syringes and disposable hypodermic needles, there is evidence of recent resterilization and reuse of needles and syringes. Electrocardiograph machines are probably present on all of these vessels, but the vintage is unclear, and the reliability questionable.

The servicing of X-ray machines is a complex task (for most physicians' offices and hospitals it is a time-consuming and costly matter to keep the machines in good working order). There are no trained X-ray personnel on board any of the Russian ships to provide this service. Often the machines are out of service for much of the year because of needed repairs. Three of the ten vessels are known to have an X-ray facility; unfortunately, because of technical factors, they are basically limited to X rays of extremities. The machines are not portable, and the taking of X rays and the development of films is a long and cumbersome process. Rarely are X rays taken of the Russian crew, and because of the many limitations present, they are not used frequently when needed for passengers. Therefore, the skill of the Russian physicians using this equipment is marginal at best. The training and approach to medicine of a Russian physician is basically different from that in the West. Too often western physicians have observed that the Russian physicians consider themselves specialists in areas where they have had minimal training. It appears that their motivation to be a ship's physician is a higher salary than they would earn working in a hospital in Russia.

An illness or injury becomes a complex frustration when the Russian doctor speaks little or no English or other languages. Finding an interpreter is often difficult, especially one who can translate a medical history. In an emergency or in the case where multiple people have been injured, this has been a disaster.

In early 1997 a tourist aboard one of the smaller Russian ships in the Antarctic consulted the Russian physician because of discomfort in his chest. After the briefest of examinations, he was told that the pain was due either to adhesions from his recent coronary bypass operation or intestinal gas. He was advised to take an enema. When he got seasick on the return across Drake Passage, the doctor put acupuncture needles in his ear. Fortunately, the passenger has a good sense of humor and he remarked, "At least I didn't get worse." On reaching South America at the end of the voyage, his first priority was to get "real medical care."

However, there are instances of some Russian physicians being extremely helpful as well as being most capable. A consistently high level of care, however, is conspicuously absent.

Six of these ten Russian vessels carry thirty-six tourists and two carry approximately seventy tourists. As of late 1997, the tour companies that charter these vessels have relied totally on Russian medical care.

Obviously, these tour companies, chartering and subchartering these smaller vessels, are relying on the fact that they are being used for short trips down the Antarctic Peninsula and the nearby islands or up in the Arctic, and only where trips last about seven to ten days. Somehow the idea is that what is available medically on these vessels will suffice for these short cruises.

Two of the Russian ships are diesel icebreakers and one is a larger cruise ship; each of the three carries approximately a hundred passengers. All three have an X-ray facility with the limitations previously mentioned. The two icebreakers have a somewhat larger medical facility, but the examining table

A Russian polar research vessel used for tourism that did not *carry a western-trained physician as of late 1997.*

is inadequate and theoretically it would also serve as operating table, but no general anesthesia is available.

The reader must put this all in the perspective of the medical care available in Russia today. In the spring of 1996, a CBS *60 Minutes* television program stated that 20 percent of Russian hospitals lacked running water and 50 percent had no hot water. Frequently medicines were found to be unavailable, unless purchased by patients on the black market. Alcoholism is rampant and this also involves health workers.

Western physicians who have worked on the two older non-Russian vessels that ply these waters state that X-ray machines are not on board, and the medical facilities are poor. Of two large ships involved in Antarctic tourism the larger, the *Marco Polo,* is known to have a physician and three nurses.

The large Russian diesel icebreakers and their nuclear icebreakers each carry two helicopters. This has proved very helpful for emergencies, but these aircraft are not equipped to carry sick and injured people. Because of the vast distances to be covered, the short range of the helicopters limits their use.

Probably all of the vessels have, in addition to telephone, a telex capability and fax machines.

In the Arctic, many of the same ships are involved in tourism. The great trips to the North Pole across the Northern Sea Route and across the Northwest Passage are usually made by the Russian-registered ships or several of the other vessels that are involved in Antarctic tourism during the astral summer. The largest number of seaborne tourists in the Arctic are in the Scandinavian area where there is good access to ports, communication, and transportation to proper medical facilities. In addition, there is one Russian nuclear icebreaker with a medical facility that surpasses the others that have been discussed. Similar problems with equipment exist, but medicines are in better supply. The Murmansk shipping company that runs the nuclear icebreaker fleet is probably one of the premier corporations in Russia today. It appears because of that status, the ships get what is necessary. None of the dispensaries on the ships, however, have a medical library. If one looks about, the best that is found are several tattered and old books on medicine.

It is all too apparent that there is no consistency in medical care available for Arctic and Antarctic tourists. The AIM study confirmed that in 1994 the tour and shipping companies did not wish to see medical standards for personnel, supplies, and equipment, but this thinking may be changing. Over the long term, safety and preventive medical measures will not only save lives but will be healthier for the tourist industry.

CHAPTER 6

Safety on the Ship, on Zodiac-type Craft, and on Helicopters

All our hoped-for explorations and perhaps discoveries seemed slipping away from us. I do not like to contemplate any further accidents, although in our position almost anything might happen.

—George W. DeLong, Lt., U.S. Navy, Commanding the *Jeannette* expedition's quest for the North Pole, 1881

The best medicine is preventive medicine. Safety aboard ships, helicopters, and Zodiac-type craft can prevent most of the major accidents one sees in the polar regions—be it in field research, expeditions, or tourism.

ONBOARD SAFETY

Prior to 1970, several different ships were chartered for tourist travel to the Antarctic and the Arctic. They were certainly not appropriate for this type of travel. Naval and merchant craft from many countries traveled these same routes, and they too often were ill-prepared for the Arctic Ocean and the Southern Ocean. In 1970, the *Lindblad Explorer,* an ice-strengthened ship built specifically for polar travel, first went to the Antarctic, and in 1984 was the first tourist vessel to transit the Northwest Passage. In the past twenty-seven years, many other ships have made these types of voyages, and with increasing frequency the ships have been specifically designed for polar travel. More recently the choice has been diesel- or nuclear-powered icebreakers.

Lindblad Explorer *with leopard seal in the foreground off Antarctic Peninsula.*

Passengers embarking on these ships should be physically, emotionally, and intellectually prepared for the trip. It would be reasonable to expect that each tour company will send, in addition to background information about the voyage, information about shipboard activities and "the do's and don'ts." Hopefully, too, each passenger will have studied appropriate references in order to be prepared for the area they are visiting. In July 1996, Quark Expeditions, Inc. published an "Expedition Leader's Handbook," which has set a standard for the industry. Most tour companies are using this or a variation thereof, to offer guidelines for the expedition leader covering his or her areas of responsibility. Undoubtedly, this handbook will be enlarged over time and modified from experience.

An initial briefing should be held during the first day of the voyage and safety issues stressed. The doctor should be introduced and he or she should detail his or her availability and give some advice on the more common problems such as motion sickness and the danger of fractures. The ship's surgeon also must be deeply involved in all safety issues.

Worldwide regulations by Safety of Life at Sea (SOLAS) and the Intergovernmental Maritime Organization (IMO) govern safety issues for all ships carrying passengers. On all passenger vessels, it is required that passengers go as a drill to the emergency station and abandon ship station within twenty-four hours of sailing, but this may not be soon enough! The Russian passenger ship *Admiral Nakhimov* sank in 1986, only one and a half hours after sailing from the port of Novorossisk on the Black Sea. Over four hundred passengers drowned. Reading instruction manuals before boarding and holding the required drills as soon as possible would be most prudent. The master of a ship may establish any emergency signals in addition to the international routine, but everyone should be prepared for emergencies by the time they leave port. *Survival Guide for the Mariner* by Robert J. Meurn, which is listed in the chapter references, is an excellent book for those who wish to go deeper into the subject.

Great care is necessary in moving about a ship. Passengers should wear shoes with appropriate nonskid soles. Decks can be slippery from rain, snow, or ice, and it is easy to trip over the high transoms of the weather doors. Ships may pitch and roll to extreme degrees, and during rough weather passengers should not go out on deck. Adequate handrails should be placed strategically about the entire ship, including passenger cabins and bathrooms. Straps should be available in order to keep a person from being thrown from his or her bunk during heavy seas. Some of the worst fractures seen have occurred in passenger cabins. Doors should always be kept fully open or completely closed and they should be opened and closed by the handle only. Fingers in a doorjamb can be a complete disaster. The decks should have a nonskid or high-friction type of surface in the areas commonly used by passengers. Walking on helicopter decks is extremely dangerous as there are no railings. On a moving ship it's best not to go anywhere where you can't have one hand on the ship at all times.

SAFETY ON ZODIACS

Zodiacs are U.S. Coast Guard–approved motorized landing craft developed by Jacques Cousteau for use in worldwide expeditions. These sturdy and very stable craft are constructed of high-performance, plastomer

Passenger using proper hand-to-arm grip when boarding Zodiac (note side gate design of gangway).

Boarding Zodiac from gangway platform at bottom of ship's ladder, Antarctica.

fabrics, with several separate airtight compartments. They are virtually unsinkable, and accommodate twelve passengers. Although various manufacturers make similar craft, "Zodiac" has become a common name for these boats.

The Zodiac-type inflatable watercraft are without doubt the best craft to transport passengers from ship to shore and back. A safe gangway access from the ship to the Zodiac is accomplished by the following: 1) side-gate design where entry to the Zodiac-type craft is made directly from a platform at the lower deck level onto the pontoon of the Zodiac or 2) gangway platform at the bottom of the ship's accommodation ladder from which one goes on the Zodiac craft. Two skilled crewmen should be available for loading and unloading passengers. Life jackets are necessary at all times, and passengers must have both hands free for getting on and off the craft. Cameras are best carried in a plastic bag in a backpack,

Loading platform at bottom of ship's ladder on an extremely dangerous day with heavy seas rising and falling up to 10 feet, Antarctica.

and large hand-carried items must be passed to the crew so the passenger has both hands free to use the forearm grip when going aboard. (Several years ago in the Antarctic, one frail woman slipped behind the crew member who was loading and was going to re-board the platform on her own when a great swell caused everything to lurch. Fortunately, a crewman grabbed one of her arms as she went completely under the water; otherwise she would have been lost.) Passengers should never jump from the platform into the boat; they may injure others as well as themselves. One should never step over the stern of the Zodiac, as the slightest motion of the craft could bring the wooden transom and engine down on your leg. The operator of the Zodiac will instruct the passengers to slide along the pontoon to the bow and there, by simply swinging their legs around, they can stand up in the water and be helped ashore. Everyone should walk, not run. There may be rocks that are slippery with ice, algae, or guano, making maneuvering tricky. Young passengers fall just as hard as the older ones, so everyone must be very careful. Smoking is never permitted on these gasoline-powered craft.

Aging, collapsed iceberg with multiple entrances and channels.

The responsibility for passengers transfers from ship's officers to the expedition leader once they have boarded the Zodiac craft, and it is the staff's responsibility to ensure that safety guidelines are adhered to ashore.

It is also interesting to note that insurance coverage changes when passengers board a Zodiac and again when they step ashore! Remember, that when the weather is too bad the Zodiac should not go. A passenger who is not sure about his or her own capabilities should not go either!

Extremely dangerous Zodiac trip under the collapsing iceberg.

Even though the Zodiac craft with its multiple inflatable compartments is one of the safest types of watercraft known, some basic items must be carried. There should always be two paddles to be used in case of engine failure, an anchor, several lines, an extra tank of fuel, tools for motor repairs, a first-aid kit, and a compass. The driver of each Zodiac craft should be experienced in driving a vessel under various conditions of wind and water, and he or she should always have a VHF radio for instant communication with the ship and other Zodiac craft.

In the last several years, Zodiac-type craft have literally become lost for hours to a full day in the Arctic and the Antarctic because of extreme fog. In some areas compass readings are very inaccurate because of being near the magnetic pole, and finding the expedition ship has proved to be extremely difficult. Radar reflectors carried on the Zodiac may be helpful for the ship to advise them how best to return, but probably the safest and simplest method is use of the satellite-based global positioning system (GPS) built and operated by the Department of Defense of the U.S. government. Over 275,000 GPS receivers are currently in use among civil maritime users. This popular navigation system can provide 10 feet (3 meters) or better accuracy anywhere in the world, and the cost of the receivers has now dropped to below $150 each. All twenty-four GPS satellites are now in orbit 11,000 miles above the Earth. Considering that Zodiacs should always be traveling in pairs at any real distance from the ship, at least one of each two should be equipped with the GPS hand-held system.

Concern about safe operation of these small watercraft is real. Both drivers and passengers must realize that discreet distances must be maintained between icebergs and glaciers, such as the Ross Ice Shelf, and the Zodiac. Failure to do so can result in complete disaster if large areas of ice suddenly and unpredictably break off or if an iceberg suddenly capsizes. The photo below, taken with a telephoto lens, shows an iceberg that the passengers were most eager to have the driver, Keith Shackleton, approach much closer. He adamantly refused to do so, and some minutes later as the craft sped away, there was a rumble and the entire iceberg capsized and the penguins scattered unpredictably. Being next to that when it happened might have cost a number of lives.

Iceberg that turned over only minutes after photo taken!

Large flashlights and a number of visual distress signals should be on both Zodiacs and helicopters, and a bucket for bailing should be aboard each Zodiac in case of a leak or a large amount of water being taken over the side. In addition to passengers wearing inflatable life jackets, an inflatable life raft should be able to be deployed from each helicopter.

SAFETY ON HELICOPTERS

Many countries have used helicopters in the polar regions, and Dick Smith of Australia is well known for his exploits to the poles in the late 1980s. With the advent of Russian icebreakers in the tourist trade in 1991, helicopters are now used not only for weather reconnaissance and ship's work, but also for tourist travel and overviewing polar sights. This new activity or "flight-seeing" is very exciting, but it is also potentially extremely dangerous. As with Zodiac watercraft travel, the expedition leader has the obligation to provide a thorough briefing to all passengers before any flying commences.

Ideally, passenger travel should adhere to the following guidelines:

1. All queuing and boarding of helicopters should be done only on the port side of the ship, and those exiting the helicopter should use the starboard side.

2. No passengers are allowed on the helicopter deck until the staff or crew officially commence boarding.

3. No one is allowed to approach or leave a helicopter when engines are being started or stopped, as the dip of the main rotor blade can be extreme.

4. No smoking is permitted on the helicopter deck or in the immediate area as refueling might be done with passengers aboard and with rotors turning.

5. Helicopters should always be boarded from the forward quadrant, and passengers should always stay clear of the tail rotor area.

6. Long objects, such as tripods, canes, poles, etc., should be kept horizontal so not to make contact with turning rotor blades.

7. Loose clothing that might be blown off, such as hats, scarves, etc., should not be worn.

8. If a helicopter is parked on a slope, passengers should be aware of the path of the turning rotor, and stoop if necessary when approaching or exiting. Helicopters should not be entered from the up-slope side.

9. After boarding, passengers must fasten the seat safety belt and put on ear covers or use ear plugs.

10. Inflatable life vests must be worn at all times.

11. When the helicopter lands, passengers should not open the door. A staff or crew member will approach the helicopter, open the doors, and direct the passengers toward the forward quadrant of the aircraft.

The expedition leader or the other staff member handling the expedition will be in charge of the boarding. Should the stay on shore be unusually long, as when one visits an emperor penguin colony, where most of the day might be spent ashore in order to afford passengers maximum light conditions for photography and provide maximum opportunity to experience these unusual locations, special arrangements are made. The helicopter staging location is made the base of operations and camps should be set up for safety. This facility would include a portable tent and other equipment that has been flown to the facility before passengers are flown into the area. The tent is lightweight and consists of aluminum poles that fit together and provide the framework, all of which collapses and fits back into the helicopter along with the remainder of the gear when camp is broken up.

The equipment on-site should include climbing ropes and related mountain gear, ice axe, radio, food box, water canister, etc. The intent is to provide a base of operations which can serve as a refuge for anyone in an emergency, be it medical or because of changing weather conditions that might alter the schedule for helicopter shuttling service. A snow block latrine can be constructed and all waste returned to the ship at the end of the activities at that site in keeping with the Antarctic protocol. Passengers are encouraged to bring their own food under these circumstances, normally sandwiches prepared on the ship. This is an exception to the "Guidance for Visitors" which tour operators use for activities in Antarctica. Passengers are also advised to bring extra clothing and emergency personal gear to tide them over for a twenty-four-hour period. No matter how good the weather looks when boarding a helicopter, passengers should bring parkas, boots, etc., to be prepared for any unusual events.

In addition to first-aid kits for both Zodiacs and helicopters, hand fire extinguishers are a must. The Federal Aviation Administration (FAA) regulations on U.S. helicopters, which are currently being upgraded, include additional very special requirements for all helicopters used in the U.S. Antarctic program, as well as those for many other national programs.

Probably the most frequent danger with helicopter travel has been during loading and unloading operations. Crew members who are assisting with loading must be particularly cautious of older people becoming disoriented when they disembark from helicopters. One woman tripped and fell, sustaining a dislocated and broken elbow. One man turned the wrong way and was stopped only several feet short of walking into the rear rotor blade.

Unfortunately there are not agreed-upon international safety standards for helicopters. In Canadian territorial waters, Russian helicopter flights are not allowed. In their stead, a Canadian helicopter, pilot, and mechanic are put aboard Russian icebreakers that wish to have helicopter capability while traversing the Northwest Passage. (How much of this is politics and how much is related to safety is an open question.) At any rate, the Canadian helicopters have inflatable pontoons attached to the skids that can be inflated by the pilot in the unlikely event of a water landing. Is this necessary? *The Wall Street Journal* on August 9, 1996, carried a tragic story: "A Widow Takes on FAA After Helicopter Tour Crash." The widowed tourist tells the tragic story of the crash of a tour helicopter in the Hawaiian Islands, in which she lost her husband. Her goal since the accident has been "to hasten the FAA's adoption of strict federal safety rules for tour helicopters—regulations that the National Transportation Safety Board has recommended for a decade. Most of all, she wants to ensure that helicopters are equipped with flotation devices that prevent them from sinking when they ditch into water."

Helicopter boarding for trip to Mertz Glacier, Antarctica.

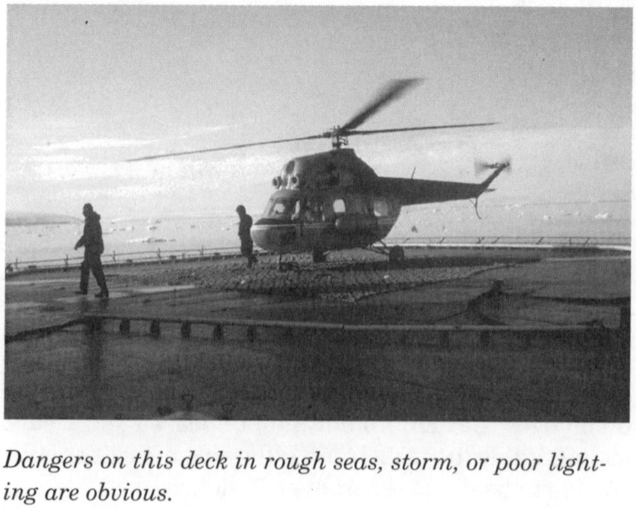

Dangers on this deck in rough seas, storm, or poor lighting are obvious.

Although the FAA planned on issuing these new helicopter standards in late 1996, there is as yet no clear understanding of the content. The accusation regarding lack of safety precautions in helicopter tourism has been made by more than one, but the FAA seems more interested in protecting the business interests of the industry than in safety concerns.

Helicopter tourism is a $375-millon industry, carrying about half a million passengers in 1996 in the United States alone. But the safety rules for tour helicopters are inconsistent. Sometimes the FAA puts out local rules and that further confuses the picture. The National Transportation Safety Board analyzed accident data between October 1988 and April 1995, and during that period there were sixty-two helicopter tour accidents with thirty-five fatalities in the United States.

Only three of the thirty-three tour operators in Hawaii use floats on their helicopters. The equipment is optional and very expensive. The latest inflatable models cost $56,000, but safety advocates claim floats greatly enhance chances of surviving a crash. So, there is clearly confusion on an important issue that can mean life or death.

Too often gross violations of safety have been seen on the refueling of Russian helicopters. The consequences of fire at sea on a polar cruise are unthinkable.

On July 27, 1996, the Associated Press reported that the *University Explorer* arrived at Auke Bay, a harbor about ten miles northwest of Juneau, Alaska, with five dead and seventy-six injured crewmen resulting from a fire at sea. This Commodore Cruise Lines ship had 730 passengers and 280 crew members. The cruise was terminated "for the safety and comfort of the passengers." Fortunately, when the tragedy occurred, the Coast Guard was able to send two cutters, a utility boat, and a helicopter to aid the ship. That sort of help is not available in the polar areas. This ship fire was the third on the inside passage waters of Alaska during that year.

Potential dangers in hillside boarding near Shackleton's Hut, Antarctica.

SAFETY ISSUES ADDRESSED

On July 13, 1995, the New Zealand Antarctic Program presented the following paper to the joint National Science Foundation/Council of Managers of National Antarctic Programs Meeting with IAATO, in Arlington, Virginia:

> SAFETY ISSUES AND CONCERNS—ROSS SEA TOURIST OPERATIONS
>
> 1.0 Background
>
> New Zealand places Government Representatives on all tourist ships intending to visit the Ross Sea primarily for the purpose of supervising the visits to the historic huts and Scott Base. The New Zealand Antarctic Program (NZAP) coordinates the placement of representatives on the ships and provides them with appropriate training and resource material.
>
> The mandatory reports produced by the representatives often raise issues of concern to the representatives and NZAP. Safety concerns are repeatedly included in the reports which have been forwarded to the tour operator concerned. However, representatives have generally observed little significant increase in safety standards or procedures over at least the last five years in the Ross Sea region. NZAP would like to take this opportunity to raise in a constructive manner some of the more significant safety issues it is aware of. Discussion and comment on the issues raised below is welcomed by NZAP.
>
> 2.0 Specific Safety Concerns Raised by New Zealand Representatives
>
> 2.1 Small boat operations
>
> The loading and unloading of passengers at small gangway platforms into Zodiacs continues to be a concern. A number of incidents at the gangway have been reported by representatives that had potential for serious injury.
>
> Survival equipment is not generally carried in Zodiacs. Passengers stranded ashore could be placed in a perilous situation without any aids to survival. Minimum standards for safety/survival equipment could be developed to guide operators.
>
> The numbers put ashore at any time could also be limited to the number that can be transported by the available helicopters/Zodiac fleet in one single movement (unless adequate survival equipment is made

available to those left ashore). All night operations should be avoided.

2.2 Helicopter operations

In general there is a lack of information available to passengers about helicopter safety, in and around the aircraft. Information sheets could be distributed to passengers on basic safety requirements and/or posters could be placed at suitable locations around the ship. Any information should be in multiple languages.

As with Zodiacs, helicopters do not carry even basic survival equipment.

There appears to be a general lack of procedures for dealing with helicopter ditching or other incidents. Little attention appears to have been given to providing adequate backup of another helicopter or Zodiacs at the ready during helicopter operations.

Helicopters have been observed to fly over open water and considerable distances from ships with no other helicopter aboard. Without backup of another helicopter aboard the ship, or in close proximity, there is no search and rescue capability in the event of an accident or malfunction if out of Zodiac range. Single helicopter operations should be reviewed by operators.

2.3 Clothing

Passengers have frequently been observed wearing inadequate clothing for the conditions. More stringent checking of clothing could be considered to help avoid a serious cold-related incident occurring ashore.

2.4 Staff Training and Guiding Ratios

A great variance in the ability and knowledge of Zodiac drivers has been observed. Skills have often proved inadequate especially under poor weather and heavy beach conditions. Adequate training of staff in this area is essential to ensure the safety of all passengers.

Expedition staff, although expert in their particular field, were often noted as having inadequate training and/or knowledge about how to deal with emergency and survival situations. For example, many lacked basic first aid qualifications or snowcraft skills. Increased attention to the application of risk management principles may help to alleviate this problem.

Guiding ratios ashore are often inadequate especially when guides are directly involved in landing and Zodiac operations. This is both a safety and environment issue that should be addressed.

2.5 Charts and information

Some charts used on tour ships have been observed to be unreliable and do not include updated information available through "Notices to Mariners." An example of this was the uncharted underwater obstruction which the *World Discoverer* grounded on and was holed near Cape Evans during 1990. Most ships operating in the Ross Sea in 1993/94 were unaware of this obstruction. A hazardous warning advisory service to ensure timely communication of information relating to hazardous conditions to all ships in Antarctica could be established.

3.0 General

NZAP appreciates that some Ross Sea tour operators place great importance and emphasis on safety issues during their visits. However, it is obvious to NZAP, though representative feedback, that attention should be given to reviewing and expanding present safety procedures to ensure that a serious incident does not occur in the Ross Sea.

The development of a comprehensive safety and operations manual for operators is suggested as an important step to ensuring that the concerns raised above are adequately addressed.

PASSENGER CONCERNS

As mentioned earlier in this chapter, the main difficulties in Zodiac and helicopter tourism occur in the loading and unloading processes. Once ashore passengers quite routinely keep out of trouble. One constant concern, however, is passengers walking across areas of very smooth ice and the possibility of their falling. Some passengers bring ski poles to help them as they walk, which is an excellent idea. A collapsible ski pole as part of a polar tourist's baggage might be put to good use on the ice.

The "backpack" is an essential for the polar traveler to carry several extra items of clothing (including a pair of gloves), a few Band-aids, and personal medicines if the person should get caught ashore for the night. More than once tourists have been stranded overnight at a polar station. This same backpack should be considered the "abandon ship bag" and kept ready in the cabin at all times.

On shore excursions it is usual for the ship's surgeon to set up a small base of operations so in the event of a problem he can be called on his VHF radio and report to the spot where help is needed.

In the high Arctic, particularly near Franz Josef Land and Svalbard, sighting polar bears should be expected. On all land excursions or walks on the ice, several crewmen are posted with shotguns to protect against the "ice bear." There are many documented cases of the polar bears being found swimming many miles from the nearest ice shelf or shore and their unpredictability is legendary. Helicopters have been very helpful in spotting them and chasing them away from tourist groups. Watching the great curious carnivores from the deck of an icebreaker is great fun and the safest way to do it.

On Antarctica there are no land predators. The leopard seal at sea is deadly for penguins but on land or an iceflow may truly be harmless. However, there are stories of men being chased across the ice by the savage looking seals, so it is prudent to maintain your distance as they can move rather rapidly.

It is clear from the details given above that polar tourism has decided risks. For example, on the morning of February 11, 1972, the *Lindblad Explorer* was off King George Island about 550 miles (885 kilometers) southeast of Cape Horn when the passengers were awakened by a series of bumps. This was more than the sound of crunching ice, and when the bumping stopped so did the motion of the ship. Soon, the captain's voice came over the loudspeaker system to advise all that the ship had run aground on uncharted rocks and the propeller had been knocked out.

Passengers were told to dress immediately in their warmest clothing and prepare to take to the lifeboats and Zodiacs. The passengers, who were directed to go the lounge to receive life jackets from the crew members, could glance out of the lounge window and see that the ship was indeed on the rocks. On the starboard side they were close to a rocky shore, on top of which rested a high vertical ice cliff; to the port side was open water. A driving snowstorm and six- to eight-foot swells added to the grimness of the picture. At 4:00 A.M. the captain ordered everyone to abandon ship. The lifeboats and Zodiacs were lowered on the lee side of the ship, which was now listing 30 degrees. With no confusion, because they had had drills on this type of thing, the passengers filed down the icy, steeply sloping gangway and into the boats. There were three huts about two miles (3 kilometers) away in which they might have taken shelter, but it was decided that landing would be dangerous. (In 30° Farenheit water, you can live only a few minutes.)

Around this time there was good news: the Chilean naval transport *Piloto Pardo* had received their distress call and was on the way to them. So all of the boats and Zodiacs were lashed together in the lee of the ship and there they rocked and rolled and waited with the wind and snow whipping severely into their faces. Because of the high winds and seas the rescuing ship was delayed for several hours.

In the meantime, the captain of the *Explorer* decided she was not about to capsize, so they were allowed to go back aboard to eat and pack their luggage. At 1:00 P.M., some ten hours after the *Explorer* ran aground, the *Piloto Pardo* emerged from the blinding snowstorm and anchored a mile away. Once again, the passengers filed into their lifeboats for a run through heavy seas to a gangway that was even steeper and icier than that of the *Explorer.* Some of the older people literally had to be pushed or carried on board.

Eight days later the passengers arrived at Punta Arenas, a Chilean town of about four thousand population on the Straits of Magellan. There they were given a hero's welcome. With the Chilean navy band blaring, each woman was given a dozen red roses.

Two days after the shipwreck, a pair of tugs failed to pull the *Explorer* off the rocks. It took a German salvage ship from Capetown, South Africa, five thousand miles (8,045 kilometers) away, to do it. Eventually, the *Explorer* was towed all the way to Norway to be repaired. But she was back in service the next year and has been doing yeoman service in both the Arctic and the Antarctic ever since. Other ships have foundered in polar waters since then; ships have always had a way of doing this. While a passenger's chances of getting in a situation like this are extremely rare, it is certainly best to be prepared.

CHAPTER 7

Communications, Disasters, and Evacuations

It is no use saying, "We are doing our best." You have got to succeed in doing what is necessary.

—Winston Churchill

Communications are undeniably a vital part of all polar activities. Mawson first used radio on September 25, 1912, to link Antarctica to Australia, but, there was a much earlier system in which polar expeditions left their messages in cairns. Nothing more than a pile of stones, these cairns could be recognized as manmade, and were used as a place to store food and supplies for an emergency or as a place to leave messages. Messages might have been left in a cairn for relief ships coming around in the next season, but this type of communication obviously was not of much help in a medical emergency.

HISTORY OF POLAR COMMUNICATIONS

Cairns are still found along the coast of Ellesmere Island. In 1980 a colleague of the author was walking along the beach there and saw two boulders, one piled on top of the other. When he lifted up one of the large boulders, he found a folded piece of paper underneath it. It had been written by Thomas Dedrick, who was a physician on one of Peary's expeditions. Fortunately, it did not describe a medical emergency!

At the Scott Polar Research Institute some interesting examples of emergency communication are displayed. When Richard Collinson took the *Enterprise* to search for Franklin's party, he experimented with various clever ideas to try to make contact with the survivors. One of these was a balloon that dropped leaflets, which was tried over London and worked extremely well. A fuse attached to the balloon allowed the leaflets to fall as it burned down. However, when the searchers got to the Arctic, the bosun pointed out that lighting a fuse near a hydrogen balloon was not a very good idea. Another concept was putting collars with messages attached onto captured Arctic foxes, hoping that some Franklin survivors might see the fox, and then find the position of the relief ship. Mawson used the radio to try to recall the *Aurora* when he arrived at his home base in the Eastern Antarctic a bit late, but the ship was already sailing away. Mawson would have been better served, of course, if he had had a radio up on the ice cap when his companions were dead and dying. What if Scott had a radio, or Shackleton on Elephant Island, or Greely in the Arctic?

Mawson used a HF (high-frequency) radio link. Since that time there has been a tremendous increase in the types and methods of communications; satellites, the most recent to appear, may eventually transform the entire communications system.

In the early sixties, the Morse key was still in use, and doctors could be contacted, and questions could be asked; for example, "We've got something wrong with someone. Can you help?" And the doctor would reply, "Look on page 34 in the ship's officer's medical guide. Take out pill #32. Give it to him three times a day."

NEED FOR GOOD COMUNICATIONS TODAY

Despite the sophisticated communication systems of today, however, many polar areas are still "poorly supported by telecommunications." Distances between operators are very often extreme, and environmental conditions may make contact difficult. Only the largest operations can be relatively self-supporting, so reliable communication networks are essential.

The exponential growth of "exotic" and "expedition" travel in recent years has placed increasing numbers of travelers at risk of illness or injury in remote areas, far removed from centers of medical care. This is particularly true in the higher Arctic and the Antarctic where the absence of airport landing strips and population centers makes the situation even more perilous. An additional challenge has been the absence of a communication system accessible to all in the polar areas. Lastly, one must realize that there is an understandable reluctance on the part of government agencies to involve themselves in treatment and evacuation measures, given the climate of litigation and their reduced sources of funding.

In the more than fifty years since the beginning of continuous occupation and scientific exploration in Antarctica, there is still no agreed-upon communications network in place, nor is there a continent-wide search-and-rescue cover. A great deal of international cooperation will be required to organize this, but some progress has been made. Currently, almost all of the ships carrying tourists operating in the Southern Ocean have telephone and fax capability, a distinct advancement over telex. The INMARSAT satellite system covers most, but again not all, of the distant areas in which these ships operate. Frequencies are assigned all ships entering the Antarctic waters, and communication is encouraged between 1900 and 2100 hours (7 and 9 P.M.), so that all might be made aware of problems potentially requiring assistance.

In the Arctic search-and-rescue (SAR) exists in some countries, but what is needed is to extend the coverage to all countries. In some areas, northern Canada, for example, communication networks are very good. In the far east of Russia, however, it is extremely poor. People are surprised to see an airplane radio operator still using a Morse key, which seems a bit antediluvian, but it probably is more effective in bad communication conditions than voice. Historically, there has been a tendency for tourist ships requiring assistance with medical diagnosis and treatment, or even medical evacuation, to turn to available government resources, such as the Canadian coast guard in the high Arctic Island reaches of Canada, or to the Antarctic bases of the various nations stationed there.

In the far north, the Canadian coast guard and their cohorts in American and Russian waters still remain the primary resource because of the scarcity of any other support. The SAR division of the Canadian coast guard explains that such efforts are coordinated through Ottawa and involve the use of helicopter retrieval from remote areas and transportation via C-130 thereafter to Halifax, Toronto, or other more distant medical facilities as warranted. The cost of such evacuations is subsequently passed on to the tour company rather than the evacuee. It should be noted that a few manned base facilities exist in the high Arctic, such as the Polaris mining center on Little Cornwallis Island and the government hospital at Sachs Harbour on Banks Island. All ships traveling these waters should have a complete list of all such facilities, the services or supplies available, and the direct means of communicating with them.

Further communication networks will have to precede polar search-and-rescue systems, because these systems will depend largely on a good communications network. It would be enormously helpful for the polar establishment to set up a high-frequency communication network. In the Antarctic, this would be the responsibility of governments through various committees established by treaty. In the Arctic, seven diverse governments would need to work together to form a unified system. As stated earlier, the tendency is for governments to shy away from these new commitments, and it is also unfortunate that Britain and the United States have been reducing coast guard coverage, which was once quite extensive.

Irrespective of the achievements, or lack of, at government level, every expedition, cruise, voyage, or trip can make a key step in establishing communications networks by preparing a communication plan before sailing. While this would seem to be self-evident, many major program investments have been made without considering safety communication networks.

What is required for a good communication plan? What is needed? One concept is a larger call-up communication system to allow contact with the home base and between elements of the expedition; the capability to seek assistance and/or medical backup; and the capacity to arrange evacuation and start a corporate response chain. Consideration must be given to the speed of the response required. If an immediate response is not necessary, then why spend a small fortune using a sophisticated expensive system. An alternative, especially for trips with limited satellite time, would be e-mail forwarding. With this system, you send your message off and someone answers it later by either satellite or by high-frequency radio. However, it is necessary to have someone listening at the other end or watching the computer for e-mail.

In the Falkland Islands, a popular landing place is Westpoint Island, where cruise ship landings are made on the beach. Passengers go up a long hill and down the other side to a seabird colony. The colony is in tusset grass, which is a delightful environment for the birds, but unfortunately people tend to fall over and occasionally become injured in this grass. On one tourist expedition, the ship was very well organized. They had a crewman up the hillside who could do a line-of-sight communication back to the ship or to the shore. On the following expedition, however, there was nothing like that setup. Only one staff man took a radio to the colony. It took a quarter of an hour for the expedition to get over the hill, and when there, no one on the ship or shore could be heard by radio. At least no one answered. If there had been an accident at the colony, it would have taken a long time to have obtained help.

Reliability is extremely important in communications systems; however, communications are only reliable when regularly and frequently used, thus establishing the communications channel. The most reliable is the satellite, but this is by no means a guaranteed channel. With current technology, and with cost-effectiveness in mind, the most reliable system probably is still a good high-frequency link and a radio operator who knows how to make the best of the system.

Thus, not only should the purchase of suitable equipment be considered, but also obtaining permission to use components of other networks in the region, and the knowledge of other systems and their frequencies. Good communications, especially at the local level between members of a group, can play a significant role in preventing accidents from occurring in the first place. Simple VHF-UHF handheld transceivers are readily available and can be relatively inexpensive. There is now no real reason for tour groups or Zodiac parties not being in good communication with each other.

In some ways, the situation in the Antarctic is the easier of the two polar regions. For a start, there is only one organization, the Antarctic Treaty and its associated committees. Secondly, there is a general appreciation among Treaty states of the difficulty of working in the region, and so the desire exists, albeit expressed differently in different countries, to work together. Nevertheless, the Antarctic has a nebulous setup. There are no strict requirements to obtain permissions or to comply with specific safety standards.

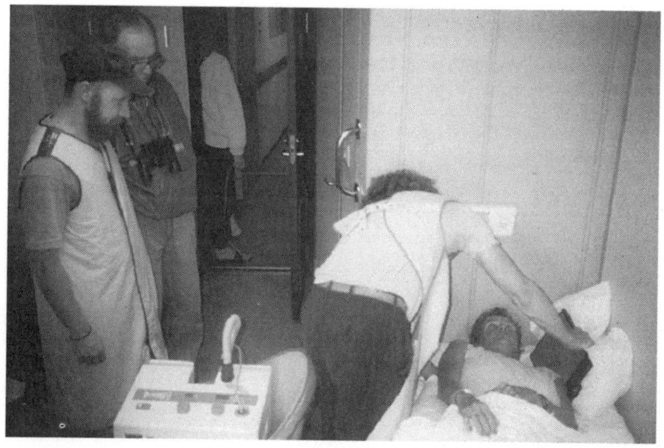

Portable X-ray machine used in tourist's cabin to study for possible neck fracture.

Portable X-ray machine from Australia's Macquarie station arriving on the Kapitan Khlebinkov.

However, since passing of the Antarctic environmental protocol for environmental protection, many countries have enacted, or are in the process of doing so, a licensing requirement for expeditions—and this includes tour operators—to be granted by the relevant authority. In most cases, the license is granted after environmental review of the activity. In Britain, the polar regions section of the Foreign and Commonwealth Office handles such inquiries. In New Zealand, it is the Minister for Foreign Affairs and Trade. In the United States, it is the National Science Foundation, but only in consultation with the Environmental Protection Agency.

In all cases, the powers granted to these bodies are surprisingly wide. The licenses may not be granted if any part of an activity is liable to lead to an adverse environmental impact. This impact could be the result of inadequate emergency contingency planning. The problem is that everything is done at governmental or agency level and suffers from the civil service approach of "red tape." Typically, the approach is often not helpful, and it varies from country to country. Sometimes managers of national Antarctic programs exhibit strong resentment and antagonism toward these expeditions, tourists, and commercial operators.

RESPONSES TO ANTARCTIC COMMUNICATIONS PROBLEMS

Fortunately, this attitude is beginning to break down. The net result is that there is some degree of international coordination among the various Treaty states, which has led to glacially slow, but significant, progress on networking and search-and-rescue efforts.

Two examples should be mentioned. One is AFIM (Antarctic Flight Information Manual), a publication of Antarctic air operations. The manual includes sections by each nation, and recently an international airline was invited for the first time to submit entries even though the organization has been flying to Antarctica for over ten years. Part of each entry in the manual details search-and-rescue capability. One element of this, agreed at Treaty level, is a TIBA (traffic information broadcast by aircraft) procedure. In this system each aircraft entering a delineated airspace, in this case south of 60° south, broadcasts various critical details at predetermined intervals to aid air navigation. This practice has been in operation since 1990 by fixed-wing aircraft, and also should be performed by cruise ship helicopters.

Another example is the Antarctic Communications Manual (ATCOM). With less degree of urgency, but with pressure from the World Meteorological Organization, a similar process to the Antarctic Flight Information Manual has commenced for radio communications. In fact, it began well before the Flight Information Manual, but not much progress has been made. The key elements of this protocol are identification of aeronautical distress channels, standardized radio procedures for distress calls, recognition for the International Maritime Distress System, recommendation that all mobile craft should have internationally recognized emergency rotation radio beacons, recognition of the need for all mobile and fixed Antarctic stations to be able to transmit and receive on 3023 kHz. In addition, all Antarctic stations, aircraft, and ships are supposed to keep radio watches commensurate with available equipment and personnel. Unfortunately, many do not listen.

AFIM and ATCOM demonstrate the Treaty nations' willingness to provide a communication network over Antarctica, but there is still much to be done to ensure that all cruises, expeditions, and tourist activities send information into and participate in the communications net. Unfortunately, the committees running this, the Council of Managers of National Antarctic Programs (COMNAP) and the Standing Committee of Antarctic Logistic Operations (SCALO), are not welcoming or encouraging manned governmental trips. However, this should not put planners off from seeking advice from and informing the relevant groups of their intentions.

At the July 1996 IAATO meeting, the organization formally accepted the medical emergency contingency plan developed by Adventure Network International (ANI) for emergency medical evacuations from the Antarctic. ANI maintains a twenty-four-hour radio watch and has an airplane on permanent standby. This service will no doubt be a great relief to the Americans, Australians, and British and the other bases that have frequently been called upon for assistance. However, there is still the question of proving the ability and willingness of the patient to pay for the assistance before takeoff, as the Danish authorities do in Greenland. A tour group cannot go to Greenland until they have a permit, and they do not get a permit until the Danish government knows who will pay for search-and-rescue if needed.

The EPIRB (emergency position-indicating radio beacon), which can flash the position of mariners in distress, has led to many dramatic rescues. In January 1997, the solo sailing fraternity in the Vendee Globe race had three dramatic rescues in the Southern Ocean. An additional racer was declared lost after a weeklong search by diverted cargo ships, several Vendee racers, and satellites found no trace of him or his boat. An international committee will decide by January 1998 about moving race courses further north in the Southern Ocean.

Despite the diplomatic dividends of the dramatic rescues by the Australian Navy, there is growing concern about the cost of these operations. On New Year's Day 1997, the Aussies conducted a three-million-dollar rescue to save a female yacht captain in the BOC (British Ocean Challenge) race in the Southern Ocean. The U.S. Coast Guard saved about 4,500 lives in 1995, following the centuries-old tradition dictating that nations rescue mariners in distress, whatever their nationality or the cost. Taxpayers in many countries are questioning the "911 culture" and many feel adventurers should pay their own rescue costs.

The newly adopted IAATO medical emergency contingency plan is a big step forward. Large areas of the Antarctic are still out of range of search-and-rescue and some 10 percent of the tourists go to these more distant areas. At any rate, the IAATO plan is an excellent start.

The basic points of the IAATO medical emergency contingency plan are as follows:

1. Recognizing the need for self-sufficiency as called for in Recommendation XVIII-1, and formal procedures to assist IAATO-member passenger vessels in the Antarctic with critically injured or sick passengers, IAATO has developed a medical emergency contingency plan in cooperation with Adventure Network International.
2. In brief, member vessels in the Antarctic will take advantage of Adventure Network International's expertise in aviation logistics and medical evacuation. The

office of Adventure Network International in Punta Arenas, Chile, will act as a twenty-four-hour emergency station from October through mid-February each season. In practice, this medical emergency evacuation plan will apply to vessels sailing in the Antarctic Peninsula region, which covers some 90 percent of tourism in the Antarctic.

3. Furthermore, IAATO members are committed to thorough medical disclosure by their passengers with an accompanying report from the passenger's home physician. This medical questionnaire and report will be available to the attending physician aboard each vessel. Passengers will be advised that sophisticated medical care is unavailable in the Antarctic.

4. IAATO members are further resolved to strongly recommend that its passengers take out comprehensive medical insurance, which will reimburse passengers for the cost of medical evacuation in the event of an emergency. (See Chapter 14 for further details about this plan.)

CURRENT CONDITIONS IN ARCTIC COMMUNICATIONS

The position in the Arctic is very different. There is no overreaching authority, such as the Antarctic Treaty, which governs activities in the Arctic. Each of the states surrounding the Arctic Ocean has its own national legislation, which to a large extent is formulated by the needs of its people and activities in the industrial centers to the south. Where these national conventions have been signed, their compliance varies from state to state. Much of the Arctic falls within the footprint of INMARSAT communications satellites, and it is only the high Arctic which suffers from a lack of cover. As in the Antarctic, areas above 70° lack coverage.

Communications networks in the Arctic depend to a great extent on where you are. In northern Canada and in Alaska, there is relatively good coverage. Settlements are regularly served by scheduled air routes, and commercial activity is so great that there is generally good medical backup because of good communications. In other areas, notably east Russia and north Greenland, coverage is poor except during their expedition season.

In the Arctic, organizing an expedition requires contact with the relevant government department. Some countries require permission to be granted before an expedition can take place. This may be a formality, as in Canada, or it may be a far more arduous task, as in northern Greenland. One of the problems of northeast Greenland is that you have to show the authorities there is someone willing to mount search-and-rescue missions in your area. Then you must get your insurance company to agree to indemnify you. In Greenland, the Danish state requires that your party be indemnified to the tune of 900,000 kroner (about U.S.$137,000), and that each individual in the party is covered for 250,000 kroner (about U.S.$38,000). The result is that the passengers on many of these trips have to pay approximately U.S.$185 for insurance for two weeks in Greenland.

A very different attitude toward expeditions and tourists exists in the Arctic as compared to the Antarctic. In part, this may be due to the interest shown by states in these activities in the more populated southern areas of their territories. It is also partly due to the much longer period that commercial operations have been going on in the Arctic, so there is not the overbearing civil service type mentality towards cooperation and access to information that is found in the Antarctic. In many ways, to the seasoned Antarctic traveler, this is the most refreshing part of Arctic travel. The downside is customs control!

Many areas in the Arctic also benefit, from the point of view of medical emergency coverage, from being overflown by frequent scheduled air routes. For example, in Greenland emergency location beacons can almost be guaranteed to work, as an aircraft is nearly always within radio view, and the authorities insist that expeditions carry beacons as standard equipment. These are very small and easy to carry, and there is a very good chance that the signal will be heard.

Attesting to the reliability of these beacons is the following story. At an airstrip in northeast Greenland in 1993, a party was parked at the airstrip waiting to fly out. One morning they were awakened at 0400 by a Danish air force jet roaring low overhead. They heard it had taken off from an airfield on the other side of Greenland in response to signals coming from a beacon, and the jet followed the signal to this airfield. So the expeditioners went to their crates, which were parked by the airstrip waiting for loading, opened them up, and found their radio beacon, untouched by human hands. Some unknown force had set it off! The only way they could stop the transmission was by snapping off the aerial. This piece of equipment probably cost about U.S.$15,000, about the same as the cost of the jet's trip. Their insurance company would not pay because there had not been a rescue. The manufacturer of the beacon could not be sued because it had gone bankrupt and was out of business. Technology does have its drawbacks.

The beacon, however, is ideal for backpacking trips since an HF radio weights 16 or 18 pounds and you may not want to carry it. However, with the HF radio, you do have voice communication, which is a distinct advantage. These communications are improving yearly. In 1994, using a mobile satellite, expeditioners talked directly from South Georgia to the Kodak labs in Los Angeles.

Why, with such technological advances, do communications remain such a problem? To be sure, all sorts of bureaucracies are part of the equation, but one must also remember that much of the polar regions is beyond good satellite communications. The magnetic poles can adversely affect HF communication, which today is the only other viable long-range competitor for satellite communication.

PROBLEMS ENCOUNTERED IN POLAR TRAVEL

To appreciate the problems of poor communication, medical care under extreme conditions, and evacuation, one should study some of the serious problems that have been encountered by tourist ships and aircraft. In the summer of 1994, the icebreaker *Kapitan Khlebnikov* was off the west coast of Greenland near Qaanaaq. A very vigorous woman slipped on the deck in calm weather and sustained what proved to be a severe fracture of the ankle. She had broken the bones on the outer side of the ankle and on the inner side of the ankle and back of the ankle. Fortunately the diagnosis was easy to make clinically, as the X-ray equipment on board the ship gave a very ghostly, foggy picture, and it was impossible to tell anything for certain from the film. Most of the available plaster on board the ship was used to cast the ankle and

Driving an icebreaker through heavy seas may send water crashing down from heights of over 80 feet.

leg in an attempt to put her bones back in the proper location. Because she did not carry specific evacuation insurance, it would have cost the woman about U.S.$47,000 to be returned by air to her home in Vancouver. The physician on board discussed matters with her and assured her that she would be well served by being casted on the ship and arranging for surgery on her return home. She elected this approach. The ship's doctor contacted her physicians at home and talked to an orthopedic surgeon. She was flown with a nurse from Toronto to Vancouver, where she went directly to a hospital for surgery. Everything worked out very well. This illustrates the kind of problems one can run into far away from a real hospital facility.

On the physician's next trip, a major problem occurred at the end of the Northwest Passage. The *Kapitan Khlebnikov* is, as are all icebreakers, a round-bottomed ship. Going through the passage had been uneventful; the very experienced crew did a competent job throughout. When the ship came around Banks Island and finally got out in the Beaufort Sea and the Chukchi Sea above the Bering Strait, she ran into a severe storm. Initially, the ship was unable to get to the Bering Strait because the captain worried that the ship would roll too severely and cause drastic problems. Therefore, the ship sailed instead along the northern coast of Siberia about 100 miles west of the strait. When the wind seemed to abate a bit, the ship turned around and headed south to the Bering Strait. The night before, the passengers were warned that during the turn itself there would be considerable rolling of the ship. The morning of the proposed turning people were warned again. A half hour before the contemplated turn, they were warned for the third time over the ship's radio. Five minutes before the turn, people were warned once more; they were told to go to their cabins and to hold on to something substantial, as the severe rolling would be for a very short period—maybe a minute or two.

Regrettably, at that time some of the passengers had headed to the bridge. The Russians are extremely good sailors, but they are rather new in the tourist business, and they were anxious to please. Therefore, they did not close the bridge; they did not feel it was their job to tell the passengers what they could and could not do. Hearing this, the ship's surgeon hastened to the bridge, arriving just before the turn, and found many people with video cameras preparing to photograph the action. He urged them not to do this and advised them to hold on tightly. The ship made its turn and rolled twice, starboard, port, starboard, port, in a very good roll. The captain said it rolled to about 52°! Surprisingly enough, it was relatively easy to hold on, but some people were too busy taking pictures and were thrown about. And when they did get thrown, they became like bowling balls, rolling across the bridge and taking other people down. In fact, most of the injuries occurred to people who were standing doing exactly what they had been told to do. The net result was that there were thirty-eight people who required medical attention.

One of the fortunate things was that there were several physicians in the tourist group. As a social courtesy the ship's surgeon usually makes a point of meeting the other physicians who are passengers aboard. The preceding week the surgeon had invited these physicians to dinner, and subsequently taken them to see the "hospital," where they met the Russian physician. He was certainly a qualified physician, but his standards of medicine were not up to western standards. The ship's surgeon was particularly fortunate when the accident happened to have the western doctors aboard: one was an orthopedic surgeon who was also a hand surgeon and another was a neurosurgeon.

Immediately after the accident occurred, the physicians set up a triage system. A woman who had previously worked as a nurse was appointed as the triage officer to determine which people needed treatment as opposed to those who were shouting most loudly for treatment. The western "staff" took over the "hospital" and started taking care of the injuries that were most significant: a man with a broken back and another with a broken leg. One man lost a finger when he was trying to grab something while sliding along the bridge area. Many people had lacerations. The next eighteen hours were spent nonstop caring for the injured. All the suture material on board was used up. Early on, the local anesthesia was also exhausted. Working as a team the western staff was able to give reasonable care to all the injured.

One of the considerations in traveling with the elderly population is that many of these people are on anticoagulants or use aspirin regularly. The previous night during the storm, a woman was thrown from her berth and lacerated the back of her head. As one might expect, because of her medications she bled profusely and the bleeding would not stop even with pressure dressings. A skin stapler came in very handy at that time. It later was implemented as part of the medical kit on that ship's trips.

It should be noted it was not only the passengers on the bridge who were injured. Several people who had retired to their cabins were actually thrown out of their cabins through knock-out panels on the doors of the cabins used for fire prevention that come out fairly easily. Three people were thrown out, two of them head first, through these doors, and of course they were badly cut and damaged.

There was another western physician who could have helped, but he was one of the innocent people holding on, on the bridge, and he had his Achilles tendon ripped loose, though not severed, by one of the other passengers cascading past. One individual sustained a ruptured spleen and another had a head injury of real concern.

The ship approached the coast of Siberia a day later, and eventually an air-evac team from Nome, Alaska, came to Siberia to assist. Since the ship was in port a day ahead of schedule, nobody was allowed off the ship in Provideniya, Siberia, except for the western ship's surgeon and the two severely injured people. Fortunately, they both did well.

Considering this trip reinforces the fact that there are risks when you undertake such an expedition. Most of the people know there is risk, but emotionally they are not prepared for the risk. They have seen glossy brochures with pretty pictures that usually show the weather as fine, and the snow and ice as very clean and pristine. It all seems so exciting. There is even a club called The Century Club in the United States which encourages people to go to places so that they can "collect countries." Over a hundred countries must be "collected" for one to qualify for membership. The Arctic and the Antarctic are divided into sectors that count as countries. Many of these people are not prepared for what they find; they are only thinking in terms of their "country" collection. Some of them get into serious trouble and are totally ill-prepared to accept what is happening.

Fortunately, trips encountering serious problems are extremely unusual. But the doctor has to be prepared to deal with these situations. In the case cited, the western-supplied surgical and medical kit was excellent, but it was not set up to service mass casualties and the Russian surgical supplies were very few.

Better coordination and greater number of supplies for ships carrying substantial numbers of tourists are in order. The reluctance on the part of tour operators to spend large amounts of money on things that may or may not be used is understandable. The medicines and supplies may not be employed, and it is easy to feel that spending additional money is not necessary. Standards must be established regarding what is necessary when one is dealing with ships in isolated areas.

Being able to communicate with outside medical help is also vitally important. Doctors should have information available regarding evacuation possibilities and routes, as well as services available in the various locations to which one would evacuate patients.

Finally, in the matter of air evacuation, probably not one passenger in a hundred really understands whether his or her insurance will allow evacuation. In the Antarctic in 1993, a woman cracked her head and authorization came from Cambridge, United Kingdom, to allow air evacuation. The cost was U.S.$75,000, and the company required payment within a month. Aside from the money, if a plane is sent out to air evac someone, and if the physician flies out with the sick or injured person, he or she would not be available for other medical problems on the ship. Fuel resources could be used up that otherwise would be available for the trip. And then there's the possibility that there could be a tragedy on the air evac, too.

On November 28, 1979, an Air New Zealand tourist sightseeing flight crashed into Mount Erebus, killing all 257 people aboard. Passengers had boarded the DC-10 in Auckland for a round-trip to Antarctica, expecting to return to Christchurch. Difficult weather conditions obscured visibility, and the pilots were unfamiliar with the terrain and Antarctic flying conditions. This was also the pilot's first trip to Antarctica. In retrospect, disaster seemed inevitable. While flying low over what the pilot believed to be McMurdo Sound, the plane disappeared. No one survived. This single worst accident in Antarctic history taxed the limited facilities available at nearby McMurdo Station so severely that rescue workers commented that the passengers aboard flight 901 were fortunate to die on impact, because there was no equipment aboard to keep them from freezing in the Antarctic cold, and the limited ground resources would not have been sufficient to save many crash survivors.

In the summer of 1993, the Russian diesel icebreaker *Kapitan Khlebnikov* attempted to circumnavigate Greenland. The Russian nuclear icebreaker, the *Sovetskiy Soyuz,* one of the most powerful icebreakers in the world, was scheduled to be available for emergencies. Only when the expedition was well under way was the tour group chartering the vessel advised that the nuclear icebreaker had been commandeered by the Russian government to work on the northern sea route where there were extremely severe ice conditions. The icebreaker was desperately needed to assist in bringing relief supplies to areas of Siberia. Fortunately, when the diesel icebreaker became beset above Cape Morris Jessup, Greenland, another Russian nuclear icebreaker, the *Yamal,* was diverted from a tourist cruise after she had left the North Pole to come to their assistance. After four days in the ice, the *Kapitan Khlebnikov* was freed up. It was a very exciting experience for the passengers, but from the standpoint of the ship's surgeon, it could have been a disaster. Possibly the passengers could have been evacuated to Cape Morris Jessup, and hopefully from there could have been evacuated by fixed wing aircraft to the Canadian air base at Alert on the northeast corner of Ellesmere Island. From there, they might have been taken down to Resolute, far to the south, and from there, flown to major cities in Canada. The entire trip would have been thousands of miles, and there was serious question whether many of the older passengers could have handled flights of this type and the problems with exposure transferring to aircraft under these

Russian M-2 helicopter preparing for flight-seeing operation from the deck of the Kapitan Khlebnikov *in Scoresby Sund, Greenland, August 26, 1993.*

very harsh conditions. There are no evacuation plans for situations like this in many areas of the high Arctic.

To get a further perspective of the rescue by the *Yamal* and the potential that existed for relying on the Canadian air force base at Alert, consider the following. In October 1991, a Canadian air force Hercules plane was on a routine flight taking supplies to the early warning station at Alert. Only ten miles (16 kilometers) from the base, the pilot miscalculated his altitude in the dark, caught a wing on the side of a hill, and crashed. Of the eighteen crew and passengers, thirteen survived.

The injuries included broken limbs, paraplegia, massive lacerations, head injuries, frostbite, and hypothermia. The one doctor in the group was so badly injured that she was unable to provide care, and medical and survival equipment was destroyed in the crash. There were land vehicles at Alert, but they could not get to the crash because there is a canyon between the base and the crash. The nearest helicopter was thousands of miles away. A helicopter and crew made the 3,600-mile (5,792-kilometer) 40-hour journey up through northern Canada, over Baffin Island to the limits of civilization and to an area where navigational aids were useless. A sophisticated navigational plane was assigned to help them find the way, but ended up being able to tell them only in which direction to turn.

The search-and-rescue technicians were alerted and were on their way there within two hours. Unfortunately, the support that they had from the Canadian government in 1991 was pathetically inadequate: World War II design parachutes, poor clothing, radio batteries that did not work, no night vision goggles, etc. There was a momentary break in the cloud cover that enabled the SAR techs to jump into the freezing, windswept night not long before a land-based group of SAR techs pushed its way through the storm to join them. Another dismantled helicopter had been flown up in a cargo plane and was reassembled in record time, just in time to fly to the crash and evacuate the injured. Considering this saga, is it any wonder a physician would have deep concerns about the possible evacuation of the tourists on the icebreaker to Alert? There are real risks in the high Arctic, and the industry must be better prepared for them.

The situation in the Antarctic is somewhat different, because of the larger number of tourist ships and the number of permanent bases on the Antarctic Peninsula. A number of commercial tourist voyages and a number of smaller expeditions have gotten into difficulties requiring assistance. In 1994, when a passenger on *The Explorer* sustained a fractured hip, help was sought at Rothera, a British Antarctic Survey base. Base physicians concurred that evacuation and early surgery in Punta Arenas was warranted, but there was reluctance on the part of base personnel to commit to dispatching a plane. This is quite understandable from several viewpoints: the cost to the base and the taxpayer was considerable; recently a plane flying from the base had crashed after hitting an iceberg with a heavy load of fuel, with tragic loss of life as well as the specter of litigation; and consumption of fuel cached for scientific research would be expended, jeopardizing planned work. Ultimately, a decision was made in Cambridge, United Kingdom, to permit the evacuation and the surgery was performed successfully in Chile. The total cost was approximately

Nuclear icebreaker rescuing Kapitan Khlebnikov *off the northernmost post of Greenland, September 4, 1993.*

U.S.$75,000, but the entire sum was repaid to the British treasury within a fortnight.

In 1994, while crossing Drake Passage on a relatively calm day, a passenger stepped out onto a wet deck from the bridge. He promptly fell and sustained a fracture dislocation of the kneecap. Among the tourists were two orthopedic surgeons who concurred that evacuation should be undertaken so that the man might have surgery within a week to preserve the function of his knee. To the credit of the expedition leader, when he was advised by the ship's surgeon of this need, he promptly turned the *Kapitan Khlebnikov* around and headed back for Punta Arenas. Evacuation by motor launch was done as the ship approached the tip of South America, and the passenger was subsequently flown home to Paris where the required surgery was done with a successful result. Unfortunately, on a subsequent cruise of the same ship, immediately following the briefing where the ship's surgeon urged care when traveling on wet decks, a woman fell in the same place, fracturing her nose and losing a considerable amount of blood.

Evacuation of tourist with fractured patella by motor launch in Drake Passage.

POSSIBILITIES FOR IMPROVEMENT IN COMMUNICATIONS

Telemedicine technology is in its infancy on tourist ships. Many ship's surgeons have telephoned colleagues in their home country for advice and consultation. Electrocardiograms have been sent from above the Arctic Circle for consultation in the United States. Transmitted images are an excellent medium for viewing skin conditions, X rays, pathology images, and funduscopic (interior of the eyeball) findings. Rapid changes in technology make it difficult to predict the role of telemedicine in future practice; however, trends suggest that within the next few years physicians will be able to see patients at remote sites by using a desktop workstation or laptop computer and a mobile wireless configuration. A number of organizations now offer medical communications, evacuation, and care from sea and distant areas of the world. (See appendix H.) The potential for the ship's surgeon of the future is tremendous.

Even the most capable ship's surgeon needs help. It is not really fair to rely on the hope that there will be several physicians and nurses available among the tourist group if disaster strikes. It would be better to have members of the expedition staff certified in cardiopulmonary resuscitation (CPR) and have basic paramedical or wilderness medical training.

IAATO, working with ANI, apparently has a good evacuation plan for tourists in trouble in the peninsula area. But what about the rest of Antarctica? What about the possibilities of mass disaster? And what about the possibility of one of our greatest fears, fire at sea? And where is a disaster plan for the Arctic?

The real question is not whether any of these things will happen, but *when* they will happen. The search-and-rescue and communications problems have tremendous bearing on medical care in the polar world. Although IAATO is starting to assume some responsibility in this area, it is necessary to broaden this entire effort. Many ship's surgeons, explorers, and polar scientists feel the time is long overdue to establish systematic organization in all of these areas of the polar environment. IAATO is perfectly positioned to form a committee of experts in these various disciplines to study and implement all of these needed improvements. The need is obvious.

CHAPTER 8

Physician Qualifications, Medical Equipment, and Medical Supplies for a Polar Tourist Ship

> In preparing a search expedition for Sir John Franklin, the doctor found the vessel to be so small that he "declined the honor of accompanying her." In this emergency, I ventured to perform the duties that such an officer [a doctor] would be called upon to discharge. Medicine had to me long been a pleasing study; and in several merchant vessels to which I had formerly belonged, no doctor but the captain was ever thought of. A good medicine chest and medical guide was all that the skipper of those ships deemed necessary. With M'Arthur's excellent little book of directions, Reece's invaluable medical guide, and the humble skill I myself possess, I thought all would be well.
>
> —W. Parker Snow, 1850

In 1970 when I assisted the ship's surgeon on the first cruise of the *Lindblad Explorer*, the medical and surgical supplies were very limited. The ECG machine didn't work, and the X-ray machine was not assembled. There were no medical reference books aboard. One was truly very much alone in the great Southern Ocean.

But times have changed. Chapter 5 detailed how the American College of Emergency Physicians Cruise Ship and Maritime Medicine Section had been grappling with medical legal issues and discussing complex medical issues such as why thrombolytic therapy should be standard on cruise ships. They recognized the tremendous interest in these issues by the cruise industry, the legal profession, physician review organizations, the media, the traveling public, and particularly the physicians who feel cruise ships can and should provide emergency care similar to that available at home. Indeed, many of their recommendations are excellent (see appendix E) and can be easily implemented for ships carrying 1,500 passengers often sailing only a few hours from evacuation to medical centers.

Conversely, most expeditions and ships in the polar regions are usually days or even weeks from medical center care. Paradoxically, in a situation where the medical needs may be the greatest, these ships have fewer trained personnel, less equipment, and limited medical supplies. Too often the physicians have not been prepared for life-threatening problems. It is apparent that a large medical disaster is inevitable.

How do we prepare for these responsibilities? Let me share what I have learned as an expedition physician, a ship's surgeon, and a medical director who has hired physicians for many cruises on small ships, and diesel and nuclear icebreakers. Most of these ships carry crews of 60 to 130, and approximately 100 passengers. On the chartered Russian ships, the Russians always provide a physician for their crew. The Russian physicians' approach to medicine is often far different from that of the western-trained professional. Their competence varies greatly, and they rarely ask for help from the western doctors on board. Unfortunately, their facilities and equipment are also of poor quality. Using their medicines is difficult due to labeling and often no expiration dates are listed. To be sure, however, some of these Russian physicians have been very competent and most helpful to the passengers and to the western doctor. Cruises on the larger of these Russian ships provide a second physician for the passengers, that is, a western physician. The smaller Russian cruise ships chartered by several different tour companies use the Russian physician for both crew and passengers. As a rule, the other (non-Russian) polar cruise vessels have a western-trained physician serving both crew and passengers.

On most cruises the expedition staff and the majority of the passengers speak English. Therefore, the ships carry an English-speaking western physician, but ability in another language is a distinct plus. Fortunately, translators seem to be found when needed. However, this has been a decided limitation in a crisis situation with many injured and triage being necessary.

QUALIFICATIONS OF AN APPROPRIATE PHYSICIAN

With a small ship, there will usually be only one physician, and no assistants. Finding the right physician is therefore extremely important. Over these years my thinking has evolved and these are the qualifications I have sought in finding cruise ship physicians:

- Graduation from an accredited medical school.
- Familiarity with drugs from the United States, the United Kingdom, Australia, and New Zealand.
- American Board certification *or* equivalent training in emergency medicine, general medicine, or one of the clinical specialties.
- Minimum of three years of clinical experience after postgraduate training. Ability to do *general* medicine and a sense of good judgment are critical.
- Certification in advanced cardiac life support and advanced trauma support, *or* equivalent experience or training.
- Active medical license and Drug Enforcement Administration registration (United States only).
- A curriculum vitae (CV) should be provided.
- In addition to and above all these qualifications, the physician must be caring, innovative, and responsible. The patient comes first, *not* the physician's travel interest. He or she must be comfortable associating with the passengers, staff, and crew. The doctor must double as a safety officer and be available and conversant with safety issues both on and off the ship, as well as on helicopters and Zodiac-type craft.

My best experience has been recruiting physicians well known to me both professionally and personally. Well-credentialed physicians who are friends of friends often are good choices. I have learned to avoid physicians whose curricula vitae indicate their areas of expertise are far away from the needs of the expedition. The first choice would be actively practicing physicians in their forties or fifties who have been to sea previously and have experienced the polar regions. Retirees are often more available, but one must be concerned about their skills and interest in the *medical* aspects of the voyage.

Physicians with unusual religious zeal, ones suspected of abuse of alcohol or drugs as well as physicians with personality disorders should be avoided. Hopefully, the well-rounded physician has a spouse accompanying him or her who has the same positive attitude and who would help the physician and expedition staff as needed.

The "super specialist" should also be avoided. One very capable emergency physician was distraught because he was without many additional drugs that he felt "would be nice to have." This same physician insisted on providing a sterile glove to each passenger to use when inserting a rectal suppository for seasickness. Although this person had functioned well in a tertiary medical center where consultants were a phone call away, I questioned how he might have coped and improvised during a real medical disaster at sea.

One must be most cautious in employing physicians whose careers have been exclusively at tertiary medical centers. They may not function well on a small ship where consultants, laboratory tests, etc., are often not available. A physician who is trained in emergency medicine and well experienced in rural general practice is usually an excellent candidate for the position. Unfortunately, these candidates are hard to find and usually are not available for long tours. Ideally, a physician should serve several tours or some months at sea, but this type of person is extremely difficult to find.

REQUIREMENTS AND ACCOMMODATIONS FOR PHYSICIANS ON BOARD

The physician on board will be on twenty-four-hour call. Either office hours are scheduled daily, or the doctor may be seen when needed. This must be worked out with the expedition leader. All serious, or potentially serious, medical problems should be reported immediately to the expedition leader and the captain of the ship. Proper medical records using the S.O.A.P. system (S = subjective findings, O = objective findings, A = assessment, and P = plan of treatment) are the physician's responsibility and on all serious cases, an additional narrative record must be kept. It is also the physician's responsibility to send with disembarking passengers, copies of medical records that may be important for their ongoing care and pertinent X rays. The expedition leader will want copies of any records of a serious nature, as will the medical director of the tour company. Obviously, the physician should also keep copies of all patients' medical records to refer to for any future events.

On polar cruises it is customary to provide the physician and his or her spouse with one of the regular passenger cabins. Unfortunately, in a number of instances, physicians have been placed in the most undesirable accommodations on the ship. Not only is this difficult for the physicians and their spouses, but it is also an extremely inadequate place to have a doctor's office. Each physician hired should have a firm understanding with the tour company regarding accommodations. All meals should be provided, and there should be an allowance for the laundry and bar bill.

Transportation from home to the ship and return is often provided for cruises of over one month, and spousal transportation if the physician serves for two full months. The physician personally never bills for professional services, and many ships do not charge passengers for medical or surgical supplies. Not only is this a usual U.S. standard, but a similar standard has been in effect for hundreds of physicians who have served on small cruise ships booked out of Sweden for many years. Each tour company has its own arrangements with physicians and allowances vary. Larger ships on which the ship's surgeon may be extremely busy often have very different arrangements, and the physician may be salaried.

EQUIPMENT AND SUPPLIES

Inasmuch as types and amounts of medicine and supplies will vary based upon the number and age of the passengers and crew, the length of the cruise and ability to restock, careful planning is necessary. One must consider, in addition to the routine needs, what would be needed in case of a mass disaster with trauma at sea or an epidemic like bacterial food poisoning. Also to be considered are the availability of drugs at ports of call and the special needs in situations such as being beset in the polar ice. With an older population, the need to be able to treat acute cardiovascular disease is very apparent. Unusual and very expensive medicines may be necessary, but it is dubious that they could be used in a distant area with limited capability for monitoring. All of these problems are compounded by considerations such as expiration dates on medicines and storage conditions. To be reasonably well-equipped is a difficult and expensive proposition. To be prepared for any disaster that might occur is virtually impossible. Books such as *KURAFID,* the *ANARE First Aid Manual, Expedition Medicine,* and the *Merck Manual* all present good information on types and amounts of medicines that might be carried. Lists are available from commercial companies, and they too may be consulted in preparing the ship's medical and surgical supplies (see appendix E). A careful inventory of all medical supplies and equipment must be done by the doctor and the ship's expedition office to allow for an orderly system for resupply. This is a big problem for all small ships. The problem may be compounded further by individual differences in physicians' prescribing patterns, unexpected needs, and the problems attendant with carrying sufficient amounts of narcotics. Ultimately, however, the physician must be responsible for these supplies, as well as for the proper first-aid supplies for helicopters and Zodiac craft.

In January 1997 Rotary International held a meeting with 285 Rotarians and guests from 23 nations at an Argentine base on the Antarctic Peninsula. Equipment was donated to improve communications among the Antarctic bases. This donation was designed to enhance an earlier project by Rotarians in Argentina and the United States that assembled a list of medicines available in various Antarctic locations. The idea would have been fine—if it had come to fruition. Regrettably, recent inquiries to the headquarters of Rotary International, the individuals involved in the project, and practicing polar medical people showed that these groups were not even aware of the project.

Advances in medicine have added another problematic dimension. Some physicians want defibrillators on *all* ships, but as several cardiologists have asked, "Can you be sure the machine will be well maintained?" "Will you have a crash cart ready with all the needed supplies?" "Will there be a team trained and drilling at intervals for the emergency?" "If the passenger is fortunate enough to be the one in three that recovers, will you have the monitors and personnel to follow through?" "Do you have the laboratory needed?" Formerly, I belonged to the pragmatic group of physicians who would want portable oxygen, an item not readily available on all small cruise ships, and would be satisfied with basic drugs for cardiac emergencies. I felt there was no need to carry some of the newer anti-arrhythmic drugs that are dangerous and require special monitoring of the patient. I realize that keeping it simple and doing it well still covers over 90 percent of the cardiac problems. However, Australia's Qantas Airways, Virgin Atlantic, and Air Zimbabwe now carry defibrillators and increased medical supplies. As of July 1, 1997, American Airlines had installed about three hundred defibrillators on aircraft—mainly those flying over water routes far from land—at main terminals, and other key locations. Twenty-three hundred cabin attendants have been trained to operate these machines that administer an electric shock to the victim's heart. These defibrillators are about the same size and weight as a laptop computer and include printed and voice prompts. Some of the smaller cruise ships are being equipped in a similar fashion.

New devices that automatically detect and interpret abnormal heartbeats and deliver electrical jolts to restore normal rhythm could save many who die of cardiac arrest. These advanced versions of the defibrillators that doctors and paramedics have used for years are so automated that only minimal training is needed to use them. Automatic defibrillators have been tested by firefighters in Seattle, Washington. After only four hours of training these firefighters were able to give shock treatment to victims and greatly increase their chances for survival.

On September 11, 1996, the Food and Drug Administration approved smaller and less expensive machines that can shock a stopped heart into beating again. These new units weigh less than four pounds and cost as little as $2,700. Experts claim that a third of the 300,000 Americans who die yearly of cardiac arrest might be saved by prompt use of one of these new units. In May 1997 at the annual meeting of the Federal Aviation Administration many companies were competing in the rapidly expanding market to provide defibrillators on commercial aircraft. Simple battery-driven electro-cardiogram machines are also now available for just under $1,000. They can be attached to a simple computer printout device and permanent records obtained.

The Laerdal portable aspirating unit is another tool that has proved to be excellent. Having one of the simpler hand respirators and airways is also important. Some small ships now carry endotracheal tubes. However, in this case, a problem may arise: having established a satisfactory airway, if the physician does not have an electric resuscitator to maintain the patient's respiration and a possible way of transferring that patient to a hospital where he or she can get diagnostic and therapeutic followup care, then what has been accomplished for this patient? However, this is not to say that the ship's surgeon should not consider the advantages of the new technology, for there is little doubt that the public will soon expect this level of sophisticated care.

It is critical to have sufficient supplies of *disposable* syringes and needles as well as *disposable* suture needles. (It is hard to believe, but there are still ships carrying and *using* reusable needles which have the threat of spreading HIV and hepatitis virus.) Likewise, disposable instruments and wound staples in disposable sterile packs are very handy. In May 1997 the *Journal of the American Medical Association* announced the effectiveness and advantages of using a group of adhesives called octylcyanoacrylates for rapid and painless wound closure that may replace the need to suture millions of lacerations each year.

On the smaller ships, the physician must be able to take and interpret an ECG, as well as take, develop, and read an X ray. One may question the need of an X-ray machine with only a hundred passengers, but in the often very rough waters of the Southern Ocean, many fractures occur. The newer portable machine with a Xerox-type processor of dry film is ideal equipment for these ships.

Innovations of all types should be considered in the polar cruise environment, but probably one of the first—and most cost-effective—measures that could be taken would be to train all the members of the expedition staff in cardiopulmonary resuscitation (CPR) and wilderness survival techniques. Not only would these trained individuals be of great help to the ship's physician in an acute emergency, they would also serve a valuable role in a mass disaster.

SPECIAL CONSIDERATIONS

It is particularly helpful, as early as possible on each cruise, to identify all health professionals on board. This is very useful in consultation and can be lifesaving in a calamity. Several points are worth making. Because of the concerns of malpractice suits, many physicians travel without using "Dr." before their name. Therefore, it is best to ask professionals to identify themselves to you privately and not in front of an assembled group. As the physician for the ship, you have a liability as either an employee or an independent contractor. However, if the physician who is on the ship as a tourist is asked to assist, he or she does so under the guise of the Good Samaritan rule

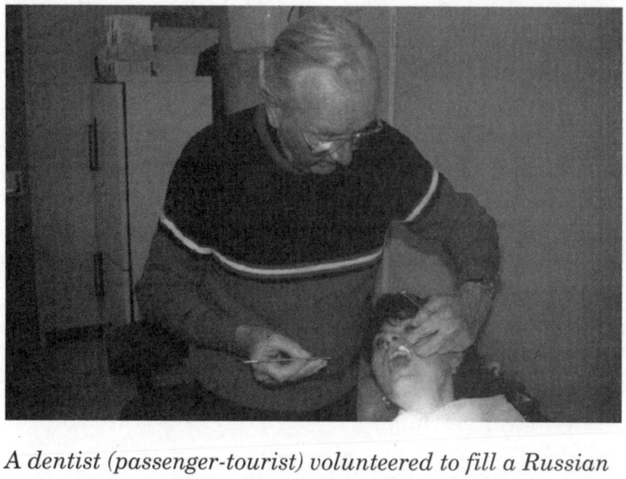

A dentist (passenger-tourist) volunteered to fill a Russian crew member's tooth at Australian Casey station.

and there should be no litigation that can be brought against that person.

The medical facilities on small polar cruise ships and icebreakers are generally inadequate. In truth, on many ships the Western physicians prefer to use their own cabins for their office because it is not only convenient, but it is clean, equipment and supplies are handy, and the physician's spouse can function as the nurse. Adequate storage space for medical equipment, supplies, and medicines is a frequent problem.

Physicians' complaints are not infrequent. Here are a few I have heard myself: "I couldn't find any sterile gloves." "The sterilizer was broken and I had to boil instruments in the kitchen." "It's very difficult to find the Russian doctor." "The meds were in a mess, and the last doctor never kept an inventory. I didn't have a lot to work with." "There wasn't an electrical plug to convert ship's power to what was needed for the ECG machine—I was lucky I didn't have anyone with a coronary." "The expedition leader was no help at all." "The X-ray film is out of date." "This is really third-world medicine!"

These problems are not new, nor are they only related to ships in polar waters. More than twenty years ago, according to a well-respected ship's surgeon, the ships' doctors of a prominent travel company were hired directly by the company because they had no medical director. Some of the doctors were very young and inexperienced, others very old and not always in the best of health. Most were Americans, some foreigners, but they did not know each other and, of course, did not feel much responsibility to their successors. Some made just one trip, considered it as a good vacation, and left the ship without any intention to return. Maybe they fulfilled their medical duties, but they often neglected organizational responsibilities and didn't take the trouble to note the duties of the ship's doctor (that is, "Instructions for the Ship's Doctor"), or make an inventory list, which resulted in lots of necessities being absent. The drug supply on one of the ships was very strange: some medicines were obsolete and a lot of necessary ones were missing. The surgical room was very dirty, the refrigerator was used to store hats and old tennis shoes, the surgical instruments rusty and unusable, and the sterilizer out of order. The X-ray machine had never been unpacked, much less mounted or used, and there was no X-ray film or chemicals for developing films. That was in 1976 on a world-class cruise ship that was very fashionable in its day.

It is obvious that to provide proper ship's medicine each ship's surgeon must have written instructions, and must read and study them *before* embarkation. Furthermore, there must be a good working relationship among the responsible ship's surgeon, the expedition leader, and the senior person serving as liaison between the ship and the travel company. Physicians who know their predecessors and their successors usually function better. Any equipment failure, communication failure, or shortage of critical supplies on these little ships cruising at the end of the world can be lethal. It is axiomatic that each tour company must have a medical director with not only the total responsibility, but also the full authority to arrange for a proper medical facility. This will cost money, but in the long run it will be cheaper than the cost of a disaster.

Each medical facility should also have a small reference library. Additional books would be a real plus. Suggestions for this library include the following (see the reference section of this book for full bibliographic information on these reference books):

- *Physicians' Desk Reference*
- *Merck Manual*
- *Current Emergency Diagnosis and Treatment*
- *KURAFID* (British Antarctic Survey Medical Handbook)
- *ANARE First Aid Manual*

The *KURAFID* and *ANARE First Aid Manual* are written for nonprofessionals, but these two books are very helpful for quick reference.

Laboratory medicine is emerging on small cruise ships. The urine dipstick and one of the blood glucose monitoring systems are advisable. Hemoglobin and hematocrit tests and pregnancy tests can also be very helpful.

It must be stressed that what each ship needs most, regardless of the state of its medical facilities, medicines, and supplies, is a skilled physician with very special judgment and compassion for life-threatening problems in the distant and hostile polar environment. Hippocrates told physicians to "do no harm." I knew a pharmacist's mate in World War II who performed an appendectomy in a U.S. submarine while under attack in Tokyo Bay. His action was heroic, yes, but clinically not clever. Unless one has the skills and can adequately work out all the details, it is probably best to use IVs, antibiotics, analgesics, and a nasogastric tube.

CHAPTER 9

Hypothermia and Cold Injuries: Relevance to Polar Tourism

by Peter Sullivan, M.B., B.S., Medical Research Officer, Australian Antarctic Division

> A cup of boiling water thrown into the air in temperatures below -60°F (-51°C) will explode into a bursting cloud of minute ice particles.
>
> —Wally Herbert, 1971

The most compelling impression the majority of people have of the polar regions is the extreme cold. This is only to be expected considering that temperatures as low as -94°F (-70°C) have been recorded in the Arctic and -129.3°F (-89.6°C) on the Antarctic plateau. Given that such low temperatures, often combined with the strong winds, are a feature of these regions, it is not remarkable that cold injuries feature so prominently in any consideration of polar medicine.

The history of polar exploration is studded with examples of "exposure" (hypothermia) and frostbite literally presenting threats to life and limb of early travelers. Even with the sophisticated facilities currently available, cold injuries still pose a risk to members of national scientific expeditions in both the Arctic and Antarctica. However, the Australian Antarctic Division's experience is that doctors in the "frozen continent" have not had to deal with a large number of such cold injuries. Rather, by concentrating on prevention (stressing adequate cold-climate training, early recognition and treatment of symptoms, and proper clothing and equipment), the number and severity of such problems can be kept to a minimum.

Fortunately most polar tourism occurs during the summer months and is largely conducted at sea level; hence, the climatic conditions are not as harsh as might be anticipated. In addition, most ship-based tourism is well controlled, with only a minimal chance of individuals being under-clothed, lost, stranded, or shipwrecked. Nonetheless, one must learn to "expect the unexpected," and it is incumbent on anyone providing medical support to polar tourism to be familiar with the conditions of hypothermia, frostbite, and nonfreezing cold injury.

In addition to the "average" escorted tourist, there is emerging a new breed of travelers—the adventure tourists. These individuals deliberately place themselves in a harsh environment to either appreciate or test themselves against the wilderness. Whether they be yachtsmen, mountain climbers, trekkers to the Pole, or simply adventure seekers, they are all at considerably greater risk of encountering one or more of the various forms of cold injury.

In order to adequately comprehend the cause, initial management, and prevention of such cold injuries it is essential to first understand something about human thermoregulation.

REGULATION OF BODY TEMPERATURE

In order to function effectively, human beings must maintain an internal body temperature within a few degrees of the "normal" of 98.6°F (37°C). This preservation of a stable temperature is achieved by a balance between heat production and heat loss and is regulated through an extremely complex set of detectors (in the brain—especially the hypothalamus—the skin, and a variety of deep body sites) and effectors (smooth muscle in the blood vessels, sweat glands, shivering, or exercising muscles).

In cold conditions, the body attempts to maintain its internal temperature, the "core" temperature, by increasing heat production and decreasing heat loss.

Heat production

Heat is constantly produced by normal body functions such as respiration and digestion, that is, metabolic heat production. Even more heat is produced by muscular activity during exercise—up to ten to twenty times above resting levels. Shivering is an involuntary form of exercise designed to increase heat production (by up to about five times) when the core temperature starts to drop.

Mechanisms of heat loss

Radiation—Heat can be lost from a warm object to the surrounding colder environment by infrared radiation. The temperature difference is obviously a major determining factor in how much heat is lost through radiation, but so is surface area. This is one reason why infants (with their high surface area to volume ratio) are more susceptible to hypothermia, and also why fingers and toes (again with a large surface area) are more subject to frostbite.

Conduction—Direct contact with surfaces colder than the body results in conductive heat loss. When standing and in dry conditions, the human body loses little heat by conduction—only what is conducted through the soles of the feet. Consequently, conduction is often not incorporated in laboratory-based formulae for thermal balance (see example below). However, the situation is markedly altered if an individual either becomes wet or lies down on a cold surface, particularly metal. Such actions result in a marked increase in conductive losses. Water in particular, with a thermal conductivity twenty-five times greater than that of air, conducts heat away from the body much more rapidly.

Convection—With convection, heat is transferred within a liquid or gas by the movement of heated particles or molecules. An example is the observation that water at the bottom of a saucepan rises as it is heated. Individuals will lose heat by convection even in still conditions; heating of the layer of air next to the skin will cause it to rise, with cooler air moving in to take its place. This cool layer will in turn draw heat away from the body as it warms up to skin temperature. Convective heat losses are much greater in windy conditions because this layer of warmed air is constantly being swept away.

Evaporation—Heat is lost from the body through the latent heat of evaporation, that is, the energy required to convert a liquid (for example, water) to a gas. This can occur through sweating, insensible perspiration, respiration, or wet clothing. Evaporation is especially significant when combined with the convective heat losses associated with wind.

Reduction of Heat Loss—The body reduces heat loss by decreasing the flow of warm blood to the skin (vasoconstriction). Compared to other animals, humans are not very efficient at such physiological heat loss reduction mechanisms, but make up for this by their ability to insulate themselves with clothing and shelter.

Thermal balance

As long as the body stays in thermal balance, that is, with neither heat gain nor loss, the core temperature will remain in a steady state at around 98.6°F (37°C). Thermal balance can be considered in terms of mathematical formulae, for example:

$$\text{Heat Balance} = M - W = Q_{sk} + Q_{res} = (C + R + E_{sk}) + (C_{res} + E_{res})$$

where all terms have units of watts per square meter WM^{-2}, and

M = rate of metabolic heat production
W = rate of mechanical work
Q_{sk} = total rate of heat loss from the skin
Q_{res} = total rate of heat loss through respiration
C_{res} = rate of convective heat loss from respiration
E_{res} = rate of evaporative heat loss from respiration
C = rate of convective heat loss from the skin
R = rate of radiative heat loss from the skin
E_{sk} = rate of total evaporative heat loss from the skin

Alternatively, thermal balance can perhaps be more easily understood by reviewing figure 1.

There are limits to both heat production and insulation, and when these prove insufficient to maintain the body's core temperature, hypothermia occurs. In

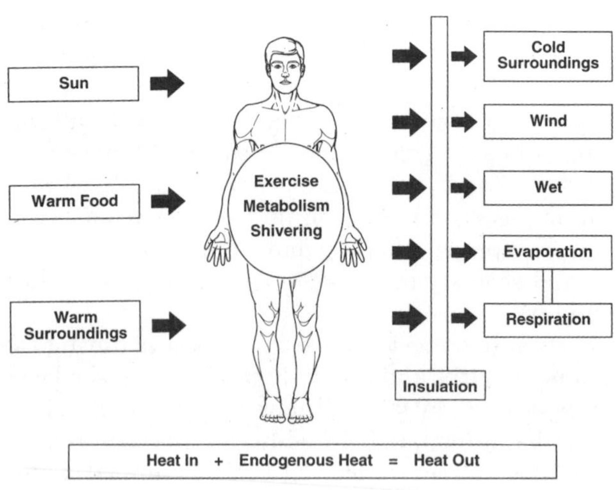

Figure 1. *Thermal balance. As long as the amount of heat lost is equal to that produced by the body (plus any heat gained from food and radiation sources such as the sun), the body is in a state of thermal balance and the core temperature will remain at approximately 98.6°F (37°C).*

addition to this generalized body cooling, attempts to shunt the warm blood to the core can mean that the extremities chill even faster, leading to local cold injuries. These problems are especially likely if the rate of heat loss from the body is accelerated, for example, by wet clothing, windchill, or by the skin being in contact with cold metal or volatile liquids.

Windchill

The phenomenon of feeling colder in conditions of even low wind has been recognized since earliest times, but was not adequately quantified until the middle of the twentieth century when Paul Siple and his colleagues conducted a series of experiments (some of them in Antarctica) into the heat loss of plastic cylinders of water. Subsequently they came up with the concept of a windchill index (WCI) and formulated an equation to estimate the rate of cooling of exposed skin:

$$\mathrm{WCI} = \left(10\sqrt{v} + 10.45 - v\right)(33 - t_a)$$

where v is wind velocity in meters per second and t_a is ambient temperature in degrees Celsius.

A variant, known as the windchill equivalent temperature chart, has been widely used to help predict the likelihood of hypothermia and frostbite. However, it is recognized that there are significant flaws in Siple's model and its application to clothed humans. An improved model, shown in figure 2, has recently been developed.

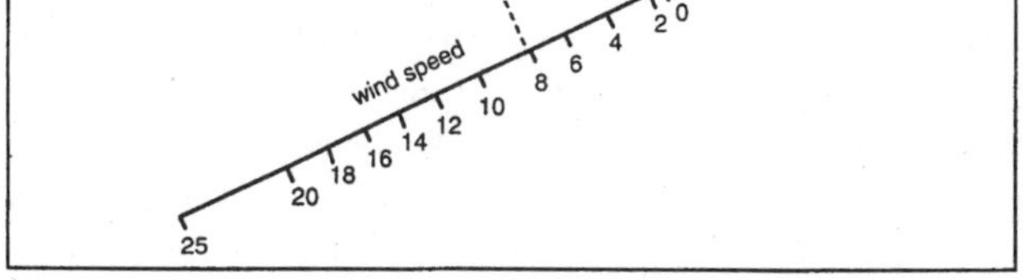

***Figure 2**. Windchill nomogram. The improved windchill nomogram based on the work of Steadman and Dixon. The dashed line shows an example of its use. With an air temperature of -4°F (-20°C) and a wind speed of 8 meters per second the effect on exposed flesh is equivalent to a temperature of -25.6°F (-32°C).*

Effect of alcohol in thermoregulation

Elevated blood alcohol levels are very commonly found in association with hypothermia. However, the exact role of alcohol in the development of hypothermia is a complex subject—certainly more complex than the often stated comment that alcohol hastens the development of hypothermia because it causes the surface blood vessels to vasodilate thus allowing more heat to be taken away from the body surface by radiation, conduction, and convection.

In fact, most laboratory studies have failed to demonstrate any significant heat loss following alcohol ingestion—at least in cold water exposure and with resting subjects in cold air exposure. There is some evidence that *exercising* subjects who have consumed alcohol may have a slightly higher rate of heat loss although, at least in the short term, most of this heat loss is compensated for by heat generated as a result of the exercise.

The main mechanisms by which alcohol intoxication can lead to hypothermia include

- decreased ability to assess risks or make properly considered judgments
- decreased perception of cold and hence a decreased requirement to seek adequate clothing or shelter
- the sedative effect of alcohol leading to sleep, which is known to cause an increase in heat loss
- impaired shivering when the core temperature does start to drop
- impaired glucose metabolism resulting, in severe cases, in decreased heat production

THE NATURE OF HYPOTHERMIA

Hypothermia can be better understood, and hence managed, if it is recognized that it is not a single condition but rather the same end result of a number of different processes. Hypothermia can come about in various ways: cold water immersion, exposure to cold-wet conditions (such as in the field) or to cold-dry conditions (such as under-heated homes), induced hypothermia for surgical reasons, or hypothermia that is secondary to a variety of medical conditions such as drug intoxication, hypothyroidism, or malnutrition. The physiological changes and results of treatment that are noted in one process need not necessarily apply to the other forms of hypothermia. In addition, assessment in the laboratory of the effectiveness of the various rewarming methods is limited by the fact that human studies are restricted by ethical considerations to cases of only mild hypothermia (core temperature above

93.2–95°F [34–35°C]) where rapid spontaneous rewarming will occur anyway. Animal studies are not always applicable and case reports of accidental hypothermia, by the very nature of the conditions under which they occur, are often not fully documented.

Classifications

Many authorities divide accidental hypothermia into categories of mild, moderate, and severe on the basis of core temperature. Unfortunately, there is little agreement as to the boundaries for each category. For the purposes of this discussion, the following limits will be used: mild (93.2–95°F/34–35°C), moderate (86–93.2°F/30–34°C), and severe (less than 86°F/30°C). While useful in a hospital situation where an accurate core temperature can be obtained (see section on "Diagnosis" below for a more detailed discussion), such core readings are often not possible in the field situation. Nonetheless a general estimate can be made based on the observable signs (see table 1).

Other authorities use duration as the criterion and employ the term "acute hypothermia" for those cases where victims have been hypothermic for less than six hours, "subacute hypothermia" for cases between six and twenty-four hours, and "chronic hypothermia" for cases of more than twenty-four hours. This has a certain advantage as far as treatment is involved, for while there may be a case for rapid rewarming (for example, in a hot bath) in certain acute cases, it is generally considered inappropriate for chronic hypothermia. In chronic cases significant fluid and electrolyte changes usually occur and actions such as rapid rewarming are far more likely to result in cardiovascular complications.

Another useful method is to categorize hypothermia according to cause, that is, "exposure hypothermia," "immersion hypothermia," "urban hypothermia," and "induced" (or therapeutic) hypothermia. This method has the advantage of ease of presentation. However, as tourists and adventure travelers are only at risk of exposure or immersion hypothermia, discussion here will be limited to those two conditions.

EXPOSURE HYPOTHERMIA

This condition should be uncommon in the "average" ship-based tourist. However, conditions such as inadequate clothing, wet clothing, injury (with the resultant loss of the ability to generate heat by walking), gross trauma, becoming lost or stranded on shore, the effects of certain prescription and nonprescription medication (for example, phenothiazines, alcohol), and extremes of age (with resulting decreased thermoregulation) carry the potential to place polar tourists at risk of exposure hypothermia—especially if more than one of the above factors comes into play at any one time.

Adventure tourists, on the other hand, place themselves at considerably greater hazard. Mountain climbers or people traveling on the Antarctic plateau experience far colder and often windier conditions. Their energy requirements are usually much greater and, if not met by high-calorie food, can result in a negative thermal balance. Finally adverse weather conditions or injury can more easily strand such travelers away from shelter, food, and evacuation.

The signs and symptoms of exposure hypothermia are often mistaken for fatigue, and even the casualty may not realize the true nature of his or her problem. The onset of hypothermia is often accompanied by shivering, apathy, tiredness, and impaired judgment. Frequently, the behavior of the hypothermic person becomes abnormal, with aggression or lack of cooperation, and the rate of progress slows. Speech usually becomes infrequent and thick, and visual abnormalities may occur. Muscle weakness, cramps, and clumsiness give way to repeated stumbling and falling until the victim eventually collapses with exhaustion and impaired consciousness, incoherence, or stupor. Companions should keep alert for "the umbles"—mumbles, fumbles, stumbles, and grumbles.

After the casualty collapses, observers may note that the victim is cold to touch, displays generalized muscle rigidity, may have a slower heart rate, and

Figure 3. *Development of exposure hypothermia. As environmental conditions of rain, wind, and snow worsen, the opportunities for heat loss increase. These losses can be countered by insulation (clothing, both windproof and / or rainproof). In addition, mechanisms for increased heat production can be called into play, namely increased exercise and shivering. However, both exercise and shivering can be exhausting and when the victim is finally forced to lie down, heat production drops dramatically and heat loss via conduction to the cold ground increases. Life-threatening hypothermia can now develop rapidly. Courtesy Dr. Tonia Cochran.*

his or her peripheral pulses are difficult or impossible to find.

IMMERSION HYPOTHERMIA

The very fact that most polar tourism is ship-based means that, at least theoretically, all such tourists are at risk of this condition. The worst-case scenario would involve sinking of a ship and multiple hypothermic casualties. Far more likely are cases such as an individual falling out of a small boat during ship-to-shore transfer or breaking through thin sea ice.

The signs and symptoms of immersion hypothermia are much the same as for exposure hypothermia, but come on far more rapidly. The thermal conductivity of water is much greater than that of air, and hence the rate of heat loss from the body is approximately twenty-five times faster in water than in air at the same temperature.

The other aspect that complicates immersion hypothermia is the likelihood of drowning or near-drowning. The muscle weakness and rigidity that accompany hypothermia can severely interfere with the victim's ability to swim or stay afloat, and the victim may drown long before hypothermia reaches a level that would be lethal in itself.

The question of how long a person can survive in water at a particular temperature is one that seems to intrigue many people, including quite naturally, passengers on polar ships.

Unfortunately, there is no ready answer to this problem, as such a wide variety of factors need to be taken into account. Among the more important considerations that determine an individual's core body temperature following immersion are water temperature, duration of exposure, insulation (fat and clothing), level of activity (swimming), weather conditions (especially wind and wave action).

A person's muscular build and the thickness of subcutaneous fat help to determine the time of onset and rate of development of immersion hypothermia. People with a heavy layer of subcutaneous fat generally fare much better in the cold than do slim people. Clothing also plays an important role in minimizing immersion hypothermia. Even conventional nonwaterproof clothing can reduce the fall of deep body temperature of immersed subjects by 50 to 75 percent (see table 2).

The amount of voluntary movement made in the water also substantially affects the rate at which hypothermia develops. This is mainly because swimming dissipates the layer of warmed water which might otherwise form around a person. Exercise will only reliably raise body temperature if the water temperature is above about 75.2°F (24°C). Hence, it is generally better to curl up into the heat escape lessening posture (HELP) than to attempt to swim any significant distance to safety (see figures 9 through 11).

THE MANAGEMENT OF HYPOTHERMIA

There is still considerable dispute as to the optimum treatment of the hypothermic victim. Each case must

Level	*Core Temperature*	*Signs and Symptoms*
Normal	37.6°C/99.7°F	"Normal" rectal temperature
	37°C/98.6°F	"Normal" oral temperature
Cold	36°C/96.8°F	Subjectively cold
	35°C/95°F	Shivering (mild to moderate)
Mild Hypothermia	34°C/93.2°F	Slurred speech
		Slowed thinking and movement
Moderate Hypothermia	33°C/91.4°F	Hallucinations and amnesia
	32°C/89.6°F	Shivering stops
	31°C/87.8°F	Decreasing consciousness
	30°C/86°F	Unconscious
Severe Hypothermia	29°C/84.2°F	Slow pulse and respiration
	28°C/82.4°F	Heart arrhythmias develop
	27°C/80.6°F	Reflexes lost
	26°C/78.8°F	Appears dead
	25°C/77°F	Spontaneous ventricular fibrillation may develop

Table 1. *Signs and symptoms of different levels of hypothermia. These are "typical" signs and symptoms at different core temperatures—individuals may vary considerably. "Normal" rectal and oral temperatures may show a diurnal variation of about 1°C. It is worth noting that there is zone between normal and hypothermia for which there is no medical nomenclature other than "being cold," that is, not everyone who is cold is hypothermic. Based on EL Lloyd (1986), adapted from Harnett et al. (1983)*

be handled on the basis of the cause of the condition, the level of hypothermia, the personnel and equipment experience available, and the availability of transport to a sophisticated treatment center. The following discussion does not claim to address all aspects of every case. Rather, it sets out a framework that provides anyone, from first aider to physician, with a clear set of priorities that can be implemented from the time the hypothermic victim is first discovered.

This six-point plan for the management of accidental hypothermia includes assessment of airway, breathing, and circulation; diagnosis; gentle handling of the casualty; prevention of further heat loss; provision of additional heat to the victim; and evacuation.

This list is not meant as a flow chart or checklist where once dealt with each item can be forgotten about and the rescuers can move on to the next point. Rather, each priority must be anticipated, rechecked, and reconsidered throughout the rescue.

Assessment of airway, breathing, and circulation

This is the highest priority in the first aid management of all emergencies. However, hypothermia is one of the few conditions in which the absence of a detectable pulse need *not* automatically mean that cardiopulmonary resuscitation (CPR) is required.

In severe hypothermia respiration may be extremely shallow, and the heartbeat can be very slow and weak. The pupils may be fixed and dilated. It may be virtually impossible to detect signs of life without an electrocardiograph. Because the chilled victim's need for oxygen is greatly diminished (by approximately 7 percent per degree Centigrade), this very low level of cardiorespiratory activity may be sufficient to maintain sufficient oxygen supply to the brain. This concept has been described by the Alaskan researcher, William Mills, as the "metabolic icebox." Attempts at CPR on such a patient may well trigger ventricular fibrillation and result in death.

The decision on whether or not to initiate CPR on a hypothermic victim found in such an apparently pulseless state is still open to debate. Some authorities such as Evan Lloyd of Scotland have cautioned that CPR should not be commenced if a person is found apparently dead unless "there is a reasonable expectation that effective cardiopulmonary resuscitation can be continued, with only brief periods of interruption for movement, until the casualty can be transported to hospital where full advanced life support can be provided." However, many recent protocols, especially those from the United States, recommend that CPR should *not* be withheld unless the victim has other lethal injuries, a frozen chest that is impossible to compress, or the situation is too hazardous for rescuers.

Similarly there is some dispute over the rate at which CPR should be performed. In some European nations it is advocated that, in order to avoid hypocapnia (a deficiency of carbon dioxide in the blood), CPR should be performed at only half the normal rate. This recommendation has only rarely been adopted in the English-speaking world.

Whatever choice is made, one thing is essential: a central pulse (carotid or femoral) must be checked for very carefully (preferably for a full minute), before any decision is made on whether or not the victim is indeed pulseless and hence requires resuscitation.

During prolonged CPR continue the rewarming process. The definition of death is failure to revive on rewarming above 89.6°F (32°C).

Diagnosis

The correct diagnosis of hypothermia is important, because, as has just been discussed, even the first-aid management of this condition differs considerably from that of other common conditions that might

ESTIMATED SURVIVAL TIME IN WATER AT 6°C

Clothing Type	*Time to Incapacity (93.2°F / 34°C), in Hours*	*Time to Unconsciousness (86°F / 30°C), in Hours*	*Time to Cardiac Arrest (77°F / 25°C), in Hours*
Light clothing	0.4–1.3	0.8–2.6	1.3–4.3
Wet-suit (4.8 mm)	1.6–4.7	3.1–9.9	4.9–16.2
Insulated dry coveralls	2.9–8.8	5.7–18.2	9.1–30.0

Table 2. *Estimated survival time (with a 95 percent confidence range) for lean subjects in rough seas at 42.8°F (6°C). It should be noted that incapacity (and hence death from drowning in an individual not wearing some form of flotation) would occur in less than one-third the time it would take for the individual to die from a hypothermia-induced cardiac arrest. An immersion suit, worn on top of high insulation underclothing, provides both flotation and a much longer survival time.*

cause altered behaviors or unconsciousness, or for which cardiopulmonary resuscitation may be required. The first clue to diagnosis is a high index of suspicion. Always consider hypothermia in the following:

- Adverse environmental conditions, such as low temperatures, high winds, wet conditions, high windchill factor.
- At-risk individuals, those who have been lost, injured, exhausted, or inadequately clothed. The young and the elderly are especially at risk.

The victim's signs and symptoms will also point to the correct diagnosis. Continual shivering, poor coordination, confusion, slurred speech, hallucinations, and dilated pupils are all indications of mild to moderate hypothermia. Behavior and the level of consciousness are the most important indicators of the victim's status; consciousness may be lost at body temperatures between 73.4°F (23°C) and 86°F (30°C). Profound hypothermia (under approximately 77°F or 25°C) may mimic death with undetectable pulse, blood pressure, and respiration; pupils that are unresponsive to light stimulus; and muscle rigidity simulating rigor mortis. Remember, never assume the victim is dead until they have been rewarmed.

By definition hypothermia is a condition in which the core body temperature is less than 95°F (35°C). Therefore, for an accurate diagnosis and proper assessment of the level of hypothermia, it is important to obtain a precise reading of the victim's temperature. But at what site should the temperature be taken, and with what sort of thermometer?

Site of Temperature Measurement—Placing a thermometer under the tongue is a time-honored method of assessing a fever and is even used in some thermal studies when the ambient temperature is not too low. However, it is almost useless for assessing the core temperature in a cold field setting.

Studies conducted at 14°F (-10°C) indicate that a subject with a normal core temperature can have an internal cheek temperature down to 77°F (25°C) if nose-breathing and even lower if mouth-breathing. While the temperature recorded under the tongue will undoubtedly be somewhat higher than these cheek temperatures such figures do indicate how an oral measurement can give a falsely low reading.

Temperatures recorded at the armpit fall into a middle ground—less reliable than rectal but more so than oral. Studies with induced hypothermia in a hospital indicate that axillary temperatures are consistently 1.0°C to 1.5°C below core temperature. Whether this finding is transferable to the hypothermic victim in the field has not yet been established. Nonetheless, as an axillary measurement is easier to take than a rectal reading, and less likely to be resisted by a conscious or semiconscious victim, it is used in some treatment centers.

A deep (5–6 inch or about 12–15 cm) rectal probe gives a reasonably accurate initial assessment of a victim's core temperature. However, during rewarming it will usually lag behind true core temperature resulting in the much-debated "after-drop" effect. In addition, it requires the loosening or removal of the victim's clothing, allowing further heat loss. Also, it is regarded as an intrusion by even semiconscious casualties. Despite all these problems it is still one of the best sites for diagnosing and assessing the hypothermic victim.

There is evidence that of all the noninvasive means of assessing core temperature, a probe passed into the esophagus via either the mouth or nose is the single most accurate and responsive method. Unfortunately, most conscious patients find it uncomfortable and practical difficulties (including the possibility of inducing vomiting) generally make it unsuitable for use in the field situation.

The ear drum or tympanic membrane shares its blood supply (the internal carotid artery) with the hypothalamus and hence some investigators argue that it can be considered a good indicator of core temperature. The earlier sensors which had to be placed in contact with the eardrum (often painfully so) have been superseded in recent years by noncontact, infrared sensors.

Choice of Thermometer—The standard clinical thermometer as usually used in hospitals and homes is designed for assessing fevers but only records down to 95°F (35°C) and hence is of no assistance in assessing the level of hypothermia.

Because of the above problem, special mercury-glass thermometers are available that record down to 68°F (20°C). However, they share the other problems common to the standard clinical thermometer: they are fragile, need to be very thoroughly shaken down for a hypothermic case, are slow to equilibrate, and may be difficult to read (for example, in the poor light of a tent).

Digital electronic thermometers are small, sturdy, easy-to-read, and accurate. As opposed to the standard mercury-glass thermometer, which takes at least

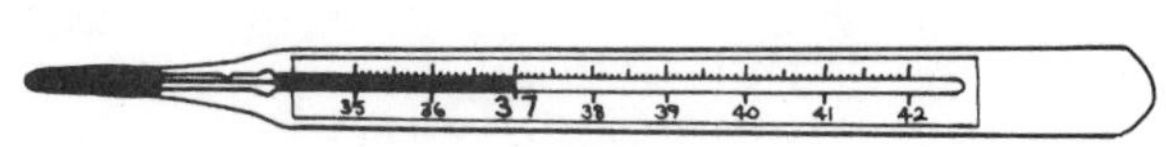

Figure 4. *Standard clinical thermometer with centigrade scale. Courtesy Dr. Tonia Cochran.*

Figure 5. *Low reading glass thermometer. Courtesy Dr. Tonia Cochran.*

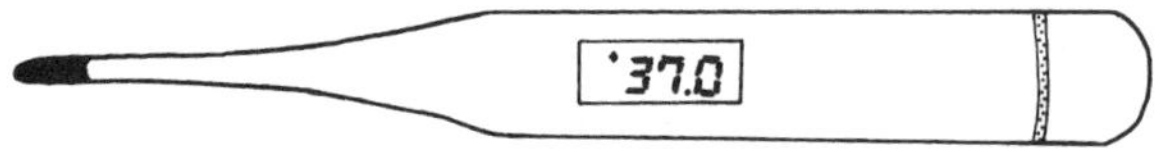

Figure 6. *Digital electronic thermometer. Courtesy Dr. Tonia Cochran.*

3 minutes to equilibrate, the electronic model gives a reading in 45 to 60 seconds. A version is made specifically for rectal use. Disadvantages include the fact that a rectal thermometer only records down to 89.6°F (32°C), can only be inserted roughly 2 inches or 5–6 cm into the rectum, and has an ambient temperature working range of 50–104°F (10–40°C). In cold conditions it must be kept warm, for example, inside the rescuer's clothing.

In many cases the thermistor thermometer is still the preferred method of monitoring core temperatures. The probe can be inserted as far as required (usually 5–6 inches or 12–15 cm) into the rectum or esophagus and does not need to be removed to be read. The only disadvantage as far as a rescue team is concerned is the bulk and cost of the device. However, with advances in electronics both of these factors have come down in recent years and suitable hand-held versions can now be purchased for a few hundred dollars.

The advantages of the infrared tympanic thermometer are that it is easy to use, almost instantaneous, and involves no undressing of or discomfort to the victim. However, there is some evidence to suggest that after the subject has been exposed to cold and windy conditions this device may be prone to providing false readings because of local chilling effects—even after some time in sheltered surroundings. Whether any such inaccuracy is clinically significant has not yet been established.

Finally, even if no equipment is available the victim's companions can make a rough assessment of thermal status by slipping a hand under the patient's clothing into the armpit. If the patient feels as warm as usual, hypothermia can be excluded as a cause of unconsciousness.

In practice, because of all the difficulties listed above, rescuers rarely get to measure body temperature in the field. In such cases the best and most reliable indicator is the patient's mental status. However, once evacuated to even a basic treatment facility, for example the surgery on a ship, the treating doctor should have access to an adequate diagnostic device, preferably either a thermistor thermometer or an infrared tympanic thermometer.

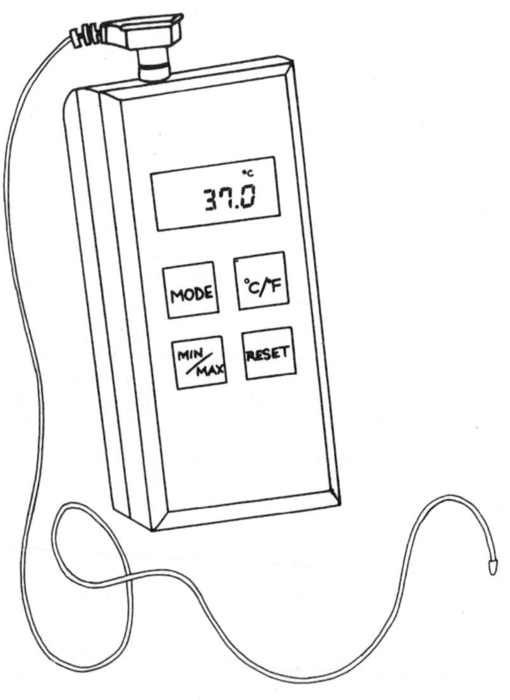

Figure 7. *Thermistor thermometer. Courtesy Dr. Tonia Cochran.*

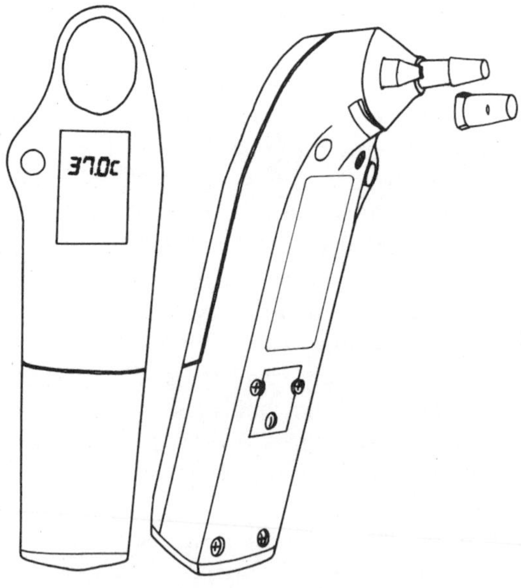

Figure 8. *Infrared tympanic thermometers. Courtesy Dr. Tonia Cochran.*

Gentle handling of the victim

The direct effect of the cold, low oxygen concentrations, and accompanying acidosis can all leave the heart muscle in a state of increased irritability. Consequently, any rough handling of the victim can trigger ventricular fibrillation and subsequent death.

This need for gentle handling must be kept in mind at every stage of the rescue. The victim must be carried to shelter with great care, wet clothes may need to be cut off, and wherever possible evacuation should avoid transport across rough terrain.

Prevention of further heat loss

This essential can be achieved in the following ways: Shelter should be provided urgently. Numerous lives have been lost when groups push on, attempting to get an obviously hypothermic victim to the comfort of a distant hut. At the earliest warnings of impending hypothermia the party should "go to ground." Even simple shelters such as snow holes and small tents have been known to save lives.

The victim should be insulated from the ground. The closed-cell foam mats commonly used by bushwalkers have been found to be very effective at decreasing conductive losses to cold ground, snow, or ice.

Wet clothing should be replaced with dry. Wet clothing allows heat to be conducted away from the body approximately five times faster than when dry. Therefore, wherever possible, wet clothing should be replaced, but only once the casualty is inside some form of shelter. The necessity of handling the patient gently means that in severe cases the wet clothing may need to be cut off.

The patient's head should be covered. A variety of figures are often quoted, but two of the more reliable studies suggest that at 24.8°F (-4°C) up to 50 percent of metabolic heat production can be lost through the uncovered head and at 5°F (-15°C) this figure can go up to as much as 70 percent.

Wrapping the victim in a sleeping bag, space blanket, or thermal recovery capsule is another way to prevent further heat loss. Space blankets are sheets of metallized plastic that were initially designed for use in outer space where most of the body's heat loss is by way of radiation. On earth the hypothermic victim can lose far more heat through conduction and convection. If space blankets are used they must be carefully wrapped around the patient so as to minimize any air movement and resultant convective or evaporative heat loss. Similarly, because of the high conductive heat loss through the metallized material, it is essential that the victim wrapped in such material be insulated from the cold ground, snow or ice. Despite these shortcomings, space blankets are often used because their small size lends itself to inclusion in first-aid or emergency supplies.

A number of thermal recovery capsules have come on the market in recent years. Some are made from various forms of space blanket (that is, high infrared reflection) material, others from high insulation synthetics. Anecdotal evidence of their effectiveness is plentiful but there are few convincing studies to demonstrate that they are more effective than a high-quality sleeping bag.

Heat loss from the respiratory tract can be minimized by wrapping a scarf around the nose and mouth, but only in such a fashion as to avoid obstructing respiration. Do not give oxygen which may have been chilled in transit to the field site unless it has been rewarmed (and preferably humidified); otherwise it can be a considerable source of further heat loss.

Provision of additional heat

This is another area of controversy with regard to the management of hypothermia. The 1992 American Heart Association *Guidelines for Cardiopulmonary Resuscitation and Emergency Care* algorithm for the treatment of hypothermia states: "Many experts think these interventions (any active form of rewarming) should be done only in-hospital, though practices vary." However, it should be acknowledged that in a remote setting, such as the Arctic and Antarctic, provision of additional heat in the field may be necessary—if only with the intention of stabilizing the core temperature rather than actual rewarming of the victim.

Therefore, the options for providing heat to the hypothermic victim are presented here in two sections: field treatment and medical treatment.

Field Treatment—Generalized warming of a shelter, hut, or tent is not a very efficient method but is often all that is required in the mildest cases. There is no need to overheat the shelter—approximately 64.4–71.6°F (18–22°C) is sufficient. The main danger to be avoided is placing the victim in front of a raging fire or radiant heater; this may result in a too rapid opening up of constricted peripheral vessels and a subsequent drop in blood pressure.

Warm drinks and high-energy food have mild physiological but strong psychological value. However, such drinks and food must only be given to a victim conscious enough to swallow with ease. Alcohol and strong caffeine drinks are best avoided.

Body-to-body contact may be helpful. A warm volunteer can strip down to the underclothes and share a sleeping bag with the similarly stripped victim. Again, this is not a very efficient method but in many circumstances it may be all that is available. It must be remembered that the volunteer will usually also cool fairly quickly, especially if the victim is severely hypothermic, and may need to be replaced after a period of time.

A variety of heat packs are available on the market. Most rely on a slow exothermic heat reaction which is initiated by exposure to the oxygen in the air. Some packs can even be recharged by boiling in hot water. They must be used cautiously as some are capable of burning the skin unless covered. They should be packed around areas such as the neck, sides of the chest, armpits, and groin.

There is some dispute about the effectiveness of attempting to rewarm a hypothermic casualty through the provision of warmed, breathing gas. Laboratory experiments have not been convincing and the mathematics indicate that, using a face mask, only a comparatively small amount of heat energy can be transferred and much of that is dissipated in the upper airways. However, what is not often recognized is that the real advantage of such a system is not the heat gain that it imparts as much as the respiratory heat loss which it prevents. There are several devices on the market that can deliver such heated and humidified gas in both the field and hospital setting.

Medical Treatment—Obviously rewarming can be undertaken more safely and conveniently in the hospital or surgery on board the tourist ship, provided the victim can be safely evacuated to the ship. In addition, the range of treatment options available on a ship will be considerably greater than can be provided in a tent or shelter onshore. With the limited facilities likely to be found on a tourist ship, the treating doctor has three main choices: passive rewarming, active external rewarming, and central rewarming. Passive rewarming is the simplest option. The patient is covered with blankets, a space blanket, or sleeping bag and kept in a warm room to rewarm by means of his or her own metabolic heat production. This is a very slow method but is often all that is required for mild cases.

Active external rewarming may be required in more serious cases (those with core temperatures below about 89.6°F or 32°C) where metabolic heat production is low and the resultant very long recovery time required by passive rewarming would put the patient at risk of cardiovascular complications. The two main variations likely to be available on board a ship are hot water bottles and heat packs (as mentioned above) and a warm bath.

Rapid rewarming in a bath at 104°F (40°C) has often been considered the standard treatment for immersion hypothermia. If used, the arms and legs should not be immersed until after the trunk has rewarmed. In recent years there has been a move away from this method because of concerns about "rewarming shock," the difficulties involved in any resultant need for defibrillation, and problems with maintaining the airway in a semiconscious or unconscious victim. This method should probably only be used in the case of the fit young conscious person with a core temperature above 86°F (30°C) who can be transported to the rewarming bath within a short time of rescue. It should be borne in mind that such cases are likely to have favorable outcome whatever mode of rewarming is used.

To physicians, the details of the central rewarming process that follow will be of interest. As opposed to external rewarming, where heat exchange occurs across the skin, central rewarming aims at preferentially supplying heat to the organs and vessels of the thorax and abdomen, that is, to the core. The three most likely options for central warming on a ship are heated inhalation, peripheral or central infusion of heated intravenous fluids, and peritoneal lavage.

As mentioned above, airway rewarming via a face mask actually transfers little heat to the patient's core. However, if delivered by an endo- or nasotracheal tube, warmed (107.6°F or 42°C) humidified air or oxygen can assist in restoring normal core temperature.

While heated intravenous fluids (104–107.6°F/40–42°C) can contribute to the rewarming process, used alone, massive volumes would be required to reverse even moderate hypothermia. Therefore it should always be used in conjunction with other means of rewarming. It is often difficult to find intravenous access in the severely hypothermic victim. If fluids are delivered via a peripheral line they are likely to cool before reaching the core; therefore, a central line is preferable. Remember, most hypothermic victims will be volume depleted so a rapid infusion of 500 mls followed by 75–100 mls/Hampton Roads may be indicated. Do not use lactated Ringer's (Hartmann's solution) as the cooled liver may be unable to metabolize lactate.

Peritoneal lavage, which is a standard technique for the evaluation of blunt abdominal trauma, can also be used as a means of transferring heat directly to the core. One to two liters (depending on body weight) of heated (104–113°F/40–45°C) isotonic dialysate can be run into the peritoneal cavity via a trocar and catheter, then removed some 10–20 minutes later. The process is repeated until the core temperature reaches 95°F (35°C).

Some additional notes on medical treatment that are worth mentioning at this stage include the following:

- Despite oft-repeated warnings that endotracheal intubation may precipitate ventricular fibrillation in the hypothermic victim, there appears to be little evidence to support this claim.
- At core temperatures of under 30°C the heart is usually unresponsive to cardioactive drugs including atropine. Not only will such drugs be ineffective but, as rewarming proceeds, they may become pharmacologically active—with undesirable consequences.
- Defibrillation is unlikely to be successful until the core temperature has been raised above 30°C.
- The high electrical impedance of cold skin may make it impossible to obtain an adequate ECG trace. Needle electrodes through the skin may be required. Similarly, shivering artifact can also make ECGs difficult to interpret.
- Common ECG findings include bradycardia, widening of the QRS complex, lengthening of the Q-T interval, and the characteristic J wave (also called Osborn wave or hypothermic hump)—a junctional point elevation at the end of the QRS complex.

Evacuation

Any evacuation plan must take the following priorities into consideration:

- It must allow for frequent assessment of the airway, breathing, and circulation.
- It must ensure that there is no further heat loss.
- It should ensure that any rough handling or movement of the patient is kept to a minimum.

If these conditions cannot be met it may well be better to take any required personnel and equipment to the victim and treat on site. Helicopter rescue facilities would appear to come closest to providing the ideal means of transport, but successful recoveries of even severely hypothermic victims have been achieved with Ski-Doos, snow vehicles, and stretcher carries. North American experience seems to indicate that if a helicopter is not available but evacuation can be accomplished in a few hours, it probably should be attempted, even though travel over rough terrain may be required. If evacuation is likely to take more than four to six hours it may be better to try to rewarm the victim in whatever shelter is available.

After recovery, severe or moderate cases should usually not be moved for approximately twenty-four hours—by which time the victim's energy reserves are likely to be replenished.

PREVENTION OF HYPOTHERMIA

Even the best equipped surgery on a tourist ship has limitations with regard to the facilities and expertise it can provide for the treatment of hypothermia. In such an extremely isolated position as an Arctic or Antarctic voyage the old adage about prevention being better than cure has even greater relevance than usual. The following steps can help to minimize the risk that tourists inevitably face when they enter the beautiful but hostile world of the polar regions.

In the prevention of exposure hypothermia, education and training is essential for both the general public and field party leaders. The following points are most critical:

- Adequate clothing should be worn or carried. Remember the layer principle.
- Adequate shelter (bivvy bags, tents etc.) should be carried at all times.
- Adequate hydration and high energy nutrition should be ensured.
- Get to shelter early—do not force the party on when any member is apparently hypothermic.
- Take special note of anyone who is injured, shivering, lagging behind, or acting strangely. Never ignore shivering.
- Learn to assess weather conditions, especially wind and approaching blizzards.

In the prevention of immersion hypothermia these points are essential:

- Avoid immersion; in the event of an abandon-ship routine, get into a covered lifeboat.
- Always wear a life jacket when there is a risk of immersion, for example, in ship-shore operations.
- Wear as much clothing as possible, even in the water, especially head gear.
- Do not exercise in an attempt to stay warm or attempt to swim more than a very short distance.
- Adopt the HELP or huddle position (see figures 9 and 10).
- Survivors of boating mishaps should attempt to get as much of their bodies out of water as possible, for example, by climbing onto a capsized boat. The convective and evaporative heat brought about by even strong winds will be less than the conductive loss to cold water.
- The victim should be recovered from the water as quickly as possible. Ideally this should be done

with the casualty in a horizontal position so as to reduce any shock or hypotension caused when "the hydrostatic squeeze" is removed as the victim is plucked from the water. This is a counsel of perfection and not always possible. However, there are both commercial and home-made devices available (called Jasons cradles) which are designed to achieve this goal.

The heat escape lessening position (HELP) is achieved by holding the upper arms securely against the sides with wrists placed over the chest. The ankles are crossed, with the legs drawn up as close as possible to the chest. However, it is almost impossible to achieve this position unless a life jacket is worn. If more than one survivor is in the water assume the huddle position. In this situation all survivors face inwards, the sides of the chest are held close together and the arms around each other. Either of these two actions can increase survival time up to 50 percent.

FROSTBITE

In conditions of subzero temperatures, heat loss from peripheral tissue may be sufficient to allow ice formation within those tissues. This freezing of the extremities and exposed areas is called frostbite. As it involves a living organism, the processes involved are much more complex than in simple freezing such as occurs when a piece of meat is placed in a freezer. Ice crystals can form either within cells (rupturing cell walls) or between cells. Growth of intercellular ice crystals draws out water from the adjacent cells, changing the osmotic pressure and causing tissue death. In addition, the cold itself damages the walls of the capillaries in the affected area, allowing leakage of plasma. Consequently, the blood flow (which has already been decreased to the body's periphery by vasoconstriction in an attempt to reduce heat loss) is further impaired. As a result, blood cells and platelets sludge and stick together causing microemboli, thus further decreasing oxygenation to the already damaged tissues.

In comparable conditions of cold, frostbite is more common at high altitude because of the decreased oxygenation of tissues. Other contributing factors include windchill, exposure to cold metals or fuel (accelerating conductive and evaporative losses respectively), constrictive clothing (for example, tight socks) which can impede the circulation to the extremities, wet clothing, injuries (for example, a broken limb with swelling from hematoma), dehydration, and general hypothermia (the body may need to "sacrifice" areas of the shell to try to preserve heat in the

Figure 9. The heat escape lessening position (HELP). By decreasing the body surface area and protecting the groin, armpits, and torso, the victim can lessen heat loss. Courtesy Dr. Tonia Cochran.

Figure 10. The modified HELP Position. In rough sea conditions adopting the standard HELP position can result in the individual rolling sufficiently to frequently submerge the head in the cold water. In such cases it is better to uncurl the legs, though keeping them crossed at the ankle. This will provide greater stability as well as some degree of heat conservation. Courtesy Dr. Tonia Cochran.

core). There is also some evidence to suggest that there is a higher risk in those who smoke or have had a previous episode of frostbite.

Theoretically, frostbite can be classified into a number of different grades of severity depending on the depth to which the tissue is frozen. Frostnip is an early, reversible stage of frostbite in which the affected tissue blanches and loses sensation; there may be minor frosting of the skin but it remains pliable. Superficial frostbite is said to occur when freezing involves only the skin and subcutaneous tissues. Deep frostbite involves the underlying muscle, nerve, blood vessels, and even bone. In practice it is often impossible to accurately assess the extent of the damage for at least several days. However, table 3 may be used as a general guide.

Signs and symptoms of frostbite

Frostbite usually appears on the exposed areas of the body such as the nose, cheeks, and ears; and on the extremities, especially the fingers and toes. It presents as firm, cold, white areas. One of the first signs is that the affected area *stops* feeling cold and painful. Remember—if an area ceases to feel painfully cold—investigate.

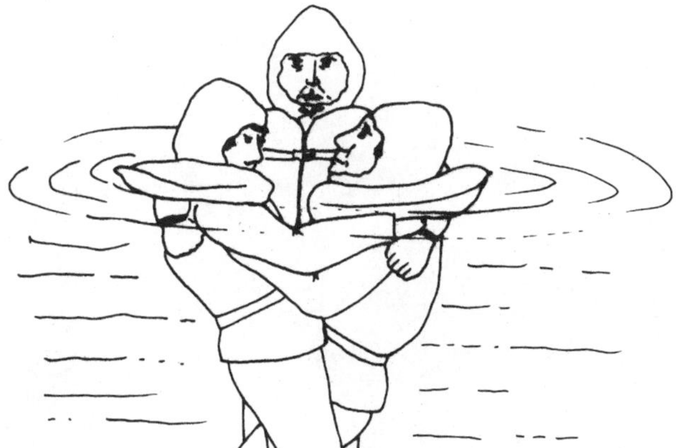

Figure 11. The huddle position. Heat loss can be decreased when members of a group huddle together, providing some reduction of convective heat loss from the torso. This technique helps keep the group together, but in real life it is difficult to actually minimize heat loss due to the unsynchronized bobbing about that results from waves. Courtesy Dr. Tonia Cochran.

In frostnip, ice crystals form only in the already dead, outermost layer of the skin. On rewarming the underlying live tissue may show an inflammatory response with redness and swelling, but no actual tissue loss. Peeling of the skin, rather like sunburn, may occur twenty-four to seventy-two hours after rewarming. Sometimes mild paresthesia may persist for days or weeks after the event. Alternatively, hypersensitivity to cold may last for months or even years.

In true frostbite the affected area is cold, hard, and anesthetic. The skin is either waxy-white or a mottled blue-grey color. On warming it becomes blotchy red, swollen, and painful. Blisters commonly develop after some hours following rewarming and may cover entire fingers or toes—especially on the dorsal side. If the blisters contain clear fluid, the underlying tissues may be still viable and, in general, tissue loss is less than if the blisters are blood-filled. After a week or so the frostbitten tissues develop a thick black covering called an eschar. Over several weeks or months this dead tissue will shrink and slough off. With superficial frostbite, the eschar may be only a few millimeters thick and when it peels off, fresh pink skin will be found underneath. With deep frostbite, far more tissue is lost; when the eschar finally separates, skin, tissue, and even bone will peel away. Long-term effects can include sensory loss, altered sweating, loss of the subcutaneous fat pad of the fingers or toes, persistent deep pain, limitation of joint movement, changes to the fingernails and toenails, and persistent cold sensitivity.

Treatment of frostbite

Treatment can be divided into three sections: self-treatment for frostnip and small areas of superficial frostbite, medical treatment on board the tourist ship for more serious forms, and field treatment for adventure travelers isolated from access to shipboard medical facilities.

Self treatment—The principal rule to impart to people who may become victims of even minor frostbite is: *Never* rub the affected area—either with snow, a gloved hand, or anything else. Similarly, dry radiant heat should be avoided.

Frostnip and small areas of superficial frostbite should be treated immediately by gently placing the affected fingers in the opposite armpit, or by placing a warm hand over a frostnipped cheek or ear. Feet can be reheated on the warm abdomen (under a

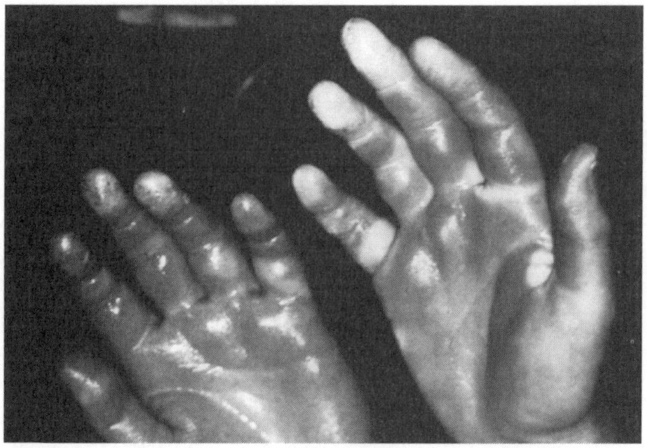

Figure 12. *Frostbitten fingers before thawing. The affected tissue is white, hard, and ice cold. Initially the affected area stops feeling cold and painful. Remember, if an area stops feeling painfully cold, investigate. On warming, the hands become blotchy, red, and swollen. Australian Antarctic Division Photo by G. Merrill.*

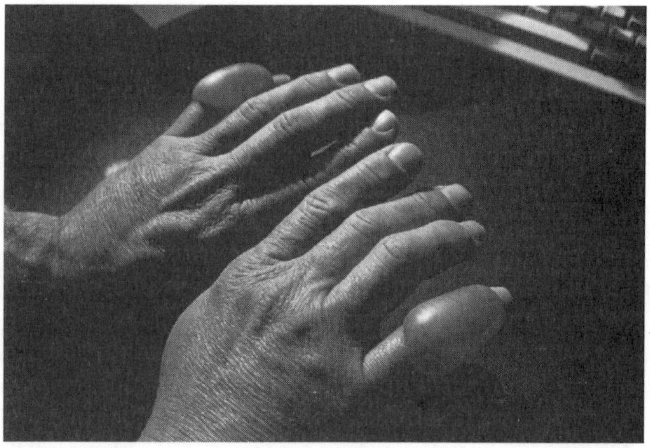

Figure 13. *In this case only the little finger on each hand has been affected. Three days after the freezing incident, blisters filled with clear serous fluid extend along the back of the fingers. If the blisters contain clear fluid, the underlying tissues may still be viable, and tissue loss is less than if the blisters are blood-filled. Australian Antarctic Photo by R. Kiernan.*

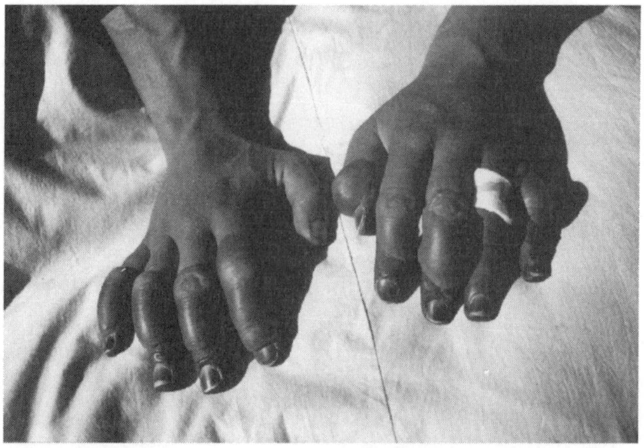

Figure 14. *When, as in this case, the blisters are blood-filled, it is usually a sign of more extensive underlying tissue damage, that is, deep frostbite. With deep frostbite, far more tissue is lost; even tendon and bone may be involved. Photo courtesy Lincoln Hall.*

Figure 15. *Some weeks after the freezing cold injury, a black carapace or eschar forms. With time the line of demarcation between viable tissue and dead, mummified tissue becomes apparent and the eschar will separate and peel off along that line. Australian Antarctic Photo by R. Burdell.*

parka) of a companion. Rewarming will be accompanied by the return of sensation—often painfully so. Once the color and consistency of the skin have been restored, the person can safely resume normal activity but must be especially vigilant against recurrence. Often the affected area may become red for several hours after thawing.

Medical Treatment—Frostbite that involves entire digits, a foot, or a hand is a serious condition and should be treated in the hospital or surgery on board the tourist ship. Most authorities agree that the preferred treatment is rapid rewarming in a water bath at 100.4–107.6°F (38–42°C) until the thawed part flushes. This often takes 20 to 30 minutes. A relatively large bath, ideally a whirlpool, should be used in order to minimize fluctuations in water temperature. (If, however, the part has been allowed to thaw slowly before arrival at hospital, the warm bath should be avoided.) The rewarming will normally be very painful and strong analgesics may be required.

After thawing, the extremities should be elevated and covered with sterile dressings. Some authorities recommend sterile aspiration of clear blisters in an attempt to limit the ongoing damage (caused by two vasoconstricting, leucocyte-sticking prostanoids—$PgF_2\alpha$ and thromboxane A_2). Both of these agents are known to be concentrated in such blisters. At the very least, such aspiration lessens the likelihood of the blisters rupturing under nonsterile conditions. There is still some dispute over whether hemorrhagic blisters should be similarly aspirated. If so, the blister cover should at least be left in place as a dressing rather than debrided.

Strong analgesia may be required for prolonged periods. Ibuprofen (400 milligrams every twelve hours) or some similar nonsteroidal anti-inflammatory should be used for both analgesic and antiprostoglandin effects. Prostaglandins are chemicals produced by the body that are involved in promoting inflammation and have been found in large quantities in frostbite blisters. Most protocols for serious frostbite also include intravenous penicillin G (500,000 units every six hours) for forty-eight to seventy-two hours.

Tetanus prophylaxis should be updated if required. Twice daily treatment in an agitated tub or bath at 104°F (40°C) may need to be continued for some weeks. Of great importance to the ultimate usefulness of the affected hand or foot is a program of early active exercise for the affected digits.

There have been a considerable number of studies to determine the effectiveness of other pharmacological agents with which to treat frostbite. Most of these have been designed to restore microcirculation, decrease microembolization and minimize cell damage. Aloe vera may be a useful topical dressing. Reserpine (0.5 mg) has been used directly into the brachial or femoral artery of the affected extremity to dilate vessels and decrease sludging. Phenoxybenzamine (10 mg/day orally, increasing over several days) may decrease tissue loss. Heparin and Dextran appear less effective. Oxygen appears to be helpful only at altitude. There is some evidence to suggest

GRADES OF FROSTBITE

Stage	*Description*	*Signs and Symptoms*
Frostnip	Only the outer layer of the skin is frozen. After thawing, skin and underlying tissue may show inflammatory changes—erythema (redness) and swelling.	Small areas of white, frosted skin. Casualty feels intense cold initially, then no pain. After thawing, mild paresthesia (itching, prickling sensation) may persist for days or weeks.
Superficial Frostbite	The full thickness of the skin is frozen. This follows frostnip when further heat loss is not prevented and freezing continues.	White, waxy-looking skin. Skin is firm to touch, but tissue underneath is soft. After thawing, blisters (usually clear) often form.
Deep Frostbite	The skin and underlying tissues are frozen, sometimes including tendons and bone. May involve an entire hand or foot.	White, waxy-looking skin that turns greyish-blue as frostbite progresses. Complete absence of sensation including pinprick. After thawing, blood-filled blisters often form.

Table 3. *The various stages of frostbite with accompanying signs and symptoms. Based on* First on the Scene, Complete Guide to First Aid and CPR, *St. John Ambulance, Canada, 1995.*

that urokinase may have a role to play in those cases that have been allowed to thaw slowly before arrival at hospital. Biofeedback training appears to show some promise during the recovery phase.

In the preantibiotic era amputation was often performed at an early stage in the treatment of frostbite. It is now generally agreed that such surgery should be delayed as long as possible, as often there proves to be more viable tissue underneath the eschar or carapace than might be initially anticipated.

Field Treatment—The decision to treat frostbite in the field can be an extremely difficult one, and a number of factors need to be considered: the severity of the case, the expected time before evacuation is possible, the facilities available, and the experience and state of health of other members of the party. The following points also should be borne in mind:

- Never thaw a part if there is any likelihood of it being refrozen. Thawing and refreezing causes far more tissue damage than continuous freezing.
- An individual with a frozen foot is not necessarily a stretcher case, but will become one once the foot is thawed, swollen, and painful.
- In general, field rewarming should not be attempted if more definitive medical treatment can be reached within two hours.

If, after taking all of the above into account, it is determined that it is appropriate to treat a frostbitten patient in the field, the following procedures should be observed:

- Set up camp or some sort of shelter so that further heat loss from the patient is minimized.
- Check to see whether the patient has a degree of hypothermia as well as frostbite. Rewarm if necessary.
- As with hypothermia, rehydration with warm drinks is important.
- Remove any constriction to circulation.
- Remove boots or gloves, but gently, to avoid further trauma to the affected area.
- Use as large a volume of water as possible; a small pan will very quickly cool below the effective temperature once a frozen extremity is put into it.
- Thawing will be extremely painful; give analgesics if available.
- Avoid using radiant heat (fire or radiator) or rubbing of the affected area.
- Do not burst the blisters unless sterile conditions are possible. There is some evidence to suggest that there are advantages in draining blisters that contain clear fluid, but such advantages are lost if infection occurs.
- Give aspirin if available, not only for its pain-killing properties but also for its ability to inhibit prostaglandin release. Although aspirin has not yet been proven to be effective it is also unlikely to do any harm and is one of the few remedies likely to be available to an isolated party.

Prevention of frostbite

In the prevention of frostbite, the following considerations are important:

- Proper clothing is vital. Well-fitting boots are especially important. Mittens are better than gloves, and in windy conditions should be secured by a harness. Adequate head gear is important for both hypothermia and frostbite. Avoid tight clothing that can restrict the circulation. Clothes need to be kept clean or the insulating layer of trapped air is diminished.
- Avoid generalized body cooling, exhaustion, and fatigue.
- Avoid sweating into high insulating clothes; use the layer principle to adjust clothing assemblage to the task.
- Cigarette smoking should be avoided.
- Maintenance of good hydration and nutrition is important.
- A windchill chart (see nomogram, figure 2) should be consulted to estimate the equivalent temperature, and then individuals should dress and act accordingly.
- Employ the "buddy system," that is, people should watch each other for the early telltale white areas on cheeks, nose, and ears.

NONFREEZING COLD INJURY

This condition (also known by the acronym NFCI) is also commonly referred to as "trench foot" or "immersion foot." It results from prolonged exposure of tissue to cold, but not freezing, temperatures. Unlike frostbite, no ice crystals actually form in the tissues but skin, blood vessels, and particularly nerves are all affected by a combination of direct effects of the cold and the accompanying circulatory changes. Development of NFCI normally takes many hours, even days, of continuous exposure to environmental temperatures below about 59°F (15°C). However, the condition can develop more rapidly if the feet are wet for prolonged periods, the circulation is restricted, or the individual is immobile or in a cramped position for long periods. For these reasons NFCI has been a significant cause of morbidity in military operations, not just during trench warfare but even into modern times. For example, in the Falkland Islands War, 14 percent of British battle casualties requiring hospitalization were admitted for this condition. Fortunately, nonfreezing cold injury is much less common in the civilian population and should very rarely pose a threat to polar tourists. However, two groups of tourists who could find themselves at risk are (1) adventure tourists (mountain climbers, long-distance skiers, manhaul sledgers, etc.) who may get snow or excessive sweat into their watertight boots with little chance of drying their feet, and (2) shipwreck survivors in life rafts sitting for days with their legs cramped and the cold of the sea being transmitted to their feet through the thin floor of the raft.

Signs and symptoms of NFCI

Both the condition and awareness of it come on slowly (see table 4). Often the first symptoms are a sensation of numbness, pain disturbing night sleep, and paresthesia including tingling or a sensation of "electric shocks" in the feet. Initially the feet are pale, numb, swollen, and the pulses are difficult to detect. However, there is no evidence of freezing of the tissues. These signs remain even after the feet have been rewarmed, either intentionally or unintentionally.

This first phase is followed (usually on the next day) by a "hyperemic" stage which is characterized by severe burning pain, return of pulses, red discoloration of the feet with increased edema, blistering, and ulceration. These effects appear to be due to vasomotor paralysis and, in less serious cases, tend to be fully reversible, slowly clearing over four to five weeks.

In the third phase swelling gradually subsides, sensation returns, increased sensitivity to cold is noticed, as is increased perspiration. In serious cases, where the nerve damage has been more extensive, recovery is much slower and the victim may be left with permanent disabilities including intractable pain.

Treatment of NFCI

Treatment consists in keeping the subject warm with the feet dry, elevated, and protected from bedclothes. Most authorities suggest that rapid rewarming in water (as recommended for frostbite) is to be avoided, as it appears to exacerbate the amount of edema that develops. Strong analgesia is often required. Aspirin may also be given for its antiplatelet and antiprostaglandin effects. Similarly, ibuprofen or naproxen could be used for both analgesia and antiprostaglandin effects.

Prevention

In preventing NFCI, consider the following:

- Ensure that boots are the best possible fit and wear with heavy (nonconstricting) socks.
- Avoid any generalized body cooling.
- Avoid prolonged standing or sitting; move about from time to time.
- Exercise the legs, or at least the calf muscles, to assist circulation to the feet.
- Take frequent warm drinks, which will help hydration and thermal balance.
- Ensure good foot care. This involves removing boots and socks twice a day, massaging the feet, and changing into dry socks whenever possible.

GRADES OF NONFREEZING COLD INJURIES

Classification	*Definition*
I	Minimal case: that showing only erythema with slight sensory changes
II	Mild case: that showing pitting edema, erythema, and sensory changes
III	Moderate case: that showing pitting edema, erythema, blisters and ecchymotic spots from ruptured blood vessels
IV	Severe case: that showing gross pitting edema, blisters, massive extravasations of blood, and incipient gangrene

Table 4. *Webster classification of immersion foot. This system is based on the appearance of the foot two to three days after injury. Based on Webster et al. (1942), as tabulated by Tek and Mackey (1993).*

CHAPTER 10

Medical Emergencies on Board

I do not want two diseases; one nature-made and one doctor-made.

—Napoleon

The material presented in this section is not intended to represent the only, nor necessarily best, methods or procedures appropriate for the medical situations discussed, but rather is intended to present an approach, view, statement, or opinion that may be helpful to others who face similar situations. The authors disclaim any and all liability for all claims that may arise out of the use of the techniques or treatment discussed, whether these claims shall be asserted by a physician or any other person.

It is recommended that medical personnel who are serving or plan to serve as physicians on board ship ensure that adequate up-to-date textbooks are available for reference purposes.

This chapter is not a rewrite of a textbook of medicine and surgery, but rather a series of anecdotes and a look at the principles of medical practice on board ship. It is not written for physicians, but rather for the polar tourist to have an understanding of how physicians approach medical problems on polar cruises.

MAJOR TRAUMA

He tripped coming out of his bathroom. The ship had been traveling for six days. He was found lying on the cabin floor by his friend. He could not get up and could certainly not bear weight on his leg. His hip was extremely painful in the groin region.

He was brought to the infirmary on a stretcher and put into a bed. It was obvious that the affected leg was shortened, and tended to fall into external rotation.

An X ray would have confirmed the hip fracture, but even without an X ray the diagnosis could be made. The neurovascular status of his leg was intact.

The leg was placed in traction with a five-pound weight dangling off the end of the bed; the weight was attached to tape which ran from the inside of the leg to the outside of the leg. He did not have to be evacuated as an emergency, but completed the trip in bed, and was taken to the hospital when the ship docked.

Sprains

Sprains are probably far more common than fractures and thus they deserve mention. A sprain implies a tearing of ligaments of a joint and may involve separation of the bones composing the joint. Many sprains are not treated. Immediate treatment is elevation of the part, immobilization of the joint, and application of ice to the joint. X rays, if available, might show a fragment of bone torn from one or the other side of the joint. Swelling due to bleeding is common; application of ice will help to diminish swelling and relieve pain.

Dislocations

Dislocation indicates displacement of one or more bones in a joint. Dislocations of all joints can occur, and diagnosis is made on clinical suspicion and confirmed by X ray. Most dislocations can be put into place by pulling on the joint after adequate anesthesia has been given. Anesthesia can be given by injecting local anesthetic directly into the joint or by injecting local anesthetic to numb the entire limb, or by general anesthesia if available.

Dislocations that occur commonly include (1) the finger joints, (2) the elbow joint, and (3) the shoulder joint. In the lower extremity, a fracture/dislocation of the ankle is probably the most common type seen.

Fractures

A fracture denotes a complete or incomplete break in a bone. Fractures may be simple or compound. A fracture is simple when the overlying skin is not broken; it is compound when the overlying skin is broken. In both types of fractures, there are many variations, depending on the direction of the fractures and the number of broken pieces involved. Diagnosis is made by clinical suspicion and confirmed by X ray. Fractures about the upper extremity occur frequently and the most common fracture in the elderly age group involves the wrist, the "Colles" fracture.

> She was seventy-one years old, and this was the trip of her lifetime. The deck was slippery and the ship was rolling and heaving in the heavy seas, but she had to go outside to feel the wind, and she slipped, putting her right hand out to break her fall. Her injured hand was extremely painful and her wrist was obviously deformed. The skin was intact, and her fingers were warm and she could move them, albeit with pain. She was brought to the physician.

If the X-ray machine had been working, it would have been obvious that she had a fracture through the distal (end) part of the radius just proximal to (in front of) the wrist joint.

The physician cleansed the skin over the fracture area with an antiseptic solution and injected local anesthetic into and about the fracture site, thus performing a "hematoma" block. Then traction was applied to the hand while someone else applied countertraction to the forearm. Very forceful pulling is necessary for one to two minutes. Forceful traction will reduce most fractures. Then a very well-padded plaster splint was applied, extending from her elbow to her hand, leaving her fingers and thumb free. She was given a sling and a packet of pain pills, and she went on to enjoy the rest of her trip. The circulatory status of her hand and the swelling were checked daily. If the swelling had become excessive, then the splint would have been split to relieve the tightness. She was asked to see an orthopedic surgeon in her home town after the trip.

If the ship's surgeon felt uneasy about the management, and if the available reference books were not satisfactory, then he or she could get on the telephone and call an orthopedic surgeon back home for immediate advice.

A fracture involving the hip (neck of femur) is unfortunately also a common fracture in the elderly population. After sustaining such a fracture the patient will be unable to walk or bear weight. The classical position of the affected lower extremity is that the leg lies in external rotation and some shortening of the leg may be noticeable compared with the other side.

If X rays are available, the diagnosis can be confirmed. The immediate treatment consists of bedrest and application of traction to the affected limb. About five pounds of weight is usually applied to the limb, and this helps to reduce pain and muscle spasm. A simple way of applying traction would be to apply Elastoplast or tape from the outer side of the lower leg to the inner side of the lower leg and the tape can be held in place with an Ace bandage. A loop of tape should be left below the sole of the foot for application of rope which can be passed over a pulley and then attached to a five-pound weight. These fractures can be comfortably immobilized in this position for a number of weeks, and if evacuation is not easily available, no harm will be done in relation to the fracture if the patient is kept in this position. Of course, there are other potential problems like deep-vein thrombosis, which can occur after a fracture of the lower extremity.

Some fractures and dislocations are emergency problems, and some can be treated on a more conservative basis. Compound fractures are emergency situations, and compound wounds should be thoroughly cleaned and debrided as necessary. This can be done under local anesthesia when general anesthesia or regional anesthesia is not available. Fractures should be splinted, and even if the fracture is not confirmed on X ray because of unavailability of equipment, then merely on the clinical suspicion the injured part should be immobilized with splints or plaster of paris. The immobilized extremity should be well-padded with cotton or any other soft material available.

Dislocations should be reduced; most can be reduced using sedation and/or local anesthetic infiltration about the dislocated part, or an injection of local anesthetic into the dislocated joint. Most dislocations are reduced by very heavy traction, followed by immobilization. Therefore, the physician may need to pull very hard on the injured part.

After reduction of the fracture or dislocation has been carried out, check X rays should be taken. However, in the case of fractures, if the reduction is not perfect and the physician does not have the expertise to obtain a perfect reduction, then he or she should accept the reduction as is, immobilize the fracture, and wait for definitive treatment of the fracture by a competent orthopedic surgeon. Most fractures can wait for up to two weeks to be reduced, so there is rarely an indication to evacuate a patient because of a fracture that is not perfectly reduced.

A fractured clavicle (collar bone) can usually be diagnosed on clinical grounds. There is usually much swelling and tenderness about the clavicle. Provided the neurovascular status of the involved extremity is normal, the treatment is merely to apply a sling to the affected side, and if available, to apply a figure-of-8-type bandage or a clavicle harness to help immobilize the clavicle.

A fracture of the humerus is common, especially in the elderly population. It is usually the neck of the humerus that fractures, that is, the junction between the shaft and the top of the bone. These fractures can be simply treated by immobilizing the arm in a sling. Definitive treatment can be undertaken within two to three weeks.

Dislocations about the elbow can certainly occur. They are usually very clinically apparent, because the olecranon process (tip of the elbow) is driven backwards, and the deformity is obvious. These dislocations are treated by manipulation, but because of the pain involved, the joint can be infiltrated with local anesthetic solution. This usually provides excellent anesthesia and the joint can be reduced and then immobilized in a plaster splint or sling. Since these can re-dislocate, the patient should be followed closely.

Dislocations about the shoulder can occur and the dislocation is usually anterior (to the front). If a dislocation is suspected, then obviously an X ray should be taken, but if X rays are not available then the physician will have to rely on clinical acumen. The dislocated joint can be infiltrated with 20 to 30cc of local anesthetic, and the dislocation reduced in an appropriate manner.

Fractures of the radius and ulna (the two bones of the forearm) can occur, and this usually will require open reduction and internal fixation with plates and/or rods. Thus, the appropriate emergency treatment would be to reduce the fracture as best possible, and then to immobilize the arm in a long arm splint or cast. The physician will use lots of padding and will be aware of compartment syndrome.

The fracture of the wrist end of the radius (the forearm bone on the thumb side) is probably the commost fracture occurring in the older age group. This is the Colles-type fracture. If this is suspected, then reduction can be carried out by traction on the hand and countertraction on the forearm. The forearm and wrist are immobilized with appropriate splints. However, these fractures do not require evacuation of the patient. Fractures about the hand usually involve metacarpals and phalanges. Again, these are not emergency situations and can be splinted initially, and taken care of definitively some two weeks later.

Hand injuries usually will be far more common among the crew working with their hands than among the passenger population. Lacerations and wounds involving the hands should be treated by stopping the bleeding. This can usually be done by direct pressure over the bleeding part. If bleeding cannot be stopped in this way, then a tourniquet should be applied to the upper arm. This can be done by applying a blood pressure cuff, inflating the cuff to a pressure of 100mm above the systolic pressure, and holding the pressure at this level while the wound is explored. Obviously, some form of anesthesia will have to be used. Again, local anesthetic infiltration can be used or a wrist block can be simply performed by infiltrating local anesthetic about the nerves at the wrist and elbow. With a tourniquet elevated about the upper arm, there will be no bleeding. The wound can be cleaned and inspected, and bleeding vessels clamped and tied off. A hemostat and clamp cannot be inserted blindly in the hand or forearm, as the vessels usually run with nerves, and crushing a nerve may damage that nerve forever. Hand wounds should be cleaned and skin closure obtained if possible. Antibiotics can be used prophylactically. Definitive repair of injured hand structures should ideally not be undertaken on board, but can quite safely be carried out two to three weeks later, if necessary. It is far easier to repair tendons and nerves two weeks later than to try to redo an inadequately performed repair done as an emergency situation. Therefore, unless the physician is very qualified to do definitive repair of structures in the hand, he or she should not attempt to do it, but rather clean the wound, close the wound if possible, use antibiotics, and if indicated, give tetanus toxoid. The injured hand can be elevated and kept in a sling. Ice can be applied to try to reduce the swelling.

An amputated hand or finger can be replanted, provided that it was not a crushing injury, and if the possibility for evacuation to a tertiary care center can be carried out, then it might be worth considering. If this is to be done, then the amputated part should be placed on ice, not on dry ice.

In summary, there are very few hand injuries that need to be taken care of as an emergency situation, other than the cleansing and closure of wounds. Anesthesia should be used, and a tourniquet employed if the wound is going to be explored. Anesthesia can be used in the form of infiltration anesthesia or nerve block anesthetic. In the same fashion for fractures involving the upper extremity, infiltration anesthesia can be used in the region of the fracture which will provide excellent anesthesia. If in doubt, the physician should go to the radio operator and call a hospital or call an orthopedic surgeon.

Crush injuries

These injuries are characterized by massive swelling with skin and soft tissue bruising. There may be concomitant loss of skin. If the circulation of blood to the part is affected, then the problem will be further compounded.

A "compartment syndrome" may occur when the pressure within the limb may be increased to such an extent that irreversible tissue damage may occur. The appropriate management is first to recognize the condition and then to treat it by relieving the pressure surgically. The procedure is a fasciotomy.

When the urine is tested in this condition, the products of muscle breakdown may be found (myoglobinuria) or even the products of blood breakdown (hemoglobinuria).

Burns

Tissue injury caused by heat, chemicals, or electrical insults results in severe damage and swelling. Body fluids may be lost because of leakage from damaged blood vessels and lymphatic channels.

With superficial burns, regeneration occurs rapidly from uninjured skin elements, and little scarring results unless infection occurs. With deep burns, there is destruction of the skin and much of the deeper tissues. The healing process is slow, and excessive granulation tissue forms before being covered by new skin. Such wounds generally contract and develop into disfiguring or disabling scars unless treated promptly by skin grafting.

The severity of the burn is judged by the quantity of tissue involved, represented by the percentage of body surface area burned, and by the depth of the burn. Often, the distinction between deep second- and third-degree burns can be made only after three to five days of observation.

Injury to the lungs can occur due to inhalation of the incomplete products of combustion. In electrical burns, injury results from the generation of heat up to 5,000°C. Progressive tissue death and sloughing are usually greater and involve deeper tissues than the original lesion would indicate. Electrical injury, particularly from alternating current, may cause immediate respiratory paralysis or abnormal cardiac rhythms or both.

Chemical burns may be due to strong acids and alkalis or other materials.

The initial treatment of the burn victim is to remove that person from the burning process. All smoldering clothing or chemical-laden material should be removed to prevent additive injury. Administration of oxygen may be necessary. Ventilation injuries, if severe, can be treated by inserting a breathing tube into the windpipe (trachea). Pain from burns needs to be relieved. A tetanus toxoid booster may be necessary. Antibiotics should be administered whenever the skin is broken. Immediate volume replacement should be started when shock is anticipated in third-degree and in extensive second-degree burns involving more than 25 percent of the body surface area of adults, or more than 30 percent of the body surface area of children. Reference to the rule of nines will help to make a determination of the extent of the body surface burned. A burn diagram is available in the *Merck Manual.* The extent of the burn can be compared with the diagram using the rule of nines. The head and neck is nine percent of the body surface area, each hand and arm is nine percent of the body surface area, etc.

Hopefully, any burns that will be encountered will be superficial burns involving a small body surface area, and without inhalation injury. These burns can be treated by wound cleaning and removing the burning agent. Topical therapy can be used once the wound is clean, and a topical agent like silver sulfadiazine cream may be applied. One layer of the cream is applied with sterile technique, and the wound is covered with gauze bandages. Medications may be necessary for relieving pain and antibiotics may be necessary. Burn patients should be assessed often and wound care should be administered daily.

DERMATOLOGICAL CONCERNS

> He had spent most of the day out in the open walking over the hard packed snow. The sky was bright. The weather was cool and pleasant. He had not worn a hat and was not wearing his gloves. That evening he appeared at the infirmary with erythema (redness) of his face, scalp, and hands. He had failed to apply any sunblock preparations. The diagnosis was obviously sunburn.

Most skin diseases can be diagnosed by physical examination alone. Except for obviously localized diseases, the patient should undress for a complete examination. The mouth, anogenital area, scalp, and nails also often provide clues to the diagnosis. The history is invaluable for assessing physical findings.

The principal types of skin lesions include flat red spots (macules), raised red spots (papules), distinct hard areas (nodules), small blisters (vesicles), blisters containing pus (pustules), large blisters (bullae), large raised red areas (wheals), and collections of prominent small blood vessels (telangiectasia). Any of these may appear as the first manifestation of the dermatitis; they are then known as the primary lesions. They may eventually change in appearance either because of the natural history of the process or because the patient scratches the irritated area causing ulceration. This may become infected or the skin may become thickened producing lichenification. These altered appearances are known as the secondary lesions. Skin may become paper thin or atrophic.

There are certain distinctive arrangements of skin lesions that may help in diagnosis. Acne occurs on the face, neck, chest, and upper back. It can involve the entire trunk. Atopic dermatitis typically involves the inside of the elbow, the back of the knee, the face, neck, and hands in children and adults. Erythema multiforme involves primarily the palms, soles, and mucous membranes but may be widespread. Erythema nodosum affects the lower legs, principally on the pretibial (area in front of the shin bone) surfaces. Lichen planus occurs in the mouth, flexor surface of wrists, trunk, and genitalia. Psoriasis occurs most commonly on extensor surfaces of elbows and knees, scalp, back, anogenital region, and nails, but may appear on flexor surfaces or even on the tip of the penis or on the palms.

Most dermatologic conditions that will be seen on short trips are not emergencies and can be treated symptomatically if a proper diagnosis cannot be made. Medications applied for topical treatment include absorbents, anti-infectives, anti-inflammatory agents, cleansing agents, and skin softeners. Locally acting agents have the following uses: (1) they cleanse, debride, and protect the skin; (2) they destroy causative agents like bacteria or fungi; (3) they attempt to relieve symptoms (itching, burning, pain); and (4) they reduce inflammation and promote healing. The topical formulations that are available include ointments, creams, lotions, and solutions. Powders are often used to protect intertriginous areas (between the toes and between the buttocks, armpit, groin, and beneath the breasts). Sunscreens help shield the skin from ultraviolet light.

Topical corticosteroids are the most effective topical anti-inflammatory agents and many preparations are now available. Itchy, inflammatory dermatoses usually respond very well to locally applied corticosteroids. However, they may worsen some conditions like acne or rosacea, and some fungal infections.

Sunburn results from overexposure of the skin to ultraviolet rays. Symptoms and signs appear in one to twenty-four hours, and skin changes may range from mild redness with subsequent scaling, to pain and swelling, skin tenderness, and blisters from more prolonged exposure. Constitutional symptoms of fever, chills, and weakness similar to a thermal burn may appear if a large portion of the body surface is affected. There may be symptoms due to heat stroke or heat exhaustion.

Simple precautions will prevent most cases of severe sunburn. Exposure to the sun should be limited. Even in winter and in the cold environment, the greatest danger of sunburn and snow blindness comes during foggy days that may be deceptive and have almost as much ultraviolet rays as clear days; the danger is increased at high altitude. Many sunscreen preparations are available, but they take about thirty minutes to bind strongly to the skin and therefore should be applied thirty to sixty minutes before sun exposure. Sunscreens are now rated in the United States by the FDA sun protection factor numbers. The higher the sun protection factor number, the greater the protection. Sunscreens with sun protection factor numbers greater than 15 are usually recommended. The treatment of acute sunburn is to avoid further exposure until the acute reaction has subsided. Early treatment of extensive and severe sunburn with a systemic corticosteroid (prednisone 20 to 30mg orally twice a day for four days for adults) will decrease the discomfort considerably.

A variety of unusual reactions may occur after only a few minutes of exposure. Many factors may contribute to increased photosensitivity: (1) systemic or cutaneous lupus; (2) ingestion of a variety of drugs (sulfonamides, tetracyclines, thiazides, griseofulvin); and (3) external application of or contact with various substances including toilet waters and certain perfumes. Other than sunburn, most dermatological conditions are not emergencies; they can be treated symptomatically.

CARDIOLOGIC PROBLEMS AND EMERGENCIES

> He had suffered a myocardial infarction three years previously. An angioplasty had been performed. He was really doing well and was symptom free. It was with his cardiologist's blessing that he undertook this trip. But he happened to feel his pulse, and he knew that it should be a regular beat. But something was wrong—he was skipping occasional beats. So a visit to the ship's physician was in order. The ECG confirmed that the irregularity was due to occasional premature ventricular contractions (PVC). PVCs will produce an irregular pulse which may be normal. Reassured that all was well, he enjoyed a wonderful trip.

Three factors make consideration of the diagnosis and treatment of heart disease important in the context of adventure travel and tourism in polar areas.

The first of these is the remoteness of Arctic and Antarctic locales, which forces the physician to make certain decisions and act upon them without discussion and consultation with colleagues in the field. The second factor is the absence of sophisticated, yet customary, tools such as pressure-monitoring lines and scans. The physician is dependent on the thoughtful eye, the stethoscope and the ECG machine. The third factor is the makeup of the passenger list, with a higher than normal proclivity to cardiovascular disease because of their age, diet, and lifestyle.

There are also three major groups of problems that might confront the physician under these circumstances: cardiac arrhythmias (irregularity of heart rhythm), congestive heart failure, and acute myocardial infarction. While problems may arise regarding control of hypertension or dosage of anticoagulation, these tend to be more chronic situations and will respond to modification of dosage of drugs the passengers are already taking. Relative to this, information should always be solicited from passengers regarding their current drug regimen prior to departure, and they should be strongly urged to bring these medications with them in quantity to last the entire trip. Polar expedition ships are not traveling pharmacies and a complete array of all commonly used drugs cannot be stocked. When passenger health forms are returned, a careful perusal by the physician might suggest certain additions to the standard pharmacopoeia.

Arrhythmias are generally brought to the physician's attention because of the passenger's symptomatic complaints. The corollary to this is that many asymptomatic cardiac irregularities of rhythm occur, most of which are nonthreatening and discovered incidentally on examination. If brought to the passenger's attention, the information should be accompanied by reassurance. When passengers do report symptoms of cardiac irregularity, they are usually accurate regarding onset, degree of irregularity and sequelae. To this the physician can add, by examination, the arterial pulse, the neck venous pulse, and the ECG. As with the asymptomatic arrhythmias, most are of no hemodynamic importance and bear no prognostic significance. Drug therapy is the mainstay of treatment when required.

Atrial ectopic beats are almost never a problem, but the incidence of these is higher than normal and is probably related to the increased intake of tea, coffee, and alcohol (as well as cold remedies) associated with polar travel. They often respond to cessation or modification of intake.

Atrial fibrillation usually does produce symptoms such as palpitations or breathlessness. The primary treatment is with digoxin. While the loading dose is related to many factors, it is usually somewhat higher in arrhythmias than in congestive heart failure. This will usually prove effective in controlling the ventricular rate with no other drug therapy necessary. A history of mitral valve disease or left atrial enlargement raises concerns about embolism, and aspirin administration should be considered. Failure to respond to digitalization might suggest the use of a beta-blocker such as atenolol (Tenormin).

Atrial flutter is much less common than fibrillation, but the hemodynamic consequences and the treatment approach are essentially the same.

There are many other heart rhythm irregularities that the physician can diagnose with physical examination and ECG. Some are very easily treatable. One type known as supraventricular tachycardia may respond to pressure over a particular area in the neck. Ventricular ectopic beats are usually discovered by accident, are isolated and of no consequence. Like atrial ectopic beats, they may be related to stress, alcohol, and caffeine and often respond to management of these. In the presence of heart disease, ventricular ectopy is of significance, but treatment of these has no effect on the underlying problem which requires treatment beyond this scope.

Ventricular tachycardia with rates over 120 is potentially lethal and requires immediate treatment with intravenous lidocaine. Ventricular fibrillation, of course, requires immediate institution of cardiopulmonary resuscitation.

The second major category of cardiac problems include those related to congestive heart failure. The physician will be able to establish the reason for the heart failure and will be in a position to institute appropriate treatment.

The principal problems are inadequate contraction of the heart (myocardium) and retention of fluids—in the lungs producing pulmonary edema and in the periphery leading to swelling of the ankles. Myocardial contractility improvement is primarily promoted by the use of digoxin. The patient should rest to decrease demand upon the myocardium. Extraneous factors challenging the pump, such as thyrotoxicosis (excess thyroid hormone) or high blood pressure, should be treated and any arrhythmias present attacked. Vasodilators, with their impact on both venous and arterial beds, are of help and the most likely available source aboard ship would be sublingual nitroglycerine, in a dosage of 0.6mgm.

Concomitantly, fluid retention should be addressed. Furosemide 40mgm (initially and twice a day with increased doses as warranted) is the key drug here. Sodium restriction should be started at the same time, while hypokalemia (potassium depletion) may require the need for potassium supplements. Morphine and oxygen are other modalities that might be employed if indicated.

The third and most threatening problem likely to confront the polar physician and his patient is acute myocardial infarction (AMI) or heart attack. Many of the secondary problems associated with AMI, such as arrhythmias and myocardial failure have been discussed above, but a general treatment plan is of value. The main goals are to limit heart muscle loss, reduce pain, and prevent complications. Morphine sulfate 2–4mgm IV is quite effective in pain relief and may be repeated as needed. Oxygen should be given and slowing of the heart rate and irregularity of heart rhythm treated with atropine 0.5–1mgm IV and lidocaine IV respectively. A number of adjunctive drugs have been shown to be of statistical worth and should be employed. The most important of these is aspirin in a dose of 325mgm (non-enteric-coated); the second key drug is a beta-blocker such as atenolol 5mgm IV followed by 50–100mgm daily by mouth in the absence of gross failure or bronchospasmic disease. IV nitroglycerine has been advised in the absence of severe low blood pressure.

The cardiac problems faced by passengers are often very frightening to them, but treatment is usually straightforward and most often successful.

It would be most comforting for the physician to have a defibrillator on board should such an emergency arise. However, maintenance of this equipment is essential and it is important that this and any other electrical equipment be checked regularly to make sure that it is in good working order. Defibrillators are already available on Qantas flights. The American College of Emergency Physicians feels that it should be a standard on the larger ships that defibrillators be available.

OCULAR EMERGENCIES

Since the majority of the cruise participants will be elderly, the acute eye problems are more likely to be of a vascular or degenerative nature. Sudden loss of vision in the elderly may be due to a vascular occlusion (blockage) of the retinal vessels, retinal detachment, and temporal arteritis.

A vascular occlusion of the retinal vessels, which may involve the central retinal vein or the central retinal artery, can present with sudden loss of vision without any pain, and fortunately, the involvement may be in one eye only. In the polar environment on board ship, there is no available treatment, but even with the best facilities in western cities, little can be offered in the way of treatment.

With a retinal detachment, there is a separation of the retina from its supporting tissue. This may occur spontaneously in the older age group. It can also occur due to direct trauma to the eye. It can occur with diabetes and following ocular surgery. A small tear in the retina allows fluid to insinuate itself in the subretinal space causing a retinal detachment. The signs and symptoms are associated with the patient's perceptions of floaters in the eye and by viewing the retina with the ophthalmoscope. This condition is treatable in major centers.

Temporal arteritis is a chronic inflammatory disease of large blood vessels occurring primarily in the elderly. The arteritis most often involves arteries of the carotid system, particularly the arteries of the brain. It causes marked thickening of the innermost layer with narrowing and blockage of the vessel. The symptoms and signs are diverse, depending on the distribution of the arteritis, but typically include severe headache, scalp tenderness, and visual disturbances. The sedimentation rate is a useful simple blood test in the investigation. It may be markedly elevated above the normal level of 20mm, often above 100mm during the active phase. Diagnosis can be made clinically, but should be verified by temporal artery biopsy because of the need for prolonged corticosteroid treatment. However, because of the danger of blindness, a patient with a clinical diagnosis of temporal arteritis should be treated regardless of the biopsy findings. Most patients will respond to prednisone, 60mgm per day, and upon return to a major center, further treatment can be undertaken. Usually, ophthalmoscopic examination of the eye does not show any abnormal findings in this situation.

Glaucoma

In glaucoma, the fluid substance in the eyeball is under higher pressure than normal. The glaucomas are probably the most common cause of blindness in the United States. Primary glaucomas develop without known cause, while secondary glaucomas may develop as a result of damage from previous injuries or inflammations of the eye. With chronic open-angle glaucoma, the condition involves both eyes, is insidious, and slowly progressive, and accounts for about 90 percent of glaucomas. With narrow-angle glaucoma, there is acute obstruction to aqueous outflow. The eye is extremely painful. There is acute visual loss and the cornea may become cloudy. The increased ocular pressure is related to increased intraocular aqueous humor production and decreased outflow of aqueous humor from the eye leading to optic nerve degeneration. The diagnosis is made by noting the increased intraocular pressure and by visualizing the retina to see if there is optic disc cupping. Peripheral visual field testing may help make the diagnosis. Treatment involves decreasing the intraocular pressure through eyedrops, multiple doses of pilocarpine (2 percent to affected eye) and if Diamox is available, 250mgm immediately. Surgical treatment is available, but only in major centers.

INFECTIOUS EYE DISEASES

The most common infectious eye diseases that might be encountered on board ship include blepharitis (infection of the eyelid margins), conjunctivitis (infection of the conjunctiva), sties (infection of the glands in the lid margins), and more rarely keratitis (infection of the cornea).

Blepharitis is an inflammation of the margins of the eyelid with redness and thickening plus crusting that resembles dandruff. There is itching and burning, loss of eyelashes, tearing, and sensitivity to light. Nonulcerative blepharitis may be caused by allergies or associated with dandruff. Ulcerative blepharitis is a bacterial infection, usually staphylococcal, of the glands on the lid and follicles of the eyelashes.

Treatment for the nonulcerative type involves the elimination of dandruff and application of a bactericidal ointment to the lashes at the lid margins. For ulcerative blepharitis, hot compresses may be applied and a bactericidal ophthalmic ointment may be used.

Conjunctivitis may be bacterial with conjunctival redness with purulent discharge, while viral conjunctivitis usually causes a thin watery discharge with conjunctival redness. Allergic conjunctivitis produces a clearer conjunctival discharge.

Corneal inflammation may be associated with ulcers that arise from abrasions or other injury. A scratch from a finger or a contact lens may erode the corneal surface to set the stage for an infection that leads to keratitis. Foreign bodies should be removed. When fluorescein drops are applied to the eye, the foreign body can be seen with a small penlight, preferable with a blue filter attached. If there is an abraded area, this will also be easily seen with the fluorescein drops. Local anesthetic applied to the eye will make it possible to remove the foreign body with a hypodermic syringe and needle, preferably under some degree of magnification. Antibiotics are indicated for the abrasions, and ideally broad spectrum antibiotics should be used. Herpetic ulcers will not respond to regular antibiotics, but require Vira A, which is specific for the herpetic virus infections.

Thus, eye medications should be part of the medical list for a shipboard physician. Instruments to carry include an ophthalmoscope for viewing the interior of the eye and a penlight with a blue filter. This, together with fluorescein, is a big help in diagnosing foreign bodies, abrasions, or ulcers of the cornea.

For many years, there have been reports of much blindness amongst the Eskimos, and this had been attributed to "snow blindness." However, until 1949, no thorough evaluation of these cases had been performed. At that time, a team of four ophthalmologists studied 350 Eskimos in Alaska, and rather quickly determined that the cause of their blindness was corneal scarring. This is called phlyctenulosis, and is evidenced by tongues of vessels growing into the cornea from inflammatory disease. These periodic attacks leave scarring in the area of the vascular intrusion and cumulatively cause corneal scarring and loss of vision. The team was able to determine that this was due to tuberculin sensitivity and the Eskimos had little resistance to tuberculosis or particularly to white man's disease. The treatment was local steroid drops applied to the eye, and following this evaluation, the various school nurses and teachers were instructed to put steroid drops into red eyes of children. This quickly aborts the inflammatory invasion of the cornea and thus prevents the subsequent scarring and blurring of vision.

Snow blindness is caused by excessive exposure to ultraviolet light, causing a sunburn to the eye. The risk is as great on overcast days as in sunny conditions. Snow blindness can be avoided by being aware of snow and water reflection and wearing sunglasses or goggles. Several hours after exposure, the eyes begin to feel gritty and the discomfort rapidly progresses and can become very painful. The eyes tear profusely, the conjunctiva swells and reddens, and there may be a deep-seated boring pain behind the eyeball. Light causes pain (photophobia), the eyelids may go into spasm, and there is a general malaise. The symptoms will settle without treatment within forty-eight hours as the damage to the eyes heals, but this very painful condition can be treated by resting and protecting the eyes from light, and applying three to four drops of Amethocaine to each eye. The eyes must be padded for at least four hours after instilling the drops. Cold compresses will give additional comfort and reduce swelling. Analgesics can be used to relieve the pain. Snow blindness affects both eyes. Therefore, if the presentation is of grittiness, and pain in only one eye, it is unlikely to be due to snow blindness.

GENITOURINARY AND GYNECOLOGICAL EMERGENCIES

> She had been complaining of abdominal pain and vaginal bleeding. She was a member of the crew, and had been at sea for a few weeks. She consulted with the crew's physician and was told to go back to her cabin to rest. We do know a full examination was not carried out. We do know her hemoglobin level was not checked. We do know that she was found dead in her cabin the next morning, having bled massively. This unfortunate incident, which happened in 1992 on a foreign-registered cruise ship in Arctic waters, should never have occurred.

The standard of care at sea for the "acute abdomen" no longer includes white-knuckle appendectomies in nonsterile suboptimal conditions. Only in such conditions as blunt trauma to the abdomen, organ damage, ruptured ectopic pregnancy, or aortic aneurysm, where loss of life from hypovolemic shock is imminent, should laparotomy with general anesthesia be considered. Even then, it should be undertaken with great caution and only after radio contact has been made with consultants in major centers. The key role of the physician is to differentiate between these conditions, treat as conservatively as possible, and explain to the patient and the family why the chosen form of treatment is desirable and what the risks and options are.

Abdominal pain is a common symptom. The ship's surgeon must differentiate between a surgical abdomen and a nonsurgical abdomen. As always, a detailed history and physical examination must be undertaken to make the diagnosis. The physical examination may include a rectal and/or vaginal examination. If laboratory facilities are available, then they can be used to do a urinary examination and some blood tests.

Ships are not equipped with radiology departments, and even a plain X ray of the abdomen may not be achieved at sea. Certainly, sophisticated highly technical examinations like CAT scans and MRIs are not available. Blood is not available. No cruise ship is able to carry a blood bank. In dire emergencies, there is a walking blood bank available in the form of other passengers who are willing to donate their blood and, hopefully, know their blood groups and types. The blood typing equipment may not be available, and it may be more hazardous to transfuse mismatched blood than not. Intravenous fluids are usually available and can be used to maintain the normal fluid volume.

The Australian National Antarctic Research Expedition manual outlines the treatment regimen for conservative management of most "acute abdominal pain."

1. The patient should rest and not be allowed to eat or drink. Nasogastric suction, or the passage of a nasogastric tube, if available and convenient, can be used, especially if the patient's abdomen is distended and bowel obstruction is a consideration. There is certainly a higher frequency in the older population with previous abdominal surgeries, who may have adhesions from these previous surgeries.
2. Intravenous antibiotics are recommended. There should always be a supply on board to maintain the patient for up to ten days.
3. Intravenous fluids should be administered to keep the patient well hydrated, and should certainly be used if the patient is not eating or drinking.
4. Analgesics, in the form of narcotics or non-narcotics, should be used to keep the patient quiet and comfortable.

Appendicitis, acute cholecystitis, and diverticulitis are conditions which may be subdued or subverted with appropriate antibiotic therapy and metronidazide.

An ectopic pregnancy is a gestation that implants outside of the uterus. It represents a serious hazard to a woman's health and reproduction potential, requiring prompt recognition and early aggressive intervention. There are no distinguishing symptoms of ectopic pregnancy, but the classic symptom triad consists of amenorrhea, vaginal bleeding, and abdominal pain. The abdominal pain is usually in the lower abdomen. Missed periods or a history of an abnormal last menstrual period occurs in 75 to 90 percent of ectopic pregnancies. Thus, it is important to have a pregnancy test on board to help make this diagnosis. Making the diagnosis of an acutely ruptured ectopic pregnancy is fairly straightforward. The patient has symptoms of increasing abdominal pain, abdominal distention, and blood pressure changes. Sometimes, shoulder pain may be present from blood in the abdominal cavity irritating the diaphragm. The diaphragm and the shoulder have the same nerve supply—thus the patient may not be able to sense that the pain is from the diaphragm. Other possible diagnoses include threatened or incomplete abortion, a ruptured corpus lupeum cyst, and acute pelvic inflammatory disease.

The patient should be treated with fluid resuscitation to prevent shock. Evacuation of the patient, if possible, should be undertaken. Obviously, if this is not available, and the patient is in extremis, then a laparotomy (abdominal operation), with removal of the ruptured tube, might have to be undertaken.

Pelvic inflammatory disease comprises a spectrum of inflammatory disorders of the upper genital tract, including endometritis, salpingitis (inflammation of the fallopian tube), tubal ovarian abscess, and pelvic peritonitis. A detailed history should be taken and full examination including a pelvic examination must be carried out to confirm the diagnosis. A blood count, including a sedimentation rate and urine analysis, can be carried out to rule out urinary tract infection. A pregnancy test may be important. The differential diagnosis must include acute appendicitis, urinary tract infection, adnexal torsion, endometriosis, bleeding corpus lupeum, and ectopic pregnancy. Treatment consists of appropriate antibiotic therapy.

A device should be available on board to check the hemoglobin level. This is important when assessing a patient with menorrhagia (abnormally profuse menstrual flow) or any condition where it is suspected that bleeding is occurring.

Acute cystitis can be extremely debilitating and unpleasant, with the patient running to the bathroom every ten or fifteen minutes. Cystitis implies inflammation of the urinary bladder. Patients with cystitis usually have symptoms of lower urinary tract irritation, such as dysuria (burning on urination), urgency and frequency with small amounts of urine, suprapubic discomfort, and at times urinary incontinence and hematuria. Management consists of rest and hydration, acidification of the urine, urinary analgesics, and appropriate antimicrobial therapy.

The passenger population is usually older, and among the males there is usually a high incidence of benign prostatic hypertrophy. Certain medications may produce the urinary symptoms. Thus, when treating upper respiratory tract infections, or particularly when antihistamines are administered for seasickness, the physician should remember that these medications may precipitate urinary retention. Thus, it is prudent to have urinary catheters on board. If it proves impossible to pass a urinary catheter and if the bladder is very distended, then it may be necessary to do a suprapubic catheterization by passing a tube into the bladder through the abdominal wall.

SEASICKNESS

In his 1858 work *Life on a Whaler,* Nathaniel Taylor describes the scourge seasickness as follows: "Seasickness is an inverted peristaltic action of the muscular coat of the stomach and intestines. The feelings are beyond the power of language to describe and are only known by those who have experienced them."

> He had traveled all the way from Italy to see the Antarctic. The trip from the Falkland Islands started off in a relatively calm sea and all was well. Within four hours of entering Drake Passage, the seas became choppy and then huge waves began breaking over the ship's bow. The ship rolled and pitched, and he began to feel nauseous and went to bed. Eventually, his vomiting became so frequent that he lay in bed with a bucket by his side. Rectal suppositories were administered, but he continued vomiting until intramuscular Compazine was given to him. This kept him comfortable for the next twenty-four hours and as soon as the sea calmed down, he was feeling wonderful. He and his wife came ashore on the Antarctic Peninsula and they soon forgot about the seasickness experience. They had the most wonderful time of their lives exploring the Antarctic Peninsula. But on the return trip, once Drake Passage was encountered, the seasickness began again and was fortunately controlled by intramuscular medication.

Seasickness is a motion sickness caused by repetitive angular and linear acceleration and deceleration, and characterized primarily by nausea and vomiting. Excessive stimulation of the inner ear by motion is the primary cause. Individuals' susceptibility varies greatly. It also appears that there is a genetic predisposition, with Orientals being especially troubled by seasickness. Visual stimuli (for example, moving horizon), poor ventilation, fumes, smoke, and carbon monoxide, and emotional factors, for example, fear and anxiety, commonly act in concert with motion to precipitate an attack. Nausea and vomiting are characteristic of this condition. This may be preceded by yawning, hyperventilation, salivation, pallor, profuse cold sweating, and somnolence. Aerophagia (an abnormal swallowing of air), dizziness, headache, a general discomfort, and fatigue may also occur.

Once nausea and vomiting develop, the patient is weak and unable to concentrate. However, with prolonged exposure to motion, individuals may adapt and gradually return to well-being. But symptoms may be reinitiated by more severe motion or recurrence of motion after a short respite. Prolonged motion sickness with vomiting may lead to hypotension, dehydration, and depression. Motion sickness can be a serious complication in patients who are ill from other causes.

There are many treatment regimens available. Susceptible individuals should minimize exposure by positioning themselves where there is the least motion; for example, amidships or in airplanes over the wings. A supine or semirecumbent position with the head braced may help matters. Reading should be avoided. A well-ventilated cabin is important, and going out on deck to sit in the fresh air is helpful. Alcoholic or dietary excesses before traveling may increase the likelihood of seasickness. Small amounts of fluids and simple food should be taken frequently during extended periods of exposure. There are many medications available, and the medications should be given before nausea and vomiting occur. One hour before departure, susceptible individuals may be given diphenhydramine, meclizine, or cyclazine. Promethazine, diazepam, or scopolamine can be used to try to minimize or prevent symptoms. A smaller dose of scopolamine can be delivered via a dermal patch applied about four hours before departure, and small amounts are released over the ensuing three days. At this writing, the patches are not available.

In the older population, there may be problems with urinary retention as a side effect of antihistamine medications. Many of these medications are available by injection, and it is useful to have Compazine or phenergan suppositories available. There are many other remedies, including aromatherapy using peppermint oil and ginger. Ginger root capsules are available and may provide relief. Acupressure over the wrist in the region of the radial artery may be helpful. There are also wristbands available that provide pressure in this area.

After vomiting begins, medication must be given rectally or by injection to be effective. With prolonged vomiting, intravenous fluids and electrolytes may be required for replacement and maintenance.

DIARRHEA

Diarrhea is unpleasant and can interfere with a vacation, especially when adequate toilet facilities are not available as in remote places. No body function is more variable and subject to extraneous influences than is defecation. Normal bowel habits vary considerably from person to person, being modified by age, individual physiologic factors, and dietary, social, and cultural patterns. Normal bowel frequency ranges from two to three times per day to two to three times per week. Changes in the stool frequency, consistency, or volume, or blood, mucus, pus, or excess fatty material in the stool may indicate disease. Diarrhea is debilitating. The electrolyte loss of sodium, potassium, magnesium, and chloride, and fluid loss may consequently cause dehydration, and vascular collapse may occur.

The clinical features may vary, depending on the cause, duration, and severity of the diarrhea, on the area of bowel affected, and on the patient's general health. The physician should inquire about associated abdominal pain or vomiting, the presence of overt blood in the stool, and the frequency and timing of bowel movements. Diarrhea is a symptom. If possible, the underlying disorder should be specifically treated, but symptomatic treatment may also be necessary in the form of codeine phosphate, or paregoric (camphorated opium tincture), or loperamide.

Severe acute diarrhea may require urgent fluid and electrolyte replacement to correct dehydration, electrolyte imbalance, and acidosis. An oral glucose electrolyte solution may be given if nausea and vomiting are not severe. Fluids containing glucose or sucrose, sodium chloride, and sodium bicarbonate are rapidly absorbed and easily prepared. If nausea or vomiting is present, oral intake should be restricted, but water and electrolytes must be replaced. Intravenous therapy with electrolyte fluids can be administered. The sources of infection are usually contaminated food and water. The agents responsible for the diarrhea are usually bacterial enteropathogens, like E. coli, shigella, or campylobacter, and viruses and Giardia. When sanitation is in doubt, diarrhea might be prevented by eating only steaming hot foods or eating fruits that can be peeled by you. Bottled water, boiled tea, and coffee can be drunk instead of using tap water or ice cubes. Thus, fluids should be replaced. Drugs can be used to reduce diarrhea and to combat the causative agents.

In February of 1996, a study was done to determine the incidence of cruise-associated diarrheal disease outbreaks since 1985. Among cruises of three to fifteen days, Centers for Disease Control staff found 1.4 outbreaks per thousand cruises. An etiologic agent was implicated in 68 percent of investigated outbreaks, 21 of 31; bacterial in 12; viral in 9. A specific vehicle of transmission was identified in 16—undercooked scallops (three outbreaks caused by enterotoxigenic E. coli); eggs (two outbreaks caused by salmonella serotype Enteridites, one by Norwalk-type virus); and food items provided by caterers during onshore excursions (three outbreaks, one caused by Shigella sonnei).

The researchers concluded that observance of four simple precautions could have prevented almost two-thirds of the investigated outbreaks on cruise ships: (1) cooking seafood thoroughly, (2) using pasteurized eggs, (3) prohibiting food handlers from working while suffering from gastrointestinal illness, and (4) avoiding the use of onshore caterers for off-ship excursions.

DENTAL EMERGENCIES

If there is a dentist on board, then the physician's life will be made much easier, and it is certainly worthwhile looking through the passenger list to find one. For, as Shakespeare wrote in *Much Ado about Nothing,* "there was never yet a philosopher that could bear the toothache patiently."

Toothache

Pain localized to a particular tooth and provoked by sweets or cold is usually caused by caries that has not yet involved the dental pulp (nerve). Because this type of pain is usually fleeting, the patient should avoid provoking stimuli, use mild analgesics, and seek proper attention as soon as possible. If facilities are available to apply a temporary filling, then this can be done.

With an abscess or irreversible pulpitis, there is usually localized pain and the patient can identify a problem tooth. There may be swelling localized to the gum or more generalized swelling involving that side of the mouth. The patient usually has a foul taste in the mouth. Emergency treatment usually consists of antibiotics like pen VK or Cleocin, and pain medications for short term.

A periapical abscess that has spread beyond the alveolar bone and causing swelling and fluctuation in adjacent soft tissue requires incision and drainage. Extraction of the tooth may be necessary if it appears that the tooth cannot be restored.

Cellulitis of the mouth may produce diffuse hard swelling and trismus (lockjaw). There may be generalized pain in the mouth. The fear is the development of a respiratory obstruction.

Treatment consists of high doses of antibiotics like Cleocin. The area can be incised and drained, and if necessary, the tooth should be extracted.

Less common causes of acute perioral swelling include periodontal abscess, infected cysts, allergy, salivary gland obstruction infection, peritonsillar infection, or skin infection.

Fractured and avulsed teeth

If a small portion of a crown of a tooth is fractured and the dental pulp is not exposed, analgesic medication and a topical covering of a tooth is appropriate. If the pulp is exposed or the tooth is mobile, then antibiotics should be given as well. Partially avulsed teeth should be repositioned and stabilized. If a tooth is completely avulsed, it may be possible to save it by immediately replacing it into the socket without washing and with minimal handling. If it is to be washed, then physiologic saline can be used. If replacement is delayed a few minutes or the tooth is excessively handled, it may be retained for a few months, but the prognosis for indefinite retention is poor. Obviously, a soft diet will be used to prevent jarring the replaced tooth until it has settled in.

Dislocated jaw

The dislocation may cause intense pain and trismus, and the patient maintains the mouth open and is unable to close the mouth. This is treated by reducing the dislocation. Injecting a local anesthetic agent in the joint area and in the area of insertion of the lateral pterygoid muscle may allow the mandible to reduce spontaneously or with minimal manual effort. Downward pressure is applied lateral to the molars or on the occlusal surfaces.

Fractured mandible

The jaw may be fractured after a blow to the jaw or after a fall striking the jaw. The patient may notice that the bite is off. There may, in fact, be gross displacement of teeth and bone. Obviously, an X ray is advisable. Treatment consists of fixing the mandible with archbars and wires. It is important to restore normal occlusion of the jaw. While the jaw is wired, a soft diet will be used for about four weeks while the mandible heals. The diet can be taken through a straw. Antibiotic prophylaxis is also important.

EAR, NOSE, AND THROAT EMERGENCIES

Epistaxis (nosebleed)

Nosebleeds may occur secondary to local infections such as sinusitis, rhinitis, or vestibulitis; drying of the nasal mucous membrane or trauma to the nose may also be responsible. Bleeding may be due to hypertension or may be due to bleeding tendencies. Patients who are on blood thinners like Coumadin or aspirin may bleed with minimal trauma to the nose.

Bleeding may be controlled by pinching the nasal alae together for five to ten minutes. If this fails, then the bleeding site must be found. The bleeding point may be cauterized. Bleeding can be controlled temporarily by applying pressure over a cotton compress impregnated with a vasoconstrictor such as phenylephrine and a topical anesthetic such as lidocaine until the site is anesthetized. Electrocautery or silver nitrate can be used. If the nosebleed is due to a bleeding tendency, Vaseline gauze is used to apply pressure as atraumatically as possible to the bleeding point. Cautery is not used, since the periphery of a cauterized area may begin to bleed. If bleeding cannot be controlled this way, then a posterior pack may have to be used. A Foley catheter can be used as a nasal pack. Antibiotics may be necessary if the bleeding is of long duration.

Internal otitis media

The symptoms of internal otitis media consist of earache and hearing loss. Examination of the eardrum with an otoscope reveals a red, bulging eardrum and the light reflex is displaced. Treatment consists of antibiotics and decongestants. Sympathomimetic agents and antihistamines can be used in allergic patients.

With external otitis media, the symptoms are those of itching and tenderness and pain in the ear. There may be discharge from the auditory canal. Treatment consists of topical antibiotics or corticosteroids and cleaning of the ear canal.

Sinusitis

Sinusitis is an inflammatory process in the paranasal sinuses due to viral, bacterial, or fungal infections or allergic reactions. The area over the involved sinus may be tender and swollen. Maxillary sinusitis causes pain over the cheekbones, toothache, and frontal headache. Frontal sinusitis produces pain in the frontal area and frontal headache. Ethmoid sinusitis causes pain behind and between the eyes and a frontal headache that is often described as "splitting." Malaise is usually present. Fever and chills suggest an extension of the infection beyond the sinuses. The nasal mucous membrane is red. There may be a seropurulent or mucopurulent discharge from the nose. Treatment consists of antibiotic coverage, decongestants, and steroid nasal spray.

Tonsillitis and peritonsillar abscess

The symptoms include sore throat and pain. There may be fever and malaise. Usually, there is difficulty or pain on swallowing. With a peritonsillar abscess, there may be trismus or even inflammation in the back of the throat.

Treatment consists of antibiotics and analgesics. Fluids should be maintained as the patients usually do not feel like eating or drinking. In the presence of a peritonsillar abscess, incision and drainage may solve the problem.

PULMONARY EMERGENCIES

Pneumothorax (collapsed lung)

The symptoms of pneumothorax include sudden shortness of breath with rapid breathing and chest pain. Examination reveals absent breath sounds on the involved side; neck veins may be distended, and the windpipe may be deviated. This occurs because of the free air in the chest between the collapsed lung and the chest wall. An open pneumothorax occurs when a penetrating chest wound allows outside air to enter the pleural space, causing the lung to collapse. In closed pneumothorax, the chest wall becomes airtight after penetration (for example, by a needle, or by a fractured rib, or after a stab wound). Air may also leak from a ruptured bronchus or perforated esophagus into the chest cavity. If an X ray can be performed, the X ray is usually characteristic, showing air without lung markings.

A small spontaneous pneumothorax requires no special treatment; the air is reabsorbed in a few days. A larger pneumothorax may take two to four weeks to heal. The course can be shortened by the introduction of a chest tube with water-sealed drainage. In a tension pneumothorax, quick removal of air may be lifesaving. Air may be removed simply by inserting into the chest a large needle attached through a three-way stopcock to a large syringe. This can be done until a chest tube can be inserted. While chest tube drainage is taking place, antibiotics are necessary.

Bronchitis and pneumonia

These two conditions can occur after an upper respiratory infection. Usually, there is fever and muscle aching and malaise and chills. Examination of the chest may reveal wheezing and shortness of breath. Treatment consists of bedrest and adequate fluids, analgesics, and antibiotic coverage. Physical therapy to promote deep breathing may help speed recovery. Coughing is also encouraged.

Asthma

Asthma is a lung disease characterized by airways obstruction that is reversible (but not completely in some patients), airways inflammation, and increased airways responsiveness to a variety of stimuli. About ten million asthmatics live in the United States. Symptoms include respiratory distress, rapid breathing, and rapid heart rate. Wheezing may be audible. Usually, the patient is sitting up to try to make breathing easier. The patient is anxious. Inspiration is short and expiration is long. Sometimes, this is accompanied by a cough. Hopefully, the patients on board will have brought their own medications. Treatment usually consists of the administration of beta-agonists and an aggressive steroid regimen. Oxygen therapy is useful, and antibiotic coverage may be necessary.

Anaphylaxis

Anaphylaxis is an acute, often explosive, systemic reaction that occurs in a previously sensitized person who again receives the sensitizing agent. The most common causative agents are foreign serum, injected enzymes, blood products, beta-lactam antimicrobials and many other drugs, desensitizing injections, and insect stings. Beta-adrenergic blockers, even in eyedrops, may aggravate anaphylactic reactions.

Usually, within one to fifteen minutes, the patient feels uneasy, becomes agitated and flushed, and complains of palpitation, tingling, itching, throbbing in the ears, coughing, sneezing, raised skin rash, and difficulty breathing owing to laryngeal swelling or bronchospasm. Nausea, vomiting, abdominal pain, and diarrhea are less common. The manifestations of shock may develop within another one or two minutes. Primary cardiovascular collapse can occur.

Patients with the greatest risk of drug anaphylaxis are those who have reacted previously to that drug. Therefore, it is very important to take a history of allergy.

Immediate treatment with epinephrine is imperative. Antihistamines may be administered. It may be necessary to start an intravenous fluid line. For more severe reactions, airway management may become important. Cardiac arrest may occur, requiring immediate resuscitation.

CHAPTER 11

Confessions of a Ship's Surgeon

Most realize death is inevitable. Many Americans seem to feel it is optional.

—Anonymous

The "confessions" that follow are the anecdotes and issues raised by a retired general practitioner who since the late 1980s has made 37 trips on 7 different ships carrying between 30 and 130 passengers per cruise. His medical background and his sensitivity to his passengers made him an excellent choice for a ship's surgeon. His story is fascinating.

The "medical department" in my experiences ranged anywhere from a fairly decent room on the *World Discoverer,* which had a place you could actually have the patient lie down to be examined, and a fairly adequate medical supply area, to what was no more than a bolted-on medicine chest in the room the physician was supposed to live in on another ship. To see a patient on the second ship you had to see them in their room or wherever else you could commandeer.

"I THINK I'M GOING TO DIE" AND OTHER CASES

This first case occurred on my first cruise to the Antarctic. He was a ninety-four-year-old Iowa farmer. I first saw him in the airport in Miami, but I didn't know who he was. I just saw an old man who was just as white as a sheet, sitting in a wheelchair with crutches on the back, and I thought, "Aw, what a shame! This poor old guy, there's nobody around him. Here he is in Miami. . . ." The next time I saw him was in Santiago, and I thought "Oh, no." The next time I saw him was in Punta Arenas and I knew I was doomed. Sure enough, he was to be on our voyage, and he was unable to get into the jeep that was to carry him to the ship. He had to have help up every step of the gangway into the ship. I knew that I would be insane to let him go on this trip, but it was my first voyage. I had no idea how to handle these things. There was no one around to ask. I was out there very much alone. They had told me a few things, but of course not the things I was going to encounter.

I finally decided that I wasn't going to let him sail with us. First of all, he was two floors below the dining room. He couldn't climb two stairs without assistance, and the ship was not set up to handle his special needs. It was the former *Lindblad Explorer,* which was then known as the *Society Explorer,* and they were not equipped to serve people in their rooms. And besides that, we were going across the Drake Passage, and one good lurch of the ship and this guy was going to go down and he would break at least two hips and his back and his neck.

So I told him I wasn't going to let him sail. He had a hard time with that because he had never been off the farm in ninety-four years. This was to be the first and only trip of his life. And then he told me he booked the trip over a year ago, and within the last four months he realized that he was going downhill and was going to die, and he said "As a matter of fact, I think I'm going to die on this voyage." And I thought, I'm not ready for that!

The second case had to do with a fifty-four-year-old Swiss Ph.D. who seemed to be fine. She had come on the ship and nobody had said a thing about any problem until we had left Punta Arenas and were across the Drake Passage, and she came in with painless jaundice and ascites (accumulation of free fluid in the abdomen). What's the problem? Who knows? And who can find out, because there isn't any laboratory equipment to do any testing whatsoever. The diagnostic possibilities ran from gall bladder disease to cirrhosis of the liver, any one of dozens of reasons to have secondary cancer of the liver including cancer of the ovary. And she knew she was coming down with jaundice before she even boarded the ship. But nothing was going to stop her!

The third case was a thirty-year-old woman from Utah who had had multiple hospitalizations for psychiatric illness with depression and multiple personalities. She looked like she had come out of a concentration camp. She looked *awful,* and it had quite an impact on the passengers who were there for a vacation, because she just looked ghastly. The problem was that one of her multiple personalities was such that she fancied herself as an olympic athlete. So all my admonitions not to exert herself, not to go out and toboggan down the snow on the Antarctic Peninsula, and please don't go into the Deception hot tub situation, where you have hot springs there that are quite hot, mix them up with cold water, get in and get your picture taken. . . . Don't *do* those things. But she wouldn't listen to anyone. She wouldn't listen to anyone whatsoever. And each time she had to be brought back in a state of collapse, in fact, even carried back to the ship.

Her sister was a graduate nurse who was traveling with her and that was the only fortunate thing about it. At night she became psychotic and periodically was screaming and raving in her stateroom most of the night, and she'd go from that into a catatonic state. And her sister filed a complaint against the ship that we did not carry thorazine on board; because if we had, that would have brought her back to real life, and that's all she needed. We were at fault for not having it.

The next had to do with a fifty-year-old psychologist who had been to South America on the Amazon River and had gotten a case of Leishmania tropica, which is a skin form of Leishmaniasis. He wasn't well yet, and the doctors were having a hard time treating it. They had tried everything. They finally sent him to the Centers for Disease Control and put him on some new experimental medication, and it seemed to be working, except for one thing. That is, it was affecting his liver function tests and his pancreatic function tests. There was concern that if it did have a profound effect on these organs that he might be in real trouble. We were going to an area of the world where there were no medical centers and certainly no laboratory work could be done on board the ship to see how he was doing and monitor the situation. The company asked whether I thought he should go on the trip and I said, "No! Why not postpone it until this skin thing is healed up." I talked to him and said, "I don't think it's a good idea. I don't think you should go. It's too much of a risk. You shouldn't take these chances." And the company said, "Go." So he went. . . and fortunately he did all right.

Then there was a seventy-two-year-old retired engineer with such a severe form of Parkinson's disease that he was constantly in trouble. He would often fall over, and when he fell it was like he was made of wood and someone just pushed him and he went right down on his face and chest. I ended up sewing him up. He must have fallen twelve or fifteen times in various places on and off the ship. But he was a headstrong guy. His wife was a nurse, and he wouldn't listen to her either. He was determined to do *everything* that he had paid to do; he even wanted to go snorkeling with the sea lions. You just knew, this guy would die! The snorkeling idea was negotiated, fortunately. We worked out a deal which put him into a better stateroom nearer to the dining room so he wouldn't have the stairs to climb if he agreed not to go snorkeling, and it worked out. The upgrade was at no charge to him, by the way.

The next case was that of a fifty-year-old who was traveling with her attorney husband and two canisters of oxygen for continual use day and night. This was up in Alaska. The problem was I had no replacement for the oxygen, because the ship was a German ship, and all the fittings for the oxygen were German fittings and would not accept any other source of supply to replenish the oxygen in Mexico, the United States, or Canada, because they just wouldn't fit. There was nothing we could do about it. It turned out that she knew a great deal about how to calculate her usage of it, so she rationed the use of the oxygen and did very well. There were no problems at all.

Of very special interest was the seventy-year-old woman who fell out of bed one morning. I'm not sure why, but she seemed to be fine. She came down after breakfast and said her wrist hurt a little bit. I checked it out, put a little wrap around it, and gave her a little TLC (tender loving care). She participated in all the activities during the day; she had lunch, she did the morning excursion, the afternoon excursion, she had dinner, and she went to bed and was fine. I didn't give it a thought.

At 2:00 A.M., she was in shock. She had a distended acute abdomen. She didn't have a lot of pain, but she did have some. She also had a strong history of gall bladder disease, and my best diagnosis was that that was the problem. But I knew I had to offload her, because she was, as I say, in shock, and I didn't know what was the matter with her. I really didn't have any way to find out, either, on board the ship. There were no laboratory facilities to assist me, in these situations. On the ships that I go on, you fly by the seat of your pants. A diagnosis is made by history and physical examination alone. You try to remember all the things they taught you in medical school and what you picked up from Dr. Jack Lange's medical publications.

Anyway, I called as we were down in the tip of Baja California Sur, Mexico. I asked that we be met by an ambulance when we pulled into Cabo San Lucas and that a doctor be there. I needed so many things. I needed oxygen, and I needed help. This lady was going to die if she didn't get it. Well, they showed up with not exactly a pickup truck—it was covered, and you could slide a gurney in there—but there was no oxygen on board. This was their idea of an ambulance, no oxygen on board. They did send two physicians who happened to work in the clinic where she was taken. I don't know, they must not have been too busy. They drove the ambulance. But there was nothing for the other one to do; there was no blood pressure cuff, no stethoscope, no oxygen, no equipment, no nada. So they took her to their clinic and they did a CBC (complete blood count) and a blood sugar, and that was all they could do. Then they couldn't get the X ray done as the machine would not do abdominal X rays. We realized that she was going to have to be air-evacuated back to the United States if she was to survive. They had to send a plane down from Albuquerque, New Mexico, down to the Baja California Sur, to bring her back at the cost of about $16,000. When she got back to a major medical center in Albuquerque, they did a CAT scan and they found out she had a ruptured spleen. Surgery saved her life.

THE NEEDS OF THE TOUR OPERATORS

What does the cruise line want? They want revenue. That's what makes a company run. And besides, the doctor's on board. They think he can handle whatever goes wrong. They want satisfied customers. They want to look good for investors. Above all, they want to make a profit. And so, when I tell them this person is ninety-four years old and shouldn't go on this trip, they don't really want to hear that, and they're not likely to tell him he can't go. In most cases, he's paid somewhere between $8,000 and $16,000 to go down there (to the Antarctic), and if he's traveling with a companion, there's a similar amount of money, and they're not going to let that slip through their fingers without a fight.

THE DOCTOR'S NEEDS

What does the ship's doctor want? You want the wherewithal to diagnose and treat most basic medical problems when they arrive; you want to look good, you know; you're a doctor. And you want the wherewithal to manage a major catastrophe if and when it happens, and it *will* happen if you do this work long enough. You want to have a vacation. You don't want to have to work too hard. You want to see the world, bring a friend, stay healthy. Those are the things the doctor wants.

THE PASSENGERS' NEEDS

What does the passenger want? The trip of a lifetime! Who cares if it's his last? In fact, I've run into three or four people who have said that they knew they were not well and didn't have long for this earth, and if they died while they were on this trip that was quite all right. They thought that was a better deal than, say, being strung out in a hospital or something like that. And they really don't worry about it as much as we do. And so I say, "Who cares if it is his last trip?" Sometimes it's true, they really do feel this way. Besides, "there's a doctor on board, and they can take care of everything." And besides that, they watch television and in the make-believe world of TV you just have to get on the helicopter, and they medevac you to the medical center and everybody lives happily ever after. And they want to get good pictures, videos, experiences, and stories to tell. That's what the passenger wants.

PASSENGERS, HEALTH FORMS, AND DISCLOSURE

Health history forms are an interesting subject. I wondered what would happen if you had the best health history form the world has ever seen. Would it be very valuable? Would it really help you or not? You realize that if it's filled out honestly it may be very valuable, but it often isn't filled out properly.

I'm reminded of a passenger I was hiking with, up to the top of this mountain in Baja California Sur, Mexico. He was periodically popping pills, and I'd watch him for a while and then I'd lose track of him, watch him, lose track of him, chat a little bit, and go on up. It was a hot day and we were all sweating, trying to get up to the top, to get a view of the ship and the sea. Finally we got up there and I asked, "What are you popping in your mouth all the time."

"Oh, nitroglycerin."

"Oh, yeah?"

"Yeah, I'm going to get to the top of that mountain. I came on this trip just to get to the top of that mountain, and I'm going to do it!"

I thought, "Boy, I don't know." When I got back I looked at his health history form, and he put down that his general health was "good." So I confronted him, and I said, "You're taking nitroglycerin and you put down that you're in good health. How do you resolve that?"

"Well," he said, "hell, I've had open heart surgery. I got defibrillated two months before I got on this trip. I'm here. I consider I'm in good health, don't you?" You can't argue with a guy like that, really.

Anyway, health history forms are well and good, but frequently they don't ask the right questions. You don't want to be too intrusive because if you ask too many personal questions, people will shy away from the company. They will not want to go on the trip. If you ask too many questions, they really don't want to share all the answers with you. You may get a lot of irrelevant information like "Sometimes I feel funny when I eat too much magnesium."

And sometimes there are cultural reasons why people don't answer them. For example, we have one form, on the *World Discoverer* (again, it was based in Germany, owned by Germans). Their forms are in German. I've noticed the Germans are particularly prone to answer "no" to everything; I don't know whether it's a societal thing that they just tend not to share information with you. I do know that because when I look at their form, it often says, "No, no, no, I'm in excellent health," and then you talk to them and you find out they're diabetic, and they do have some problems controlling their diabetes and things of that sort, but you don't find it out on the form. And that's true, I think, often with aging people. They're reluctant, perhaps they don't understand the questions as they're worded on the form. Anyway, the point is you don't get the information that you think might be helpful. Sometimes it's just as well. Sometimes, a person can fill up a form with every known ailment, and you can throw up your hands and say, "My God! I'm not going to leave their stateroom for the whole trip. I won't get the chance to do anything fun." But they're not the ones who give you trouble. Any physician who has done this work very often knows that the people you're sure will give you trouble when they walk on board the ship are not the ones who give you trouble. The ones who you think are in great health—look out—they're going to give you the problems.

Most people don't want to deal realistically with issues of transportation should they get sick. I don't think the cruise line wants to be very realistic about this either. Physicians need to tell passengers that "No, you cannot get flown out of the Antarctic by helicopter to South America. It's not possible."

Many passengers have unrealistic ideas about their needs. So, the recommendations I have on this is that if passengers need personal assistants, they should bring their own. I don't know how they're going to do it, but they should do it. I don't feel it's the responsibility of the ship, the ship's staff, crew, or the doctor to "special" someone who needs a lot of attention. I don't think it's fair to ask other people to do that. But other passengers will get caught up in doing it because they're sympathetic when they see the person needs a lot of attention, a lot of help getting around. But then they begin to resent it because pretty soon it's messing up their vacation. They didn't bargain for that when they paid for the trip. So I think people ought to bring their own help when they need it; they ought to bring all their own medicines, any aids like crutches, breathing equipment, and the like. They ought to carry it on board the ship, not packed in their luggage, because luggage gets lost, and the only way to be sure to get it is to carry it with you.

MEDICAL MALPRACTICE INSURANCE

With respect to medical malpractice insurance, is it necessary? Yes, it is! But the problem is how to get it. When I was still in private practice, and I started doing part-time ship's surgeon work, the insurance company that I had carried for twenty years in practice was happy to extend it to doing these new activities. But of course, I was in general practice, and that covered a great range of things, and they knew I'd done these things, so they didn't have any trouble with that. But say you're an internist, whether your insurance company will be willing to cover you with regard to orthopedic activities which you haven't done in years is another matter.

Anyway, following retirement I tried for about a year, through the AMA (American Medical Association), my state medical association, and every other possible organization, to get medical malpractice insurance for myself. I couldn't do it. I think that anyone who is retired isn't very likely to be able to get medical malpractice insurance.

However, a lot of retired doctors make pretty good cruise physicians, because they're good with older people; they've seen and done a lot of stuff, and they've got the time. For the jobs I've done in the last six years, I get a free trip and I get to take someone with me. No money changes hands. I'm not exactly an employee. I don't know if I'm classified as an independent contractor. I have a hunch that medical malpractice insurance is very very difficult to get for cruise physicians in most any circumstances. The only way I can see that it could be done would be to have the company consider the physician an agent of the company and therefore be willing to cover the physician with professional liability insurance.

I've not heard of a doctor per se being sued for medical malpractice on a cruise ship, but I don't doubt for a minute that it has occurred; I just haven't personally encountered it or seen it with people that I know. I have seen people sue the company, when they get diarrhea or vomiting or something like that. I think that's usually totally groundless, but the companies will most often settle out of court and keep the whole thing quiet.

OTHER CONSIDERATIONS FOR PHYSICIANS

There are additional considerations with regard to medical malpractice. The ship's country of registry might be different from the ship's country of ownership, which might be different from the country of the cruise line leasing the ship, which might be different from the physician who's practicing on the ship, and the nationality of the ship's officers and crew. And did the incident occur on land? In which case, can you say who owns the land? What about territorial waters? What about open seas? I'm not a lawyer and I don't know the answers to those questions.

In remote islands or in isolated Arctic villages, the native people have medical problems. They have no money; and they may have no economy whatsoever. And the doctor from the cruise ship is asked to see them. Well, the reason that happens is because the expedition leader wants to make some points with the islanders so the chief will invite the passengers to his island and show off. And that's all well and good; it makes for a good trip for the tourists. But I wonder about the ethics of giving medications to the islanders which are going to be dispensed by people with very questionable training.

I remember one island I went to in Indonesia. They had someone with asthma, and the person had an inhaler. So I said, "Let me see how you use the inhaler." She didn't shake it up, she just put it out about six inches from her mouth and went "pop" like that, just like that. I said, "No, that isn't going to work. Well, I happen to have asthma myself sometimes. Let me show you how to do this." So I showed her, I wet my lips, I put it in my mouth, I breathed out all my air, I sucked in like this.... By the time I finished that, the nurse and the patient were in hysterics. They thought that was the funniest thing they'd ever seen.

It is obvious from the "confessions" of this one shipboard physician that the relationship between passenger, doctor, and tour company is complex. If a passenger ends up in a legal battle with the tour company or ship owner, the passenger can count on going to court on the company's terms, not his or her own. That is because the U.S. Supreme Court ruled that cruise companies can have disputes litigated according to the fine print on the passenger's ticket. A woman who slipped on a deck mat during a Carnival cruise later filed suit in her home state of Washington, but a judge ruled that the dispute had to be litigated in Florida, the home of the Carnival cruise line, as specified on the back of the ticket. A federal appeals court overturned that ruling saying the woman wasn't able to freely bargain such terms. However, the United States Supreme Court upheld the original verdict.

Tour companies may be incorporated outside of the United States, but still could be sued in the United States. That is, if their main office and most of their staff, as well as the passengers were from the United States, a case could be made to make that happen.

Most of the ships carrying the polar travelers of today are of Russian registry. The companies are based in Vladivostok or Murmansk. Even if the lawsuit could be tranferred to Moscow, it appears there would be some very special problems!

Many American physicians "go bare," that is, they carry no professional liability insurance. Either they are unable to obtain this because they are retired, or the cost is prohibitive, or they make the judgment that they will go without. Probably the most common cause to sue a physician in the United States today, is that patients don't like doctors. They feel they were not treated properly, but often the only reason they feel that way is lack of attention. With the small number of passengers on a polar cruise, unless there is an overwhelming calamity, the ship's surgeon should have ample time to see his or her patients daily. Once patients view the limited medical facility and get to know the physician not only as a professional but as a friend, medical liability issues become extremely rare.

In 1995, one of the tour companies carrying hundreds of thousands of passengers yearly on cruises in the Caribbean, found that approximately 90 percent of their medical liability issues involved evacuating injured or ill patients from their ships. "Lack of timely evacuation" is a phrase that was used repeatedly. It is well recognized that on polar cruises it may be virtually impossible to evacuate passengers for much-needed medical care. Not only should the passengers be advised of this before cruises begin, but if and when a situation arises where the ship's surgeon feels that additional care is necessary and he or she cannot provide that with the medical setup aboard, the patient should be so advised, and also the expedition leader and captain of the vessel. The physician should clearly state the problem and options to the patient, and carefully note this on the medical record. Just because the doctor realizes they are too far from help doesn't mean the patient will understand and appreciate that at a later time. Documentation becomes critical.

Many passengers who are medical professionals have served as consultants to the ship's surgeon. When they do this on a specific request and do not charge for their services, they probably come under a "Good Samaritan ruling" and would be completely free of any perceived liability. Shipboard physicians and patients alike owe a debt of gratitude to those medical personnel who have assisted in emergency situations.

The physician who wrote the perspectives in this chapter stated clearly that he was not a lawyer and couldn't address the complicated legal issues involved in polar tourism. In the next chapter a qualified legal expert clarifies the rights and responsibilities of those involved in the industry and those who use its services.

CHAPTER 12

Liability Issues in Expedition and Cruise Medicine

This section was prepared by Carolyn S. Langer, M.D., J.D., M.P.H., legal editor of The Wilderness Medicine Letter. Because of her unique background in medicine, law, and public health, Dr. Langer is able to reply constructively to medical legal issues in polar expedition cruising.

The following is an excerpt from the standard "fine print" found on the back of cruise passengers' tickets:

CARRIER NOT LIABLE
FOR PASSENGER'S MEDICAL CARE

(a) *Medical Services on Vessel.* The Carrier does not undertake that a physician or medical personnel will be aboard the Vessel. If the Vessel does carry a physician or medical personnel, then they are independent contractors and work directly for the Passengers.

(b) *Consent of Treatment.* If, in the opinion of the Carrier, a Passenger in need of medical or surgical services is unable to request it, the Passenger hereby expressly consents to such treatment, if any, and to pay the cost thereof charged by the Vessel's physician or other physician or medical personnel designated by the Carrier who in doing so is acting on behalf of the Passenger.

(c) *Treatment at Passenger's Risk.* All medicines and all medical or surgical services furnished by the Vessel's physician, if any, or any other physician or medical personnel (all of whom are engaged by the Passenger as independent contractors) or ship's officers, employees or agents of the Carrier, shall be and are accepted by and at the Passenger's sole risk and expense, and the Carrier shall not be responsible for the quality, nature or consequence thereof.

(d) *Passenger's Obligation to Report Medical Conditions.* Before this Ticket is issued, the Passenger must report to the Carrier or its general agent, all preexisting illness, disabilities or pregnancy and all other conditions for which the Passenger may require medical attention during the course of the Cruise. If any such condition arises after the Ticket is issued, the Passenger must report all such conditions to the Carrier, Purser or Vessel's Master or physician, if any, before boarding, or if the Passenger has boarded the Vessel, then before the Vessel leaves port. The Carrier, Vessel and the Vessel's physician, if any, shall have no liability in connection with any such condition.

(e) *Lack of Obligation to Examine Passenger.* Neither the Carrier, nor the Vessel's physician, if any, has any obligation to examine any Passenger for any purpose prior to boarding or sailing.

(f) *Refusal of Passage.* The Carrier reserves the right to refuse passage to a Passenger who has failed to give proper notice of any disability, illness, pregnancy or other condition requiring special care, attention or treatment or who in the Carrier's sole opinion is physically or mentally unfit for the Cruise. In such event, the Passenger is not entitled to any refund of fare.

INTRODUCTION

In recent years market pressures have led to the expanded participation of the general public (including an aging population) in expeditions and cruises to more remote regions of the world. Such travel not only poses a higher risk of injury and illness, but often includes extreme environments, limited access to medical personnel and supplies, and extended patient management due to limited medical evacuation capabilities. What are the medical-legal ramifications for tour operators and trip physicians? Historically, the probability of a lawsuit was low because participants were younger, more experienced adventurers who tended to be higher risk takers with greater awareness of and willingness to assume these risks. However, the increased involvement of the general population in these pursuits has undoubtedly generated a concomitant increase in exposure to liability. To minimize their liability, it is important for tour operators and trip physicians to implement sound risk management principles for medical clearance, education, and provision of medical services to trip participants.

TORT LAW AND THE DOCTRINE OF NEGLIGENCE

In tort law, members of society owe a duty to other people to act reasonably and in ways that will not hurt another person or his or her property. In the travel medicine context, redress for a private civil wrong is typically sought under the negligence doctrine. To bring a cause of action under a negligence theory, the plaintiff (the party filing the claim) must establish the following four elements:

1. Duty: The defendant has a duty to use due care as a reasonably prudent person would under similar circumstances. For example, a plaintiff could argue that a trip physician owes the participants a duty to demonstrate "the knowledge, skill, and care customarily exercised by a reasonable and prudent physician under similar circumstances, given the prevailing state of medical knowledge and available resources."[1] To meet this duty, physicians must typically adhere to the standard of care prevailing within the medical community.

2. Breach of duty: Defendants breach their duty when they fail to conform to the duty of care or to act in accordance with norms or standards of practice. This breach may occur either through commission or omission of certain acts. For example, a physician may breach the duty of care by failing to diagnose or treat (omission) or by improperly treating a patient (commission).

3. Causation: The plaintiff must further prove that the defendant's conduct was the direct, foreseeable, and proximate cause of the resulting injuries. In other words, absent the defendant's conduct, the harm would not have occurred. Establishing causation is often the most problematic step for plaintiffs. For example, an injured traveler might allege that a trip leader or medical practitioner breached the duty of care by delaying medical evacuation, but the defendant could argue that the injury had already occurred and that any delay in evacuation neither caused nor aggravated the injury.

4. Damages: As the final step, the plaintiff must demonstrate damages, that is, harm to the individual's person, property, or interests for which the redress is customarily a monetary award. Awards may encompass special damages (out-of-pocket losses, medical expenses, lost earnings), general damages (pain and suffering), and punitive damages. Punitive damages are rare in the medical context because the plaintiff must prove that the defendant's conduct exceeded simple negligence and was grossly negligent, reckless, or malicious. Nonetheless, physicians should be aware that their insurance policies generally do not provide malpractice coverage for punitive damages.

Medical malpractice is a specific form of negligence occurring in the execution of a physician's professional or fiduciary duties. Medical malpractice can be defined as medical care that falls below the standard of care expected of a reasonably prudent physician under similar circumstances resulting in foreseeable harm to the patient. It should be noted that in all negligence suits, the plaintiff bears the burden of proof in establishing the requisite four elements under a "more probably than not" standard. In other words, the plaintiff must establish that there was a greater than fifty percent probability that the defendant's breach of duty caused the harm. Note also that in addition to federal law, each state has its own body of statutory, regulatory, and case law. Thus, while this chapter presents general legal and risk management principles, physicians should always familiarize themselves with the laws and precedents in their own state prior to implementing policies and procedures related to travel medicine.

LIABILITY CONCERNS IN TRAVEL MEDICINE

With these basic principles of negligence outlined, the remainder of this chapter will examine how these legal doctrines apply in the unique circumstances of travel medicine. Not surprisingly, the increased participation of the general population in adventure travel has led to higher—and in many cases, unrealistic—expectations on the part of the public. Some unseasoned travelers to remote destinations anticipate the same level of medical resources (including medical personnel, equipment, medications, and evacuation capabilities) to which they have access in their own large urban tertiary care medical centers. It is vital, therefore, for tour operators and trip physicians to understand the duty and standard of care to which they must adhere and to educate trip participants about the risks of travel.

DUTY TO WARN AND EDUCATE TRIP PARTICIPANTS

R.P., a middle-aged male, booked a tour to Bolivia with a travel agent. In the trip brochure, the tour operator represented itself as an experienced and reputable company and stated that it researched all locations to which it arranged tours and "would care for participants from 'portal to portal.'"[2] In addition, the travel agent inquired of both the tour operator and local health agencies regarding health requirements and necessary precautions. During the trip, R.P. developed high altitude cerebral edema after flying from Chile (at sea level) to La Paz, Bolivia (elevation 13,000 feet) in under one hour. He subsequently sued the travel agent and tour organizer for failure to warn him of the health risks associated with this travel.

In general, there is no duty to warn of dangers that are as obvious to the participant as to the organizer. Obvious dangers might include the possibility of seasickness or airsickness, substandard sanitation, and environmental conditions. Moreover, travel agents and tour operators have no duty to investigate potential vacation sites, including dangerous conditions and terrain or lower standards of medical care in foreign countries. However, they do have a duty to warn of known unreasonable risks or dangers, such as political turmoil and criminal attacks, that are *foreseeable* or likely to occur. Typically, though, to incur this duty to warn, the travel agent or tour operator must have actual or constructive notice of the hazardous condition arising from their knowledge of special circumstances, for example, prior occurrences. In addition, travel agents and tour operators may contractually expand their duty to warn through representations made in brochures or other advertisements. In the case mentioned above, for example, the court recognized that tour organizers are not insurers of the safety of tourists with whom they contract and need not warn of obvious hazards. Nonetheless, in this case, the travel organizer contractually expanded its obligation through its representations and brochures, and created a reasonable expectation on the part of the tourist that it would research the risks of high altitude travel and warn him of accompanying dangers.

Even in the absence of liability, trip organizers and medical practitioners have incentive to prevent travel-associated injury or illness. They suffer harm as well from both a financial and ethical standpoint when a tourist experiences physical or financial loss, fellow travelers are inconvenienced, or the reputation of the company or medical practice is potentially damaged. Sound risk management principles dictate that travel companies provide as much useful information as is feasible to prevent these adverse consequences. Companies lacking the wherewithal to research health hazards may benefit from the assistance of a medical adviser. Depending on the nature of the trip, some or all of the following information may be useful to participants:

1. Environmental conditions: climate, altitude, terrain
2. Activity level: type, intensity, duration, and frequency of activity or exertion required on trip
3. Specific health hazards: tropical diseases, marine envenomation, frostbite, heat injuries
4. General health information: safety of local food and water, local medical resources
5. Known risks: political unrest, high crime areas
6. Recommended immunizations

MEDICAL CLEARANCE OF TRIP PARTICIPANTS

Tour operators have *no* duty to medically screen trip participants. Travelers have a responsibility to exercise due caution for their own safety. Nonetheless, do tour operators have the right or an incentive to screen participants? Medical clearance of travelers may serve several beneficial purposes. It can function to educate participants about potential health hazards, thereby reducing their risk of harm. Medical screening affords the participant's private physician the opportunity to better manage the patient's care. It may also enable a tour operator to arrange accommodations in advance for participants with special needs. Moreover, medical clearance may also reduce the tour operator's liability, costs, and inconvenience.

On the other hand, medical screening also has its disadvantages. Some authorities believe that medical screening is wasteful because a high risk patient with a strong desire to go on a trip may nevertheless ignore the dangers and conceal any significant past medical history (or shop around for a doctor willing to grant the medical clearance). In addition, with the enactment of the Americans with Disabilities Act (ADA) of 1990, many tour operators fear discrimination suits for medically screening out disabled persons. With a proper understanding of the legal issues underlying medical clearance and the ADA, tour operators and physicians can safeguard the interests of all parties involved.

Title III of the ADA prohibits all places of public accommodation and services operated by private entities from discriminating against the disabled. Further, a public accommodation may not apply eligibility criteria that screen out an individual or any class of individuals with disabilities "unless such criteria can be shown to be necessary for the provision of the goods, services, facilities, advantages, or accommodations."[3] For example, "a cruise line could not apply eligibility criteria to potential passengers in a manner that would screen out individuals with disabilities unless the criteria are 'necessary'. . . .[4]

A public accommodation is not required to permit an individual to participate in services when the individual poses a direct threat to the *health or safety of others*. This determination that the participant poses a significant risk must be an individualized assessment using reasonable judgment based on current medical knowledge or the best available objective evidence. Although the "direct threat exception" to the ADA only permits exclusion of participants when they are a threat to others, the "safety exception" may provide grounds for excluding individuals when they pose a threat to themselves. The "safety exception" holds that a public accommodation may impose legitimate safety requirements that are *necessary for safe operations.* As an example, the regulations cite as a valid screening criterion the requirement for all participants in a recreational rafting expedition to meet a necessary level of swimming proficiency.

For screening criteria to be valid, however, they must be uniformly applied to all prospective participants, not merely to those with disabilities. Moreover, they must be based on actual risks—not on mere speculation, stereotyping, or generalizations about a person or class of persons with a particular disability. A tour organizer could not, for example, categorically exclude all persons with a history of angina from a high altitude trip, but rather must afford individuals with documented, well-controlled angina an opportunity to establish their fitness and eligibility for the trip.

Even when screening criteria are valid and the prospective participant cannot meet those requirements, a public accommodation must make reasonable modifications in policies and practices, or accommodate the disabled individual unless such modifications would fundamentally alter the nature of the goods, services, or facilities offered. For example, a cruise line could be required as a reasonable modification to provide a stateroom on the same level as the restaurant to an individual who relies on a wheelchair for mobility. However, a mountain trek would not be required to transform to a bus tour to accommodate this same individual.

In order to minimize the potential for discrimination claims, tour operators should provide physicians granting medical clearance as much information as possible regarding the physical demands of the trip. Tour organizers must provide detailed information concerning environmental conditions, specific health hazards, health and living conditions in the destination site, and availability of local medical resources. Companies should be as specific as possible in describing environmental conditions (for example, altitude in feet, temperature in degrees). Trip organizers must also delineate the type, intensity, duration, and frequency of activity; for example, bus tour, mild walking (1 to 2 miles [1.6 to 3 kilometers] per day), vigorous hiking (specify distance and terrain), backpacking (specify weight of gear), trekking to remote areas (for example, twenty-four hours from definitive medical care), climbing, swimming, canoeing, etc.

The health care professional in turn must tailor the medical history and examination to the physical demands of the trip. The physician should become familiar with the patient's past medical history, including any medications that could interact with the environment to which the patient is traveling. The medical practitioner should also advise the patient to bring along, if applicable, extra medications or medical equipment for potential complications or exacerbations (including extra eyeglasses, hearing aid batteries, anaphylaxis kit, etc.) Additionally, the physician should inform the patient of applicable first-aid procedures. The physician may also need to inform the trip organizer of special needs or accommodations.

Because patients and their physicians may be hesitant to disclose confidential medical information to a travel company, medical clearance forms should emphasize functional abilities and limitations rather than diagnoses. If medical clearance forms request sufficiently detailed information about the prospective participant's medical fitness to meet the physical demands of the trip, travel companies frequently do not need to know about specific medical diagnoses. Companies that do request confidential medical information should only disclose this information to employees with a need to know and should ensure that the company medical adviser or trip physician safeguards this information in a locked file. The company may also want to encourage high risk patients to share medical information with trip leaders or to bring along key medical records. Even though a company-employed medical adviser or private family physician makes determinations about medical fitness and medical clearance, the travel company bears the legal responsibility for excluding disabled participants or for failing to accommodate their needs.

PROFESSIONAL LIABILITY AND MEDICAL MALPRACTICE

In addition to a lack of proper health warnings, two other common claims by injured trip participants include failure to provide adequate medical services and facilities and the negligent delivery of medical care. Historically, tour operators and cruise ships have had no obligation to insure the health or safety of participants or to provide health care—particularly physicians' services—on trips. Trip organizers should, nonetheless, ascertain the appropriate standard of care for their particular circumstances by determining the medical resources that other companies have provided on similar expeditions to similar destinations. Companies generally have the duty to staff trips to remote locations with personnel who have "significant training to provide adequate first aid and medical care until evaluation can be arranged."[5] Typically, these staff members are EMT-level providers or lay people with basic first aid training. Trips to locales with readily available medical care may have a lesser obligation to furnish staff trained in first aid. In the event of an adverse medical outcome, travel company employees would be judged by a "reasonably prudent person" standard, that is, they would have the duty to use reasonable care to furnish such aid and assistance as an ordinarily prudent person or trip leader would under similar circumstances.

Several professional medical organizations, such as the American College of Emergency Physicians and the Wilderness Medical Society, are seeking to define and establish standards of care for provision of medical services on cruise ships and expeditions. In the meantime, many companies voluntarily staff and advertise physicians on their trips for the comfort and convenience of their passengers or to provide a competitive marketing advantage. Travel companies that advertise the presence of trip physicians and medical facilities in brochures, contracts, and other correspondence to participants or prospective participants contractually expand their obligation by creating an implied or express contract for the availability of certain medical services. At a minimum, it is expected that trip physicians will have the resources and capability to evaluate, manage emergencies, and, when necessary, arrange for more definitive care for the types of injuries and illnesses that might be reasonably anticipated on these types of trips.[6]

Who, if anyone, is liable when the physician commits medical malpractice? A typical custom in the adventure travel industry is to offer doctors generous discounts on trips in exchange for medical support of fellow passengers. Many of these physicians are under the mistaken impression that they are covered by Good Samaritan laws in the event of a malpractice claim. The discounted fee, however, is the equivalent of compensation, and these physicians along with those on straight salaries would in all likelihood be considered independent contractors with a pre-existing duty to render medical care to fellow participants.

This potential exposure to malpractice claims has two important risk management implications for expedition physicians. First, physicians must familiarize themselves with the medical issues that they are likely to encounter on their trips and must possess the knowledge and skills to diagnose and treat relevant medical disorders. A doctor employed on a cruise to known endemic areas, for example, must be familiar with the diagnosis and treatment of tropical diseases. A physician with a mountain trekking group, on the other hand, should be able to recognize the signs and symptoms of high altitude sickness and be proficient in the management of this condition. In determining the standard of care, a jury would expect the physician to "anticipate usual and customary medical problems" and to apply "physical examination . . . diagnostic skills . . . and first aid measures"[7] as a reasonably prudent physician would do under similar circumstances, taking into account the remote location, the extremes of environment, and the limited capability to transport medical equipment on the trip.

Second, physicians should not assume that their medical malpractice insurance policies will cover them for claims arising out of medical services rendered on trips. Many insurance policies carry limitations on coverage for care delivered outside the scope of a doctor's normal practice or beyond a certain geographic area. In these cases, trip physicians should seek extended coverage through their own insurance policies or through the tour organizer.

The negligence of a physician generally will not be imputed under a theory of *respondeat superior* (master-servant relationship) to the tour organizer or carrier. Many courts have noted that the relationship between a passenger and a doctor is not a traditional activity over which a cruise ship or tour organizer has control. Moreover, a shipping or travel company is not in the business of providing medical services to passengers and does not possess the expertise requisite to supervise a physician brought along for the convenience of the passengers. Nonetheless, once the carrier or tour organizer goes about hiring a physician, it owes a duty to participants to exercise reasonable care in the selection of a competent and qualified doctor. To the extent that the company fails to discharge this duty, it may be subject to a cause of action for the negligent hiring of an incompetent doctor. Therefore, cruise lines and tour operators should ensure that trip physicians are proficient in general medical care, emergency treatment, and medical management of diseases endemic to the destination site.

Furthermore, travel companies and cruise ships should brief trip physicians on available resources, host country medical facilities, and evacuation procedures. Finally, companies should conduct formal credentialing of prospective trip physicians, to include verification of medical school graduation, board certification, state licensure, and history of disciplinary actions.

MEDICAL RECORDKEEPING ON CRUISES AND EXPEDITIONS

Good recordkeeping is of paramount importance in the practice of expedition medicine. The medical record is both a health care document and a legal document. Although storage space and portability of medical records on trips to remote locations are often limited, trip physicians should, nonetheless, strive to be as thorough as possible in documenting medical care. The medical record functions as a complete, written, and chronological record of a patient's medical history, condition, and treatment. In medical malpractice claims, which are frequently litigated years after the alleged occurrence, these records may be the only written source for reconstructing the sequence of events and subsequent treatment. Moreover, memories fade and witnesses become less available over time. Therefore, courts tend to give tremendous weight to the written record, and will often assume that documented events occurred and that undocumented events did not occur, particularly when the plaintiff's and defendant's oral testimonies conflict.

Although the length and content of entries will vary with the specific circumstances, notes should at a minimum include the patient's chief complaint, the results of the physical examination (including negative findings), an assessment, and a treatment plan. The key point to remember in the creation of medical records is that they may be used to prove or disprove that the medical practitioner adhered to the appropriate standard of care. Therefore, physicians should record sufficient details to reflect their thought processes and to justify their care under the circumstances. Moreover, physicians should document events chronologically and as soon as feasible after the delivery of medical care. Once notes have been entered into the chart or record, the medical practitioner should never alter or write over the original notes. Nor should pages be removed or inserted. If corrections are necessary, the physician should place a single line through the error, enter the correction, and initial and date the correction. Addenda should be placed after the last entry in the chart. Notes, of course, should always be legible and signed and dated by the health care provider making the entry. Upon completion of the trip, the company should treat these medical records as confidential information and should place them in locked medical files, granting access only to designated personnel (company medical advisers or others with a need to know). Some states have explicit laws or regulations that dictate the minimum period for retention of medical records. In the absence of such laws, travel companies and cruise lines should store medical records for the period of time corresponding to the statute of limitations for tort claims in their states—usually a couple of years.

CONCLUSION

The services of physicians on cruises and expeditions are invaluable to the safety and welfare of participants. Nonetheless, the expanded participation of higher risk individuals on trips to more remote regions of the world increases the liability exposure of health care providers. Legal issues—particularly causation—become more complex when medicine is practiced in these unconventional settings. By following the risk management principles outlined in this chapter, physicians can continue to provide effective care while minimizing their own liability.

NOTES

1. Flamm, M.B. "Health Care Provider as a Defendant." In *ACLM: Legal Medicine,* 3rd ed., St. Louis, Mosby-Yearbook Co., 1995, p. 119.
2. *Philippe v. Lloyd's Aero Boliviano,* 589 So. 2d 536, 540.
3. 28 CFR 36.301.
4. 28 CFR 36, App. B.
5. Herr, R.D. "The Climb Physician: An Endangered Species?" *Journal of Wilderness Medicine* 1, 144–146 (1990).
6. Backer, H. *Wilderness Medicine Letter* (Newsletter of the Wilderness Medical Society), Vol. 6, No. 4, October 1989, p. 10.
7. Henry, G., and Stein, E.R. "Medical Liability and Wilderness Emergencies." In Auerbach, P., and Geehr, E.C., eds. *Management of Wilderness and Environmental Emergencies,* St. Louis: Mosby, 1989, p. 1045.

CHAPTER 13

Polar Travel through the Eyes of the Passengers

It was six men of Indostan
To learning much inclined,
Who went to see the Elephant
(Though all of them were blind),
That each by observation
Might satisfy his mind.

"The Blind Men and the Elephant"
—John Godfrey Saxe, 1816–1887

Persons going to the Arctic or Antarctic do so for different reasons. Many go for scientific interests, and many are seasoned travelers who come to broaden their experiences by going to the far-off lands of ice. Some go to follow the footsteps of explorers, others go for adventure. Although much can be learned by reading about polar history and absorbing the guidebooks on the areas, a very special perspective is gained by reading and contemplating the reports of seasoned travelers who have been there in the past several years. A synthesis of many observations often gives one a clearer picture. Here are a few perspectives from those who have "been there, done that."

HOW SAFE IS SAFE?

by Kathryn S. Andersen

My husband, Marvin, and I have traveled to the polar regions three times aboard Russian ships, twice as tourists seeking adventure and the last time when he served as ship's doctor. My doctorate is in organic chemistry with no involvement in medicine at all so these few words will deal with views of a layperson who enjoys a little excitement and dealing with the unexpected. My greatest concerns with safety in the past were prevention of accidents (explosions) in teaching labs and shepherding four children to adulthood.

The perception of safety and risks to life and limb are perhaps in the eye of the worrier. Actions that we view as safe and enjoyable for ourselves, we may definitely find unsafe and overly risk-laden for others. Children under the age of six, or maybe it is seven, are not allowed to hike the knife-edge trail on Maine's Mt. Katahdin. Someone has determined that it is not safe for them to do so. It has been my perception that nimble-footed children with experience in hiking and an ingrained sense of reasonableness are far better suited to climbing and sticking to the straight and narrow than some adults. They are closer to the ground and have not developed the same sense of fear that advancing years bring. A cautious and methodical adult upon looking straight down on either side of the knife-edge and seeing the narrowness of the trail ahead begins to wonder what will happen if a foot slips or is placed in the wrong spot. He or she can easily decide that the trail is so unsafe that only the foolhardy would go one step forward, and therefore the trail is not safe for anyone, children or adults. An adventuresome adult may be gripped with a few pangs of fear, but, after all, excitement and a challenge were the reasons for selecting the trail in the first place. If the surface were smooth and a guard rope or rail lined the narrowest parts, why bother to come at all?

A trip to the polar regions is not a hike on Mt. Katahdin but some of the same logic may be applied. The literature sent out ahead of time clearly states that the projected itinerary may not be followed and that landings will be attempted according to weather conditions. To my way of thinking that means that the captain is in charge of the ship and will use his best skills to take the ship where it is safe to go. With all his past experience in Russian seas, I would surely not dispute his judgment and would have faith that we should be safe aboard ship—tossed about on rough seas perhaps, or beset in the ice for a while as occurred on the attempted circumnavigation of Greenland—but safe if we behaved in a reasonable manner. Having heard horror stories of broken limbs on high seas, Marvin when he served as ship's doctor warned the passengers of an upcoming rough time on the Drake Passage and instructed them to fasten themselves into their beds and crawl to the bathroom if they had to get up during the night. He also told them to hold on while walking about. The staff warned them about icy decks and rough seas. No broken bones resulted. The passengers in most cases were seasoned travelers who were well aware of the fact that their enjoyment of the trip depended upon their physical fitness. I was never afraid of shipboard accidents among the passengers on any of the three trips I took.

Other possible areas of concern were Zodiac trips, helicopter trips, and dangers on shore, such as fog or whiteout, thin ice or crevasses, and, in the Arctic, polar bears. Zodiac trips are always optional. Thus, those who feel they are unable to cope with rough water, wet landings, or difficult disembarkation from the ship can stay aboard and be safe. As we approached Elephant Island on the last trip, wind willies (spindrift) ruffled the surface of the seas with myriad small whitecaps. I was amazed to see active preparation to get the Zodiacs into the water for a reconnaissance. I thought to myself that I would definitely sit this one out. The Zodiacs were cranked back to the deck before they ever hit the surface of the water thereby restoring my faith in the staff or staff-captain combination who make Zodiac decisions.

We did see Zodiac embarkations occur when the ocean swells were so great that the loading platform rose several yards above the top of the Zodiac before plunging well beneath the surface so that those unlucky passengers who did not jump aboard the Zodiac at the right time were soaked to the armpits. This was not an ideal situation, but I would not consider it "unsafe." Some of the Zodiac rides where we bump-bump-bumped into the wind seemed interminable but not unsafe for those of us huddled in the bottom of the boat. I often wished that they would go slower but then the misery would have been prolonged. My greatest concern was keeping the camcorder and camera equipment dry during the trips and when exiting and entering the Zodiac because both arms were given over to strong staff or crew members for assistance. Sometimes, I found these Zodiac transitions worked best when the passenger was totally relaxed while being literally tossed into or out of the Zodiac by both arms.

Before the Greenland trip, I had never been in a helicopter and was a bit put off by what looked like a flimsy craft at best. Then I thought of all the missions these Russian pilots must have flown and decided to put myself in their hands, much like the flights into and out of the Zodiac. Once the decision of faith had been made, I found the trips a delight and discovered a whole new way to enjoy the geology of the region and get a really good look at the patterns of pressure ridges, the trails of glaciers (in the Arctic), and the scope of penguin colonies. Not so much fun were landings ashore in the fog, but I still had faith. Even though the helicopter pilots seemed to have no trouble navigating in the fog (only one flew under such conditions), Zodiac drivers really did depend on line-of-sight navigation. One day in the South Sandwich Islands, a dense fog rolled in shortly after the last Zodiac left the ship. Not until I returned to the ship did I find out that Marvin was aboard and that it was lost! For two hours it prowled the shores of the wrong island (correctly identified by those on the Russian ship from landmarks described) until staff in another Zodiac with a GPS aboard led them back to the ship.

Fog and whiteout conditions on shore were handled without incident. Colorful pennants were put up at regular intervals to lead passengers from the ship to the penguins in the Antarctic. Staff may have been temporarily lost in the whiteout while seeking a rookery and placing stakes but were always found and brought back with the GPS. I would hope that future expeditions might equip all staff members with one of these devices so that they would know their positions and that of the boat or Zodiac landing at all times. In the Arctic, the polar bear patrol was always active and we were made well aware of the danger in encountering one. Thin ice and crevasses were marked in areas where we were permitted to walk ashore. One day in the Weddell Sea when we had not left the ship for well over a week, an operation was set up to take groups of passengers up for helicopter rides and drop them on ice floes way ahead of the ship for future pick-up. As the weather deteriorated, a wise decision was made to discontinue this operation for safety reasons long before everyone had "had a turn."

For his stint as ship's doctor, Marvin made every attempt to be prepared. Besides attending the Polar Medicine Conference in Cambridge, England, he consulted with three doctors in the family, a plastic surgeon, a urologist, and an emergency medicine doctor. He took along books and supplies these professionals suggested. Furthermore, he had a plan for consulting with physicians back home by phone if the need arose. I had confidence in his preparation and felt that he could handle whatever might arise, another example of faith that puts the mind at rest. A neurosurgeon whose wife slipped and injured her elbow chose to treat her himself and only needed Marvin to provide him with supplies for making a cast. By far, the largest single reason for patients to seek Marvin's care resulted from an overwhelming desire for perfect pictures and great concern for protecting their expensive equipment.

Overindulgence in photography was not discussed at the conference in England nor is it listed as a condition in any of the books Marvin took along, but that weakness led to most of the problems he saw on the trip to the Weddell Sea. After eleven days on the ship and whiteout conditions when we landed and saw our first emperor penguins, the passengers and staff could not believe their good fortunes when we arose on day twelve to see sun and lots of penguins. A senior staff member who has been active on many of these trips in the past was determined to get some magnificent penguin pictures and went without sunglasses. His resulting severe snow blindness laid him up in misery for several days. A chemistry professor who had to get the perfect picture could not do so with his gloves on and left them in his pocket for the day. His black and blistered hands were so painful and unattractive that he kept them covered for the rest of the trip except for viewings by the curious. He expected to return to the classroom in gloves so that his students would not know. An engineer tripped over a protruding piece of metal on the top deck while photographing and smashed his nose on the deck rather than risk injury to the camera. Probably nothing was broken, but he was bloody and bruised. He complained of pain for days. An elderly physician

Mother emperor penguin feeding chick at Riiser-Larsen rookery, Weddell Sea.

from the Isle of Jersey slipped on an oily patch on a lower deck while photographing and spent the rest of the trip in his cabin with a severe headache. He was fearful of a subdural hematoma which was confirmed when he reached home. Today he is fine and has no aftereffects.

It seems to me that the question of safety on these trips involves each individual's perception of personal safety. Standing in the teeming rain among fourteen million pairs of penguins, after a somewhat hairy Zodiac ride, an endocrinologist from Texas was heard to say, "I don't know how many damn fools there are in this world, but I think they must all be standing here on Zavadovski Island." Maybe those of us who take these trips are all damn fools but we personally love it and are willing to risk any twinges of concern about safety for the adventure and the unexpected.

Emperor penguin, "tobagganing."

MY FIRST, BUT IT WON'T BE MY LAST, TRIP TO THE ICE

by A.D. Van Galen

My wife and I traveled on an attempted circumnavigation about Greenland in 1993 without any concerns for health and safety. We had no significant history of illness in the past, and felt reassured by the presence of a close friend of many years who was the ship's surgeon. We gave very little thought to health or anything else. I felt that if a major medical emergency would occur, we would literally all be in the same boat!

I found the Russian crew to be very professional. My wife has some fears of cold water and had concerns about the Zodiacs. I found them to be in good condition and traveling in them went well.

Zavadowsky island, reported to have 13 million pairs of penguins!

My particular concern, however, was the helicopters. The pilots seemed well qualified, but the helicopters themselves appeared shabby, which did not inspire confidence. What really counts, however, is their mechanical condition, which I assumed to be fine. Why did we go? Because our friend, the ship's surgeon, was there. Did we enjoy it? I did so immensely! My wife had no regrets but her English was not adequate enough to follow all the lectures. We found the lectures a bit long and most of the passengers very old.

RISK IN HIGH LATITUDES

by E. Newbold Smith

My view, for whatever it's worth, about physical risks that might be encountered in polar regions is based on an amalgam of expeditions that I have taken over a quarter of a century, mostly in my own boat. Probably the most applicable excursion and the one that achieved the highest northern latitude for me was a trip on a Russian icebreaker, *Kapitan Khlebnikov,* which attempted to circumnavigate Greenland in 1993. We managed to get stuck in fast ice more than sixteen feet (five meters) thick about twenty miles (thirty-two kilometers) north of Cape Morris Jessup, the northernmost land on the earth.

Fortunately for all the passengers and crew, we had an experienced ship's surgeon aboard. Were it not for him, I am sure there would have been heightened anxiety, for we were marooned for four days and subjected to the enormous power of the floes of tons of multilayer ice that actually caused a seven-degree list to starboard. I had been many times in pack ice amongst icebergs, bergey bits, and growlers (in the Arctic and Antarctic), but never before marooned in a completely powerless position.

At the time, I was sixty-seven years old, but I worried for those much older men and women, who might have had to be lifted off a windswept, slippery deck by helicopter, taking off at an angle that was anything but optimal. I kept those thoughts to myself, and I must say that being able to see the coast had an ameliorating effect on all of us. In addition to the presence of a doctor with long experience in icy (and dicey) conditions, the sponsors of the expedition did a superb job of reassuring all hands and, most importantly, securing the help of another, more powerful, icebreaker, which came to our rescue from her location at the North Pole. Both the travel company and the ship's company did all in their power to amuse and disabuse the passengers, with barbecues on the ice and, in the case of the crew, soccer games on the surface of the Arctic Ocean.

The marooning was of unusual extremis and a self-inflicted accident to be sure. Most medical emergencies, I believe, come as a sudden surprise, like a broken leg, appendicitis, or a stroke or heart attack.

For my own part, whether I will be traveling on my own forty-four-foot (thirteen-kilometer) sailboat or something much larger, I try to consult physicians beforehand to be sure I have a proper supply of whatever I or my friends will need in the way of medical supplies. That usually includes narcotics and even surgical devices, about which I shudder at the thought of having to use, not to mention the shock of my shipmates if I were to pull out a syringe!

It should be noted that the Arctic is a much better place to have an accident or illness than is the Antarctic. Up north there are all sorts of Eskimo villages with dispensaries. Some of the settlements even have a doctor. Where none exist, at least in Canada the local Royal Canadian Mounted Police can call in help by air. In Greenland, Iceland, and Norway the infrastructure is possibly even better. In the Antarctic, well, you can talk to a penguin!

In 1994, on a sailing expedition to Hudson Bay, I contracted a cutaneous ulcer on my ankle. It was first treated at the Indian village of Chisasibi, near James Bay. Later it was treated and dressed by a paramedic at the small Inuit village of Akaluit on northern Hudson Bay. The darn thing lasted for several months, all because of original infection, probably from an insect bite.

It seems to me that the older one gets the more likely it is that a person may be attuned to his or her systemic vulnerabilities. Therefore, an ounce of prevention is always a good thing. Just knowing

Polar bear tracks, Franz Josef Land.

one's allergies can be helpful to a doctor from whom you seek medication. The same strategy, that is, caution, is even more pertinent to conditions where a bone might be broken. I am a former quadriplegic from a horse accident, so I have limitations. I take care not to slip or to attempt difficult ascents or descents. This didn't prevent me from climbing up the lighthouse on Cape Horn, so I can't complain. The point is: know your limitations.

In summation, those of us lucky enough to venture to antipodal extremities of the world should be well prepared, not just for harsher elements but for our own potential maladies. By avoiding excess one should not come a cropper. Do not cross the line between adventure and stunt. I do not, for example, applaud a solo round-the-world passage, nor someone who rows across the ocean. Both are stunts that may cost other people's lives in a rescue. By the same token, it would not be wise for passengers to venture some distance from a group on the ice sheet, where there could be crevasses. Likewise, in polar bear country up north or leopard seal territory down south it would not be wise to take chances of any sort; it will be courting disaster. A dollop of fear is a useful ingredient, and we should not fight it.

Finally, we should be thankful that there are doctors who risk malpractice litigation to make our lives safer in an increasingly litigious world.

WHOSE RISK AND WHOSE RESPONSIBILITY IS IT?

by an anonymous guest lecturer on an Antarctic tour staff

An eighty-year-old tourist collapsed on the bridge near Deception Island. The Russian doctor immediately came to the bridge and after a short examination, made a diagnosis of a "heart attack" and gave him an injection that I believe was Demerol. Several husky crewmen carried him down to the dispensary. There were two doctors (tourists) aboard who were called upon to assist. Comments by these doctors afterward were that the Russian doctor was not familiar with the defibrillator and that there was a dearth of medications that were needed to stabilize the patient.

We then proceeded to Frei Station on King George Island. We did not have the proper frequencies to contact them in advance to arrange an airborne medevac and it was not until we were within UHF range that we could speak with the station. The Chilean Air Force was very generous and capable with their help. They took the man into their dispensary and arranged a medevac to Punta Arenas. I understand that the gentleman is now back in the United States and is recuperating nicely.

I don't fault the Russian doctor too much but rather the system. The Russians have no money to properly equip their shipboard medical facilities. Perhaps it should be left up to the tourist companies to see that this is taken care of. On the other hand the patient was a man who did a lot of backwoods hiking and skiing—what would have happened if he had had a heart attack then? In other words, how much risk is the tourist willing to assume or, conversely, how sophisticated must the medical capability aboard ship be?

On the tourist cruises that I have been on in Antarctic seas we had no broken limbs, but that was sheer luck. We had tourists aboard who were lucky not to have broken a limb walking down the dock to the ship—with canes, crutches, or in wheelchairs. Some were so overweight that if they fell ashore we could not have lifted them into a Zodiac. I admire their pluck, but I do not believe that they have any business aboard these ships. If one of these passengers gets injured we are talking about a diversion of the vessel and loss of field time for every other passenger, not just an inconvenience to the one who is injured. I believe some medical standards should be set. The U.S. Antarctic Program has such standards and they refuse to take medically unfit people there no matter how important—including congressmen.

A WONDERFUL TRIP THAT DIDN'T END UP SO WELL

by Carmen Becker

As experienced travelers, my husband and I always have a medical checkup, immunizations, and whatever medicines are needed to travel. We always try to

The Bransfield *being freed from polar ice.*

have a trouble-free trip, and we were assured by our doctors that our health was excellent before we embarked on an icebreaker to the Weddell Sea in November 1993. It was our second cruise on the same ship, and we enjoyed meeting again some of the passengers and crew members we had known from the previous sailing. All went very well. As usual, the Drake Passage was pretty rough, but soon we got used to the rocking and the cracking of the ice as the trip was taking its course south. The vista was magnificent. Our main purpose for taking this trip was the landing that was planned at the Queen Maud Land sector of Antarctica. On the morning of December 9, just before landing, our dreams were shattered. My husband, Bob, did not feel very well and, after breakfast, went to our cabin to rest. When I joined him about fifteen minutes later, he acted strangely and he had a bewildered look on his face. He lay down on his bunk and soon after he was unable to speak or to get up. He did not remember what happened after that. I was really frightened and called for the ship's American surgeon, who immediately came up to see Bob, and immediately he knew what had taken place. Dr. John, as we called him, informed me at that time that Bob had had a CVA (cerebral vascular accident) and that his outlook was not very good. He suggested that we stay in our cabin as we could care for him better than at the ship's "hospital" and also this way I could care for him as I wanted to both night and day. It appeared that there was little that could be done, and time would tell.

Our ship was about 2,000 miles (3,218 kilometers) from all points of civilization—except remote polar bases. They, too, were far out of helicopter range, and we learned that the medical facilities at these bases were not equipped to diagnose and treat cerebral vascular accidents in older people. We knew of no other tourist ships in this area of the Southern Ocean where we might seek assistance. Fortunately, some knowledgeable expedition staff members arranged for a radiophone communication with the British Antarctic Survey in Cambridge, England. They obtained the radio frequency to reach the *Bransfield,* a British polar research and supply vessel that was somewhere in the area. Imagine our joy to find that the ship was only 90 miles away and our dismay when we were told it was beset in the ice!

Nonetheless our ship, the *Kapitan Khlebnikov,* headed through the ice towards the *Bransfield*, and Dr. John flew in a helicopter, landed on the ice by the British ship, went aboard a cargo net, and was lifted by a big crane up to the deck of the ship. The British ship's surgeon kindly gave him the supplies that were very critical for the care of my husband. We "paid" the *Bransfield* by breaking the ice about them and freeing them to continue on their voyage to Halley Bay near the British base.

The radiotelephone from the *Kapitan Khlebnikov* was kept busy working out evacuation plans for Bob. We found that a staged evacuation using our helicopter and then aircraft taking him to Adventure Network International's base at Patriot Hills about 670 miles (1,078 kilometers) from the South Pole, then evacuating him up the peninsula and finally across the Drake Passage to Punta Arenas in Chile could be arranged. The weather was so bad that we faced the possibility of being stranded for days in a tent at the advance base at Patriot Hills, or in makeshift accommodations at one of the polar bases. He would have had to travel without medical support, as our doctor was needed on the ship. The $100,000 cost for this transportation is understandable, and I was ready to pay this as it might save his life.

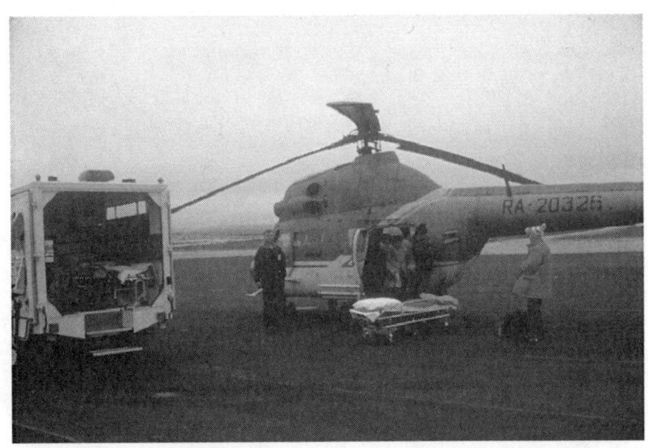

Transfer from Russian helicopter to British ambulance, Port Stanley, Falkland Islands.

The Port Stanley Hospital.

We discussed this carefully with our ship's surgeon, and he felt we should consider the unknown factors involved, the lack of supportive medical care, and that the air evacuation might only save a few days. He felt that on board the ship he had warm accommodations, good food, my nursing and his medical care, and that this was the best chance of getting him home safely. We agreed with his suggestion, and how very glad we are that we did so!

When we arrived at Port Stanley on the eastern side of the Falkland Islands, we loaded Bob and an unfortunate lady who had fractured her hip some few days earlier into an M-2 helicopter and flew to the British airfield located near the hospital. A Land Rover ambulance with well-dressed and efficient paramedics loaded us and in a matter of minutes we were at the thirty-nine-bed hospital which serves both the civilian and the military needs of the Falkland Islanders. Our doctor met with the British physician. X rays and blood studies were immediately done in that crisp and efficient but friendly British style. A few days later, we traveled by chartered aircraft to Punta Arenas where Bob was hospitalized again. With the help of a very kind lady who heads up Adventure Network International, Anne Kershaw, arrangements were made for us to fly to Santiago, and after several days of rest we flew to Miami and then on to New York. We had made it home at last! My husband had survived a dreadful experience, and I am very pleased that two and a half years later, after extensive therapy, Bob walks again, slowly but surely, and his speech is coming back. His right hand, however, is still weak. We celebrated our fifty-first wedding anniversary. Reflecting back on those grim days in the Weddell Sea, I never thought this happy day would arrive.

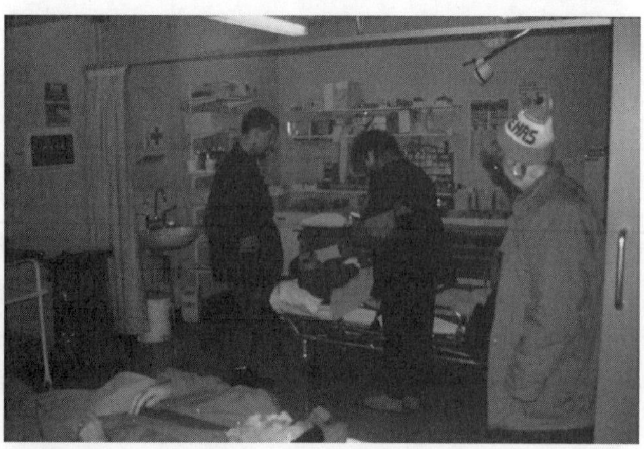

Emergency room, the Port Stanley Hospital.

We are both very grateful to the American doctor who visited my husband many times both night and day. With his good judgment and the few supplies he had, he saved my husband's life. The expedition staff and the Russian crew were all extremely helpful.

What are our travel plans? We intended to repeat the cruise to the Weddell Sea, but we felt that the Zodiac trip from the ship to the ice might be a little bit difficult. So now we're planning on some easier trips, like going to Arizona and Las Vegas. Our plans are a bit indefinite as yet, but certainly we plan on more traveling.

A PASSENGER'S PERSPECTIVE

by Ruth Ann Ger

It was my very great pleasure and privilege to visit Antarctica as the wife of the ship's physician aboard a Russian ship chartered by an American company for tourists to visit the last frontier. My background as a medical social worker, as well as eighteen years of medical office management, gave me some additional insight into the problems facing the ship's doctor. The physicians serving in these waters are often first or second timers, and don't have the experience in the polar environment that in an emergency situation is such a vital part of the safety factor.

In the small print of the company's release form a number of health and safety caveats can be found. With marvelous human selective memory, certain points are carefully noted and others are ignored by potential passengers. Do not for one moment think that the warning about bringing all medications with you is heeded by many people who have chronic but intermittent serious illnesses. A charming seventy-five-year-old man with chronic bronchitis and emphysema complicated by asthma brought no medication along. Burial at sea might be considered a joke until it becomes a looming possibility. Our gentleman patient was unaccompanied, but was fortunately befriended by some nurses who brought his deteriorating condition to the physician's attention within the first two days of the trip, enabling the physician to contact the man's doctor in California by ship's telephone. He was especially lucky that the particular antibiotic that he needed was available, because there are no pharmacies anywhere in Drake Passage. This information in the small print did not register with this gentleman quite as well as the point about the ship being "well supplied."

It may help to clarify these issues if the medical director or ship's physician sends a separate letter to each passenger, making it clear that it is their responsibility to notify the ship's doctor in advance of all and any health or fitness problems, and to bring all supplies along. Although the ship's physician was not advised of any potential problems, he found an elderly gentleman on board with multiple pathologies who could barely deal with the stairs within the ship. Somehow the young men who accompanied him managed to take him down to board the inflatable watercraft so that he could "share the experience"—despite reassuring the physician that he would remain on board.

We had an outbreak of a viral infection brought on board by a cheerful and "brave" (her mother's description) young lady who did not want to miss the trip. Unfortunately, in such close quarters, viruses have a ball, and at least half the ship came down with the same bug, leading to rumors of dirty cooking facilities. Our young Austrian chefs were distraught that such insinuations were being made, and appealed to the physician to inspect the kitchens. He did so, found them to be immaculate and reassured the dinner throng that it was a virus causing their discomfort and not negligence on the part of the staff. Some passengers were very ill, and the physician was kept very busy giving injections and encouragement.

Which brings us to another point. There was no dedicated medical facility available for the doctor to see patients. Our tiny cabin was crammed with medical supplies, forcing us to live out of our suitcases and making it extremely difficult to comfortably examine patients. Since passengers are on holiday they cannot be expected to wait in their cabins with someone who is ill, and the physician needed an escort while he examined the many dehydrating, heaving souls who awaited his ministrations. We had a singularly unhelpful manager, who was arrogant and impatient—until his pathetic moan paged the physician to attend to his own illness. He had not wanted to make the necessary accommodations for those passengers who were confined to their cabins. We had to personally check again and again to ensure that they received fluids and sustenance.

Because the physician comes on board together with the passengers there is no time to go through the bags of supplies before patients start presenting themselves. We found our cupboards crammed with bags that were unmarked and uninventoried. There was no first-aid kit set up for landings, which means each doctor reinvents the wheel when making his selections and looking for a container. A physician's presence alone is not enough, as reassuring as that might be, and appropriate equipment should be easily at hand in any emergency. Supplies should be stowed in locked cabinets, so that they can be found at a moment's notice, and inventories should be available and kept updated, with some way of knowing at what point more supplies should be ordered.

After I fell on our last landing of the trip, we made our way back to the boat to the hospital. Although designated "ship's hospital," it is the domain of the Russian physician and crew. The Joint Commission for Accreditation of Hospitals would certainly not give its seal of approval. From the mop, bucket, and IVs stored in the toilet, to the absence of safety rails to assist during one-armed, morphine-compromised trips to the bathroom during the tumultuous seas of Drake Passage, there was nothing reassuring about the hospital facility. We had met the Russian doctor earlier, but together he and my husband were unable to relocate a severe fracture of the upper arm where it fits into the shoulder joint. Unfortunately, although my husband had obtained a Russian translation of the installation procedure for the X-ray equipment that was installed earlier during our trip with much trouble by the ship's engineers, and although everything was probably functional, we could not get a picture because somehow the cassettes and films had all disappeared. These supplies are under the control of the Russian crew and not the passengers' doctor. This made it impossible to make an accurate diagnosis, although as it turned out, surgery was required and I had to wait until we reached home.

My husband decided to leave me in the hospital, thinking it would be easier to take care of me there. Now fortunately I am his wife, because there was no one else to do bathroom and other nursing duty. The physician doesn't just get to check, treat, and leave. He is IT. The Russian doctor was wonderful to me, but he spoke no practical English and his medical practices were different from our accustomed standards. Who knows: they may have been superior under the circumstances, but not appropriate for tourists with Western expectations. Passengers who visited were surprised that there was no nurse in attendance.

Landing at Ushuaia, we found the company agent to be extremely helpful, but the clinic woefully inadequate. They were temporarily without X-ray capability, but the staff was kind and considerate, although language was a problem. We were finally introduced to the traumatologist who insisted on immobilizing me in a body cast, for which I am, in retrospect, very grateful, because the flights home were very difficult. Do not expect any help from the airlines. Fortunately my physician husband was going all the way home with me, because the morphine made the travel possible. If it had been someone going to Italy, Chicago, or California, he or she would not have been able to travel unescorted. Altogether it took six days to get home.

It is now nine months since my injury. I know that nothing could be done without a proper X ray, operating room, and anesthesiologist. I still have a nonunion of the neck of humerus, and the head of humerus is compromised. The nerves are showing some signs of regeneration, but I have no strength yet and still have pain and limitation of movement. We anticipate a shoulder replacement procedure in the near future. I don't want to think about the professional liability if it had been another passenger. You see, the small print that everyone remembered stated very clearly that a fully supplied medical service was available on board. And as we all know, not only is this not so, but it is impossible.

Despite all this, would I go again? In a minute! But I'd be much more demanding of safety and preparedness standards.

CHAPTER 14

What Should a Passenger Expect?

If you have an important point to make, don't try to be subtle or clever. Use a pile driver. Hit the point once. Then come back and hit it again. Then hit it a third time—a tremendous whack.

—Winston Churchill

Planning a trip to the Arctic or Antarctic has many facets. The first question is obviously why does one wish to go? A historical interest may figure in the decision or a particular interest in the flora or fauna. Contrary to what some expect, there are hundreds of different wildflowers in the region about the Arctic Circle while only several specimens survive in unusual areas of the Antarctic. In the north, walrus and polar bear are abundant in some areas, the musk ox can still be found in a few areas, and you may get fleeting glimpses of the Arctic hare or fox. If you go to the right stop, you also may find large herds of reindeer. The seal population of the north is not frequently seen as they are rather skittish compared to the great numbers of seals one sees in the Antarctic. There are no indigenous land animals on the southern continent, but it takes no luck at all to see hundreds of thousands or even millions upon millions of penguins in Antarctica. For those who want to see the "big ice," Antarctica is the best destination. Interest in geography, seeing the areas where famous explorers have been, are also reasons people choose to go.

CHOICES ABOUT POLAR TRAVEL

It is important to carefully read the tour companies' brochures before choosing your trip. If you do not know individuals who have been there before, ask the tour company. Often they can provide someone in your locale who will speak to you and describe their experience and tell you why they enjoyed the trip. Read the guidebooks offered and consult the reading list in this book to get into the vast amount of knowledge that is available on this most exciting part of the world.

Some of the polar trips are relatively short: one can leave home in North America, visit either the high Arctic or the Antarctic Peninsula and be home within a two-week period. Going to either of these two destinations affords one the greatest economy in a polar trip, and frequently there is little change in

Weddell Seal, Ross Island.

Elephant seal, Potter Cove, King George Island.

Polar bear on ice floe in the Northern Sea Route.

the longitude with these two destinations, hence less jet lag.

Make your decision early. You may get a much better choice of cabins that way. The less expensive cabins on most cruises are on the lower decks. Paradoxically, a cabin on a lower deck, located amidships, gives one far less motion when the ship begins to pitch and roll in the polar seas. This is particularly valuable in the round-bottom icebreakers, which have such tremendous motion in the Southern Ocean. If you have an infirmity, it may be wise to ask for a cabin closer to the dining room. Some ships have elevators, but in heavy seas they may not function.

Are you fit for the trip? Should there be the slightest question, it is advisable to check with your physician and explain to him or her the rigors of the voyage. If you have any chronic health problems of concern, either you or your physician should discuss this condition with the medical director of the tour company. It is hard to conceive of anyone who can walk a mile not being fit for a polar trip. Walking a mile (1.6 kilometers) a day for some weeks before the trip should put you in good shape for the voyage.

Careful attention should be paid to any chronic health problem that could be a handicap. Smokers should realize that they are asked not to smoke except in several selected areas aboard ship, they cannot smoke on helicopters or Zodiacs, and not on the Antarctic continent. Those known to abuse alcohol and drugs do not belong on these voyages because of the obvious dangers they present to themselves and their shipmates. It is difficult to define "severe obesity," but individuals too large to go up and down multiple flights of stairs on shipboard or to use the ladder to the Zodiac may find themselves shipbound. It is inappropriate to be lifting obese passengers into a large box and lowering them by derrick onto the ice as was done from one ship several years ago. Individuals with diabetes that is well controlled certainly are candidates for the trip. Many passengers have cardiovascular disease and make the trip without difficulty. On one trip several years ago, I identified almost ten percent of the passenger list who had had coronary bypass surgery! None of them had any problems. It is wise, however, to check carefully with your physician, fill out the health forms properly, and, if necessary, discuss your condition with the tour medical director and bring a copy of your last electrocardiogram on the trip with you. Then, should there be any problems, one can be done and compared to the data that you have brought.

Some individuals require canes, crutches, or wheelchairs. The staff cannot be counted upon to give special care to individuals with these problems. There may be difficulty going up and down steps and ladders, walking on ice or in snow and over rocks. The height of the transom from the hallway to one's cabin and into the bathroom may present obstacles.

Penguin rookery on Paulet Island Iceberg, off the Antarctic Peninsula.

Walrus at sea.

These are not reasons not to go on the ship, but your difficulties should be discussed carefully with the tour company to see if arrangements that are satisfactory to you can be made. All in all, there are very few individuals who cannot safely make this trip. Lastly, if you have any special dietary need, this requirement should be discussed long before boarding ship.

The "wellness concept" has been raised at various times. It is obviously unfair to refuse passage to individuals who have disabilities. On the other hand, the person with a disability has an obligation to honestly portray his or her health situation to the tour line to work out the best possible approach to the problem. Remember, very few will find they are unable to make the voyage.

Le Marie Channel, Antarctica.

PREPARATION FOR POLAR TRAVEL

Your tour company will certainly publish advice on suggested clothing. In most all cases, informality is the rule, and neckties are not needed for men although they may wish to bring a sportcoat to wear for special occasions. Women are more often comfortable in slacks, but may wish to bring a cocktail-type dress for a special occasion. The important thing to realize is that protective clothing minimizes heat transfer to the environment. Most types of suggested clothing take advantage of the insulating qualities of trapped air to limit heat loss. The thicker the layer of trapped air, the greater the insulation. In basic English, this means "layering." You will be a lot more comfortable having the ability to wear no sweater, or one or two sweaters under your parka to achieve the "layering."

On a sunny windless day in the austral summer of the Antarctic, or the summer of the Arctic, one is frequently out on deck in a light sweater only. Usually, it is a few degrees warmer in the Arctic than in the Antarctic. As soon as the sun disappears or the wind picks up, the need for heavier clothing is rapidly apparent. A balaclava or warm hat is mandatory. Frequently the tour company will supply passengers with parkas containing a synthetic material for insulation which is extremely effective. Orange and red colors are preferred so that people can be seen on shore. Heavy pants of the Gor-Tex type can keep one dry on a Zodiac. Rubber or other suitable waterproof boots up to the knees that are large enough to let you wear two pairs of socks complete the outer garb. Many passengers bring special underwear, which is probably a wise idea, but a number do without it. Several pairs of gloves are a must, and often it takes an inner knit pair and an outer heavier glove to keep one's hands warm. Gloves with fingers are preferred over mittens for the use of cameras.

Le Marie Channel, Antarctica.

Fancy camera bags are really not needed. What is needed is a waterproof plastic bag to carry cameras, binoculars, etc. The photographic equipment ranges

Iceberg, Antarctica.

Zodiac landing on black sand of Deception Island, off Antarctic Peninsula.

from the professionals with their bags of lenses and extra film to the rank amateurs with their disposable cameras with wide-angle lens, etc. All equipment should be put in plastic bags; a backpack will keep things together and will serve to hold an extra sweater and other necessities.

Passengers should wear nonskid type of shoes (boat shoes) to minimize dangers when walking on the ship's deck.

Ski poles have proved invaluable for walking on ice or in deep snow. For easy transport to the ship, as well as on Zodiacs and helicopters, the collapsible type is recommended.

Sunglasses are a must! The eyes are extremely sensitive to overexposure to ultraviolet radiation. In the high latitudes, a sunburnlike reaction of the cornea and conjunctivae is not uncommon from even mildly excessive amounts of ultraviolet radiation. This snow blindness was a real problem for earlier explorers. Symptoms may not arise for up to twelve hours after excessive exposure; in addition to the redness, there may be increased tearing and a gritty sensation in the eye. Pain may be a severe manifestation and the doctor will direct his or her effort toward controlling this pain. The problem should be cleared up in several days.

The Kapitan Khlebnikov *breaking ice off the French station, Dumont d'Urville, Antarctica.*

Solar radiation can also be very harmful to the skin. Exposure to excessive amounts greatly increases the rate at which skin ages. Many people have seen what is known as "photo aging," the wrinkled, leathery skin seen prematurely in persons habitually exposed to the sun. Exposure to excessive solar radiation can also markedly increase the chance of skin cancer.

In 1928, the world's first commercial use of a sunscreen, an emulsion of benzyl salicylate and benzyl cinnamate, was reported in the United States. Several years later a 10 percent solution of phenylsalicylate (Solol) appeared in Australia. By 1935, lotions of quinine oleate and quinine bisulfate were available in the United States and in 1943, para-aminobenzoic acid was patented. Following the U.S. military use of red petrolatum, a variety of chemicals were introduced and various skin screen agents have come to the market. Any person who has one of the many photosensitivity dermatoses should have special counseling about requirements to protect their skin. For the average individual, agents with a skin protectant factor of at least 15 should be used, and the possibility of allergy to any of these agents must be considered. To be safe, it is wise to use one of these agents under conditions of strong sunlight to be sure that you are comfortable, and that you experience no problems before you go off to the polar regions.

What immunizations are required for going to the polar regions? This simple question has many implications. Considering the fact that you will have very little contact with the indigenous population above the Arctic Circle, and that the only inhabitants below the Antarctic Circle will be fellow tourists and healthy young men and women at polar stations who will have been properly immunized, this is not a significant problem.

Tetanus and diphtheria vaccine is used for primary immunization, and booster doses should be given at ten-year intervals throughout one's life. Although tetanus is the main concern on a worldwide basis, the diphtheria component can be very important where this disease has gained in numbers in the population in parts of the former Soviet Union. In individual cases, there may be a need to supplement coverage on poliomyelitis, and it is recommended that each person speak with his or her own physician regarding pneumococcal and influenza vaccines.

These immunizations are recommended for older individuals and people with special health risks. The rise of contracting hepatitis A virus is higher for passengers from countries where the disease is not endemic who travel to destinations where the disease is highly endemic. Preventive measures, together with advice on hygiene and dietary precautions, include passive or active immunization. Prophylaxis with immunoglobulin provides relatively cheap but short-term protection, while the vaccine (Havrix 720) offers longer-term protection at greater cost. Furthermore, a screening test with high predictive value is available if one wants to assess the presence of natural immunity before undertaking preventive measures.

One critical point is very simple. Passengers must not only consider their arrival at the polar destination, but what countries they will be traveling through. They must also decide whether they will spend enough time there to make the hazards worthy of additional immunization.

Probably the best resource for accurate and up-to-date information comes from the Centers for Disease Control in Atlanta, Georgia. Their Travelers' Health Hotline fax information number (404-332-4565) and Web site (http://www.cdc.gov) are excellent sources of information. Information on all areas that one will be traveling through with detailed recommendations can be simply obtained. This information should be obtained first, and then the problem discussed with the passenger's physician as it is difficult to expect him or her to be fully informed about day-to-day changes that may occur in recommended immunizations for travel around the world. Remember, primary immunization or boosters may require some weeks so don't wait until the last minute.

All travelers are advised to prepare a travel medical kit appropriate to their itinerary.

First, the kit should contain adequate supplies of all prescription medications that one normally takes as well as additional prescriptions obtained relevant to the trip. If you are known to get seasick, this medication might head the list. A word of caution, however, the seasickness remedy, Transderm Scop, which is a small patch placed on the skin behind the ear, is not currently available in the United States, but sometimes is found in pharmacies abroad. Possibly it will be released again with some modification. This medication, although frequently effective in preventing one from becoming seasick, has a high incidence of untoward reactions, particularly among the elderly. One poor individual was found nude at night on the helicopter deck trying to hail a taxi! Many Orientals are found to have less tolerance to medications of this type, and it was frightening to see several Japanese tourists wearing not only a patch behind *each* ear, but changing them daily rather than every three days as suggested by the manufacturer. Using one-half patch has proved efficacious for many Oriental people. The author prefers to avoid the use of this medication.

Drugs for simple self-treatment of travelers' diarrhea such as Pepto-Bismol, Lomotil, or Imodium should be carried. Many individuals can carry a supply of an antibiotic to be used under certain circumstances as directed by their personal physician. A small supply of analgesics (pain medication), antihistamines, and Band-Aids might complete the list.

Other items for the travel medical kit might be of a more personal nature including birth control medication, condoms, tampons, and any special creams or lotions one needs for medical use as well as a sunscreen lotion.

Some individuals, such as those with severe diabetes, may carry a very special "survival kit" containing a blood-glucose meter, test strips, insulin, syringe, food, and dextrose tablets—tools for control of blood sugar levels.

Another word of caution: The Halcion or Triazolam drugs used to control "jet lag" have been known to cause transient global amnesia. Imbibing alcoholic beverages can produce these episodes in very healthy subjects. Again, unless it is unavoidable, it is best to have experienced the use of any of the medications before one takes them along in the travel kit for a polar voyage. You should be able to expect that your ship's surgeon will be prepared to take care of most of your needs, but it is still best to take care of the simple ones yourself, thus avoiding many problems alluded to earlier and making your trip far more pleasant. For those interested in a commercial pack containing many of these items, there are companies like Chinook Medical Gear, Inc. (800-766-1365) that market multipurpose kits with organized bags containing items of the sort that have just been discussed.

THE CHANGING POLAR TRAVEL SCENE

As this section is being written, profound changes are occurring in how medical needs are addressed in the cruise ship industry. As has been said, specialty groups, large national medical groups, and people at all levels are demanding change. Let us consider some background information. In 1994, 377,000 people sailed on Holland America ships. Fifteen died on board; 363 were disembarked on an emergency basis.

Because of improved medical facilities, the need for air evac has been cut in half since 1992. About one-third of the passengers evacuated had heart-related problems; others had respiratory difficulties, gastrointestinal bleeding, other gastrointestinal problems, strokes, fractures, etc. Translating passenger numbers into what is seen on yearly sailings in the Antarctic, if the mix of passengers was indeed the same, one might anticipate a death approximately every other year, and each year approximately fifteen to twenty being disembarked on an emergency basis. Since good statistics are not available, I can only say that I think the rate of seriously ill disembarked may be slightly higher because of the limited medical care available on polar cruises, but the death rate of one every other year is about as projected. That is, under routine conditions, the risks are not as bad as one might imagine. However, the implications of a disaster involving many or all passengers is far greater than on a luxury ship such as those that sail the Caribbean with impunity.

Some writers claim that the forecast for the cruise industry is stormy, and sailing the high seas is becoming increasingly perilous for small privately owned fleets in the cruise ship industry. Although the number of people wanting to travel by ship appears to increase yearly, the number of new ships to offer cruises may be outpacing them. Competition has increased markedly in the past several years and Holland America, which is noted for its fine medical care, is without doubt setting a standard for cruise ship medicine. Passengers are becoming more knowledgeable and more demanding.

In June 1996, the American Medical Association approved a resolution urging the development of medical standards for cruises. Policymakers at the AMA decided that the organization would work for federal legislation or an international treaty to set minimum standards of acceptable care. Such care would deal with problems from a head cold to a heart attack. The International Council of Cruise Lines has stated that its nineteen members are developing health care guidelines and would like the medical community to give them some leeway. It should be very obvious that hospitals vary from small marginal facilities to large medical centers with fine reputations, that emergency rooms may be inefficient and ineffective or set up for triage and mass emergencies, and that the quality of physicians varies tremendously. The same is true aboard cruise ships be they for the large general tourist trade or for ships that carry far fewer to the far ends of the earth. We can't expect a medical center on every polar cruise ship, but there should be a capable, compassionate physician who is well skilled in medical and surgical emergencies and has the proper equipment and supply of medicines to handle most emergencies.

WHAT *SHOULD* YOU EXPECT ON A POLAR VOYAGE?

It is reasonable to expect that the expedition staff is composed largely of individuals who have had cardiopulmonary resuscitation (CPR) training and some paramedical training. I think you should expect that your physician be of the caliber discussed in chapter 8, and that the equipment and medicine available be of the quality and quantity needed to care for almost all foreseeable emergencies. I think you should expect that each ship's doctor be equipped with a list of ports of call, passenger agents, hospitals, and a way to communicate with these people in case of emergencies or for evacuation purposes. Similar information should be available for all polar bases. The quality of aid available at these locations should be noted, not just locations. As one looks at the ports of call just above the Antarctic Circle, excluding the ports of Hobart, Australia, and Bluff, New Zealand, and Port Stanley in the Falkland Islands, the pickings are very bleak. In the Arctic, although Murmansk or the city of Provideniya might be considered, the quality of care available is an important consideration. A thorough list of all this information is needed and it should be updated yearly.

A ship must have access to ports and arrangements for rapidly replenishing medical supplies. Portable oxygen tanks pose severe problems, inasmuch as there are few places that can supply filled tanks or have the necessary attachments to allow refilling of oxygen tanks. Most ships do not carry that capability aboard.

Not only should there be a level of expertise involving physician, equipment, medications, and communications, but the decision by some tour companies to rely completely upon the Russian physician assigned to the ship's crew to care for their passengers is a grave error. Earlier in this book we discussed the often limited ability of the Russian physicians aboard and the limitations in their equipment and medicines. In a July 1996 issue of the *Journal of the American Medical Association,* the author states, "In the former Soviet Union, the supply of personnel of even skilled professional occupations was characterized by an emphasis on quantity of output rather than quality of training." He then quotes the health minister of the Soviet Union, Sergei Burenkov, M.D., who said in 1986: "For society today, what is important is not how many there are of us (physicians) but how we work and the quality of the medical care which we provide." Until the Russian medical profession, including their equipment and supplies, can measure up to what is expected by western passengers, I think it is a serious mistake not to carry a western physician on all polar tour trips. The idea that ships carrying one hundred passengers need a western doctor, but those carrying seventy-odd or thirty-five to forty do not, is entirely fallacious. Heart attacks on polar cruise ships are not predictable, and their management is difficult at best.

The issues of safety stressed in chapters 6 and 7 on Zodiacs, helicopters, and in other situations are self-evident, and it appears that upgrading in safety in these areas is occurring each year. Passengers should make inquiries about these procedures as well as early "shipboard briefings," drills for fire, and abandon ship drills.

How does one learn that the tour group you are considering traveling with meets all of these requirements? You can speak to former tourists with the tour group, the medical director, and others with the tour company and ask frank questions. The companies are well aware of the needs that must met, and the better companies will be complying rapidly.

In fact in May 1997, IAATO reported to the XXI Antarctic Treaty Consultative Meeting at Christchurch, New Zealand, the following information:

1. The Medical Emergency Contingency Plan coordinated by Adventure Network International (ANI) as a pilot project in the 1996–97 season will continue in the 1997–98 season.
2. An outside consultant has been contacted to review the medical equipment, physician qualifications, and the medical inventories of member companies and to make recommendations for industry-wide standards.
3. As a means of ensuring safety for tour operations using Zodiac inflatable boats and helicopters, standard operating procedures include safety kits for each Zodiac and an elaborate inventory of equipment for helicopter operations.

The executive secretary of IAATO has gone on record to state that many of these initiatives had their origin in the polar medicine conference chaired by Aid for International Medicine at the Scott Polar Research Institute in October of 1995. This new positive approach may portend many constructive changes in polar medical care and safety.

INSURANCE CONSIDERATIONS

Another important item in preparing for polar tourism is travel insurance. Why should, or would, anyone buy travel insurance? Probably for the same reason you insure your car or your house, or buy life insurance. Unless you can afford to lose the cost of the expensive trip, you might best safeguard the money you have spent against the possibility that you never get to take the voyage. Really good travel insurance protects you if you become very ill and cannot make the trip or a family emergency precludes your going. But you can't collect if you simply change your mind, and it might not cover you if your flight was delayed and you missed the boat! Also, insurance of this type is not inexpensive. In most cases, a policy of this sort costs about U.S.$6 per $100 spent for the planned trip.

In the past several years, several cruise companies have collapsed. The RFD Tours of Kansas City collapsed, Domenico Tours of New Jersey closed and went into bankruptcy, and the Regency Cruise Line stopped operating in October 1995, leaving people in faraway places to do their best in finding their way back home. In contemplating the purchase of travel insurance, it is strongly advised that you read the policy over very carefully, including the fine print to be sure you will be covered for such a catastrophe.

Another form of insurance should be carefully considered by all taking a polar trip. That is, health care away from home and costs incurred with medical evacuation. First, you should review your existing insurance as your health plan may provide for emergency care away from home. However, there are usually many restrictions, and rarely, if ever, do they extend the coverage overseas. Medicare does not cover medical needs outside of the United States. Emergency medical assistance insurance covers all medical expenses incurred by a traveler when they are caused by an injury on the trip. It includes coverage for a stay in a foreign hospital or for a flight back home if the traveler is visiting a place with substandard medical facilities. This all sounds quite straightforward. However, if you are planning a polar trip, and if there are no specific phrases covering this area of the world in your insurance it is advisable to obtain an addendum to the policy guaranteeing the company will cover transportation if authorized by the ship's surgeon. You should also clarify what they mean by "substandard facilities." Some passengers have had great difficulty in obtaining reimbursement under those circumstances.

Travel insurance is so important that since January 1994, the EEC laws insist that tour operators ensure that everyone traveling with them has adequate travel insurance. That means that if you book out of England, it will be mandatory for you to purchase travel insurance at the same time you buy your ticket for the tour. A typical policy covers personal accident compensation, compensation for cancellation or curtailment of a trip, loss of baggage, personal liability, and legal advisory service. Most important, the policy may cover up to £2 million (about $3,250,000 U.S. dollars).

As of late 1996, insurance of this type was not required by most tour groups in the North American market. However, because this need is so important, the following information—though admittedly not a complete list—is provided for the guidance of prospective tourists:

Access American: 800-284-8300
The Berkely Group: 800-323-3149
Chester Profetto Agency: 800-523-8020
C.S.A.: 800-348-9505
Globalcare Insurance Services: 800-779-1017
Health Care Abroad, Wallach & Co.: 800-237-6615
Mutual of Omaha: 800-228-9792
Tele-Trip: 800-228-9792
Travel Assistance International: 800-821-2828
Travel Guard International: 800-782-5151
Travel Insured: 800-243-3174

On the North American market, coverage appears to be in the same cost range as mentioned for the United Kingdom.

TRAVEL TO AND FROM THE SHIP

A few words about flying to the ship and getting home. During a British Airways flight to Asia in 1995 a physician performed surgery with a coat hanger and an Evian bottle to reinflate a passenger's collapsed lung. In spite of his ingenuity and a successful outcome, this incident does raise some questions. Since 1986, the Federal Aviation Administration has required planes to carry medical kits equipped with drugs and supplies to treat heart attack, insulin shock, severe allergic reaction, and various other disorders. The contents of the kit expected to be administered by medical personnel are constantly being reviewed by the airlines and the FAA. Medical kits today contain a blood pressure cuff, a stethoscope, gloves, devices to open breathing airways (tracheotomy tubes), needles and syringes, dextrose for diabetes (insulin shock), benedryl for allergy, epinephrine for allergic crisis or cardiac arrest, and nitroglycerin for anginal attacks. Strong analgesics such as morphine and tranquilizers such as valium are not carried because of the danger of abuse.

Cardiac arrest from ventricular fibrillation is a common cause of death in western society and often occurs suddenly in people perceived to be in good health. The only effective therapy is electrical defibrillation. When defibrillation is applied within two minutes most victims survive. But if defibrillation is delayed beyond fifteen minutes, even with effective cardiopulmonary resuscitation, survival is rare. Semiautomatic defibrillators have been installed in all fifty-three Qantas International 747 and 767 aircraft since September 1991 and in the large Australian terminals; and all 370 flight service directors were trained in their use.

At Seattle-Tacoma International Airport, in a one-year period, 754 travelers were evaluated for medical problems. Seventy-five percent had experienced problems in the airport either before or after a flight, and 25 percent experienced problems during a flight. There were five cardiac arrests, four of which occurred within minutes of deplaning, three at the baggage carousels, and one in an aircraft preparing for takeoff.

The subject of defibrillators has been mentioned again because of its significance. With the data presented above, and the increased availability of this technique as described in chapter 8, it appears that it is necessary to have defibrillators on all polar tourist ships.

In the United States less than one flight per 100,000 makes an unscheduled landing for a medical emergency. Air travel is even healthier than these figures suggest. When dealing with such large numbers of people of all ages, some deaths are inevitable. In 60 percent of deaths in flight, there were no known precipitating risk factors. Furthermore, it is necessary to consider that a number of individuals travel specifically because they are ill, some being extremely ill.

For U.S. citizens traveling abroad, help is available through the American Citizens Services (ACS), an agency of the U.S. State Department, that has an office in every U.S. embassy and consulate throughout the world. Consular Information Sheets are available on the Internet at http://travel.state.gov or by fax (202-647-3000). A lost passport can usually be replaced within twenty-four hours. It is wise to carry a photocopy of your passport's identification page and extra passport photos to speed up the process.

The American Citizens Committee can also provide lists of medical personnel and hospitals and clinics abroad, as well as arrange emergency financial aid in serious situations. They can notify family and friends in case of illness and assist in making arrangements for commercial flights home. In case of death, they will notify next of kin, assist with arrangements for burial, and prepare a report of death. The ACS can be very helpful in cases of civil unrest abroad or in cases of natural disaster. They will not only advise your family of your situation, but also assist with your evacuation.

Should there be an emergency at home, the ACS can contact the U.S. State Department Overseas Citizens Office (202-647-5225), twenty-four hours a day for help. Although these services may be rarely needed, in a real emergency they can be lifesaving. One last word, however, if you are traveling with a tour group, on land, in the air, or on a tourist ship, do notify your expedition leader first. Coordinating efforts is the key to success.

To sum up we suggest that you get properly organized and that you carefully check with the tour company and be sure they can meet your comfort level. A trip to the Arctic or the Antarctic can be the trip of a lifetime. A good third of the passengers are on repeat trips and you may become one of them!

Lingering sunset at 2 A.M. in East Antarctica.

APPENDIX A

The Antarctic Treaty and Recommendation XVIII-1, Adopted at the Antarctic Treaty Meeting, Kyoto, Japan, 1994

The twelve nations listed in the preamble (below) signed the Antarctic Treaty on 1 December 1959 at Washington, D.C. The treaty entered into force on 23 June 1961; the twelve signatories became the original twelve consultative nations.

As of mid-1994, fourteen additional nations (Brazil, China, Ecuador, Finland, Germany, India, Italy, Netherlands, Poland, Republic of Korea, Peru, Sweden, Spain, and Uruguay) have achieved consultative status by acceding to the treaty and by conducting substantial scientific research in Antarctica. Russia carries forward the signatory privileges and responsibilities established by the former Soviet Union.

Another sixteen nations have acceded to the Antarctic Treaty: Austria, Bulgaria, Canada, Colombia, Cuba, Czech Republic, Democratic People's Republic of Korea, Denmark, Greece, Guatemala, Hungary, Papua New Guinea, Romania, Slovak Republic, Switzerland, and Ukraine. These nations agree to abide by the treaty and may attend consultative meetings as observers.

The forty-two Antarctic Treaty nations represent about two-thirds of the world's human population.

Consultative meetings have been held approximately every other year since the treaty entered into force, but since 1993 they have been held annually. Each meeting has generated recommendations regarding operation of the treaty that, when ratified by the participating governments, become binding on the parties to the treaty.

Additional meetings within the Antarctic Treaty system have produced agreements on conservation of seals, conservation of living resources, and comprehensive environmental protection.

What follows is the complete text of the Antarctic Treaty. The headings for each article were added by the National Science Foundation and are unofficial.

[preamble]

The Governments of Argentina, Australia, Belgium, Chile, the French Republic, Japan, New Zealand, Norway, the Union of South Africa, The Union of Soviet Socialist Republics, the United Kingdom of Great Britain and Northern Ireland, and the United States of America.

Recognizing that it is in the interest of all mankind that Antarctica shall continue forever to be used exclusively for peaceful purposes and shall not become the scene or object of international discord;

Acknowledging the substantial contributions to scientific knowledge resulting from international cooperation in scientific investigation in Antarctica;

Convinced that the establishment of a firm foundation for the continuation and development of such cooperation on the basis of freedom of scientific investigation in Antarctica as applied during the International Geophysical Year accords with the interests of science and the progress of all mankind;

Convinced also that a treaty ensuring the use of Antarctica for peaceful purposes only and the continuance of international harmony in Antarctica will further the purposes and principles embodied in the Charter of the United Nations;

Have agreed as follows:

Article I
[Antarctica for peaceful purposes only]

1. Antarctica shall be used for peaceful purposes only. There shall be prohibited, inter alia, any measures of a military nature, such as the establishment of military bases and fortifications, the carrying out of military maneuvers, as well as the testing of any type of weapons.
2. The present Treaty shall not prevent the use of military personnel or equipment for scientific research or for any other peaceful purposes.

Article II
[freedom of scientific investigation to continue]

Freedom of scientific investigation in Antarctica and cooperation toward that end, as applied during the International Geophysical Year, shall continue, subject to the provisions of the present Treaty.

Article III
[plans and results to be exchanged]

1. In order to promote international cooperation in scientific investigation in Antarctica, as provided for in Article II of the present Treaty, the Contracting Parties agree that, to the greatest extent feasible and practicable:

(a) information regarding plans for scientific programs in Antarctica shall be exchanged to permit maximum economy and efficiency of operations;

(b) scientific personnel shall be exchanged in Antarctica between expeditions and stations;

(c) scientific observations and results from Antarctica shall be exchanged and made freely available.

2. In implementing this Article, every encouragement shall be given to the establishment of cooperative working relations with those Specialized Agencies of the United Nations and other international organizations having a scientific or technical interest in Antarctica.

Article IV
[territorial claims]

1. Nothing contained in the present Treaty shall be interpreted as:

(a) a renunciation by any Contracting Party of previously asserted rights of or claims to territorial sovereignty in Antarctica;

(b) a renunciation or diminution by any Contracting Party of any basis of claim to territorial sovereignty in Antarctica which it may have whether as a result of its activities or those of its nationals in Antarctica, or otherwise;

(c) prejudicing the position of any Contracting Party as regards its recognition or nonrecognition of any other State's right of or claim or basis of claim to territorial sovereignty in Antarctica.

2. No acts or activities taking place while the present Treaty is in force shall constitute a basis for asserting, supporting or denying a claim to territorial sovereignty in Antarctica. No new claim, or enlargement of an existing claim, to territorial sovereignty shall be asserted while the present Treaty is in force.

Article V
[nuclear explosions prohibited]

1. Any nuclear explosions in Antarctica and the disposal there of radioactive waste material shall be prohibited.

2. In the event of the conclusion of international agreements concerning the use of nuclear energy, including nuclear explosions and the disposal of radioactive waste material, to which all of the Contracting Parties whose representatives are entitled to participate in the meetings provided for under Article IX are parties, the rules established under such agreements shall apply in Antarctica.

Article VI
[area covered by Treaty]

The provisions of the present Treaty shall apply to the area south of 60 degrees South latitude, including all ice shelves, but nothing in the present Treaty shall prejudice or in any way affect the rights, or the exercise of the rights, of any State under international law with regard to the high seas within that area.

Article VII
[free access for observation and inspection]

1. In order to promote the objectives and ensure the observation of the provisions of the present Treaty, each Contracting Party whose representatives are entitled to participate in the meetings referred to in Article IX of the Treaty shall have the right to designate observers to carry out any inspection provided for by the present Article. Observers shall be nationals of the Contracting Parties which designate them. The names of the observers shall be communicated to every other Contracting Party having the right to designate observers, and like notice shall be given of the termination of their appointment.

2. Each observer designated in accordance with the provisions of paragraph 1 of this Article shall have complete freedom of access at any time to any or all areas of Antarctica.

3. All areas of Antarctica, including all stations, installations and equipment within those areas, and all ships and aircraft at points of discharging or embarking cargoes or personnel in Antarctica, shall be open at all times to inspection by any observers designated in accordance with paragraph 1 of this Article.

4. Aerial observation may be carried out at any time over any or all areas of Antarctica by any of the Contracting Parties having the rights to designate observers.

5. Each Contracting Party shall, at the time when the present Treaty enters into force for it, inform the other Contracting Parties, and thereafter shall give them notice in advance, of

(a) all expeditions to and within Antarctica, on the part of its ships of nationals, and all expeditions to Antarctica organized in or proceeding from its territory;

(b) all stations in Antarctica occupied by its nationals; and

(c) any military personnel or equipment intended to be introduced by it into Antarctica subject to the conditions prescribed in paragraph 2 of Article I of the present Treaty.

Article VIII
[personnel under jurisdiction of their own states]

1. In order to facilitate the exercise of their functions under the present Treaty, and without prejudice to the respective positions of the Contracting Parties relating to jurisdiction over all other persons in Antarctica, observers designated under paragraph 1 of Article VII and scientific personnel exchanged under subparagraph 1(b) of Article III of the Treaty, and members of the staffs accompanying any such persons, shall be subject only to the jurisdiction of the Contracting Party of which they are nationals in respect to all acts or omissions occurring while they are in Antarctica for the purpose of exercising their functions.
2. Without prejudice to the provisions of paragraph 1 of this Article, and pending the adoption of measures in pursuance of subparagraph 1(e) of Article IX, the Contracting Parties concerned in any case of dispute with regard to the exercise of jurisdiction in Antarctica shall immediately consult together with a view to reaching a mutually acceptable solution.

Article IX
[Treaty states to meet periodically]

1. Representatives of the Contracting Parties named in the preamble to the present Treaty shall meet at the City of Canberra within two months after the date of entry into force of the Treaty, and thereafter at suitable intervals and places, for the purpose of exchanging information, consulting together on matters of common interest pertaining to Antarctica, and formulating and considering, and recommending to their Governments, measures in furtherance of the principles and objectives of the Treaty including measures regarding:

(a) use of Antarctica for peaceful purposes only;

(b) facilitation of scientific research in Antarctica;

(c) facilitation of international scientific cooperation in Antarctica;

(d) facilitation of the exercise of the rights of inspection provided for in Article VII of the Treaty;

(e) questions relating to the exercise of jurisdiction in Antarctica;

(f) preservation and conservation of living resources in Antarctica.

2. Each Contracting Party which has become a party to the present Treaty by accession under Article XIII shall be entitled to appoint representatives to participate in the meetings referred to in paragraph 1 of the present Article, during such time as the Contracting Party demonstrates its interest in Antarctica by conducting substantial scientific research activity there, such as the establishment of a scientific station or the despatch of a scientific expedition.
3. Reports from the observers referred to in Article VII of the present Treaty shall be transmitted to the representatives of the Contracting Parties participating in the meetings referred to in paragraph 1 of the present Article.
4. The measures referred to in paragraph 1 of this Article shall become effective when approved by all the Contracting Parties whose representatives were entitled to participate in the meetings held to consider those measures.
5. Any or all of the rights established in the present Treaty may be exercised as from the date of entry into force of the Treaty whether or not any measures facilitating the exercise of such rights have been proposed, considered or approved as provided in this Article.

Article X
[discourages activities contrary to Treaty]

Each of the Contracting Parties undertakes to exert appropriate efforts, consistent with the Charter of the United Nations, to the end that no one engages in any activity in Antarctica contrary to the principles or purposes of the present Treaty.

Article XI
[settlement of disputes]

1. If any dispute arises between two or more of the Contracting Parties concerning the interpretation or application of the present Treaty, those Contracting Parties shall consult among themselves with a view to having the dispute resolved by negotiation, inquiry, mediation, conciliation, arbitration, judicial settlement or other peaceful means of their own choice.
2. Any dispute of this character not so resolved shall, with the consent, in each case, of all parties to the dispute, be referred to the International Court of Justice for settlement; but failure to reach agreement on reference to the International Court shall not absolve parties to the dispute from the responsibility of continuing to seek to resolve it by any of the various peaceful means referred to in paragraph 1 of this Article.

Article XII
[review of Treaty possible after 30 years]

1. (a) The present Treaty may be modified or amended at any time by unanimous agreement of the Contracting Parties whose representatives are entitled to participate in the meetings provided for under Article IX. Any such modification or amendment shall enter into force when the depositary Government has received notice from all such Contracting Parties that they have ratified it.

(b) Such modification or amendment shall thereafter enter into force as to any other Contracting Party when notice of ratification by it has been received by the depositary Government. Any such Contracting Party from which no notice of ratification is received within a period of two years from the date of entry into force of the modification or amendment in accordance with the provisions of subparagraph 1(a) of this Article shall be deemed to have withdrawn from the present Treaty on the date of the expiration of such period.

2. (a) If after the expiration of thirty years from the date of entry into force of the present Treaty, any of the Contracting Parties whose representatives are entitled to participate in the meetings provided for under Article IX so requests by a communication addressed to the depositary Government, a Conference of all the Contracting Parties shall be held as soon as practicable to review the operation of the Treaty.

(b) Any modification or amendment to the present Treaty which is approved at such a Conference by a majority of the Contracting Parties there represented, including a majority of those whose representatives are entitled to participate in the meetings provided for under Article IX, shall be communicated by the depositary Government to all the Contracting Parties immediately after the termination of the Conference and shall enter into force in accordance with the provisions of paragraph 1 of the present Article.

(c) If any such modification or amendment has not entered into force in accordance with the provisions of subparagraph 1(a) of this Article within a period of two years after the date of its communication to all the Contracting Parties, any Contracting Party may at any time after the expiration of that period give notice to the depositary Government of its withdrawal from the present Treaty; and such withdrawal shall take effect two years after the receipt of the notice by the depositary Government.

Article XIII
[ratification and accession]

1. The present Treaty shall be subject to ratification by the signatory States. It shall be open for accession by any State which is a Member of the United Nations, or by any other State which may be invited to accede to the Treaty with the consent of all the Contracting Parties whose representatives are entitled to participate in the meetings provided for under Article IX of the Treaty.
2. Ratification of or accession to the present Treaty shall be effected by each State in accordance with its constitutional processes.
3. Instruments of ratification and instruments of accession shall be deposited with the Government of the United States of America, hereby designated as the depositary Government.
4. The depositary Government shall inform all signatory and acceding States of the date of each deposit of an instrument of ratification or accession, and the date of entry into force of the Treaty and of any modification or amendment thereto.
5. Upon the deposit of instruments of ratification by all the signatory States, the present Treaty shall enter into force for those States and for States which have deposited instruments of accession. Thereafter the Treaty shall enter into force for any acceding State upon the deposit of its instrument of accession.
6. The present Treaty shall be registered by the depositary Government pursuant to Article 102 of the Charter of the United Nations.

Article XIV
[United States is repository]

The present Treaty, done in the English, French, Russian, and Spanish languages, each version being equally authentic, shall be deposited in the archives of the Government of the United States of America, which shall transmit duly certified copies thereof to the Governments of the signatory and acceding States.

In witness whereof, the undersigned Plenipotentiaries, duly authorized, have signed the present Treaty.

Done at Washington the first day of December, one thousand nine hundred and fifty-nine.

RECOMMENDATION XVIII-1, ADOPTED AT THE ANTARCTIC TREATY MEETING, KYOTO, 1994

Guidance for visitors to the Antarctic

Activities in the Antarctic are governed by the Antarctic Treaty of 1959 and associated agreements, referred to collectively as the Antarctic Treaty System. The Treaty established Antarctica as a zone of peace and science.

In 1991, the Antarctic Treaty Consultative Parties adopted the Protocol on Environmental Protection to the Antarctic Treaty, which designates the Antarctic as a natural reserve. The Protocol, which is not reprinted here because of space limitations, sets out environmental principles, procedures and obligations for the comprehensive protection of the Antarctic environment, and its dependent and associated ecosystems. The Consultative Parties have agreed that, pending its entry into force, as far as possible and in accordance with their legal system, the provisions of the Protocol should be applied as appropriate.

The Environmental Protocol applies to tourism and non-governmental activities, as well as governmental activities in the Antarctic Treaty Area. It is intended to ensure that these activities do not have adverse impacts on the Antarctic environment, or on its scientific and aesthetic values.

This *Guidance for Visitors to the Antarctic* is intended to ensure that all visitors are aware of, and are therefore able to comply with, the Treaty and the Protocol. Visitors are, of course, bound by national laws and regulations applicable to activities in the Antarctic.

Protect Antarctic Wildlife—Taking or harmful interference with Antarctic wildlife is prohibited except in accordance with a permit issued by a national authority.

- Do not use aircraft, vessels, small boats, or other means of transport in ways that disturb wildlife, either at sea or on land.
- Do not feed, touch, or handle birds or seals, or approach or photograph them in ways that cause them to alter their behavior. Special care is needed when animals are breeding or molting.
- Do not damage plants, for example by walking, driving, or landing on extensive moss beds or lichen-covered scree slopes.
- Do not use guns or explosives. Keep noise to the minimum to avoid frightening wildlife.
- Do not bring non-native plants or animals into the Antarctic such as live poultry, pet dogs and cats or house plants.

Respect Protected Areas—A variety of areas in the Antarctic have been afforded special protection because of their particular ecological, scientific, historic or other values. Entry into certain areas may be prohibited except in accordance with a permit issued by an appropriate national authority. Activities in and near designated Historic Sites and Monuments and certain other areas may be subject to special restrictions.

- Know the locations of areas that have been afforded special protection and any restrictions regarding entry and activities that can be carried out in and near them.
- Observe applicable restrictions.
- Do not damage, remove, or destroy Historic Sites or Monuments or any artifacts associated with them.

Respect Scientific Research—Do not interfere with scientific research, facilities or equipment.

- Obtain permission before visiting Antarctic science and support facilities; reconfirm arrangements 24–72 hours before arrival; and comply with the rules regarding such visits.
- Do not interfere with, or remove, scientific equipment or marker posts, and do not disturb experimental study sites, field camps or supplies.

Be Safe—Be prepared for severe and changeable weather and ensure that your equipment and clothing meet Antarctic standards. Remember that the Antarctic environment is inhospitable, unpredictable, and potentially dangerous.

- Know your capabilities, the dangers posed by the Antarctic environment, and act accordingly. Plan activities with safety in mind at all times.
- Keep a safe distance from all wildlife, both on land and at sea.
- Take note of, and act on, the advice and instructions from your leaders; do not stray from your group.
- Do not walk onto glaciers or large snow fields without the proper equipment and experience; there is a real danger of falling into hidden crevasses.
- Do not expect a rescue service. Self-sufficiency is increased and risks reduced by sound planning, quality equipment, and trained personnel.
- Do not enter emergency refuges (except in emergencies). If you use equipment or food from a refuge, inform the nearest research station or national authority once the emergency is over.

- Respect any smoking restrictions, particularly around buildings, and take great care to safeguard against the danger of fire. This is a real hazard in the dry environment of Antarctica.

Keep Antarctica Pristine—Antarctica remains relatively pristine, the largest wilderness area on Earth. It has not yet been subjected to large scale human perturbations. Please keep it that way.

- Do not dispose of litter or garbage on land. Open burning is prohibited.
- Do not disturb or pollute lakes or streams. Any materials discarded at sea must be disposed of properly.
- Do not paint or engrave names or graffiti on rocks or buildings.
- Do not collect or take away biological or geological specimens or man-made artifacts as a souvenir, including rocks, bones, eggs, fossils, and parts or contents of buildings.
- Do not deface or vandalize buildings, whether occupied, abandoned, or unoccupied, or emergency refuges.

Guidance for those organizing and conducting tourism and non-governmental activities in the Antarctic

Antarctica is the largest wilderness area on Earth, unaffected by large scale human activities. Accordingly, this unique and pristine environment has been afforded special protection. Furthermore, it is physically remote, inhospitable, unpredictable and potentially dangerous. All activities in the Antarctic Treaty Area, therefore, should be planned and conducted with both environmental protection and safety in mind.

Activities in the Antarctic are subject to the Antarctic Treaty of 1959 and associated legal instruments, referred to collectively as the Antarctic Treaty system. These include the Convention for the Conservation of Antarctic Seals (CCAS 1972), the Convention on the Conservation of Antarctic Marine Living Resources (CCAMLR 1980) and the Recommendations and other measures adopted by the Antarctic Treaty Consultative Parties under the Antarctic Treaty.

In 1991, the Consultative Parties to the Antarctic Treaty adopted the Protocol on Environmental Protection to the Antarctic Treaty. This Protocol sets out environmental principles, procedures and obligations for the comprehensive protection of the Antarctic environment, and its dependent and associated ecosystems. The Consultative Parties have agreed that, pending its entry into force, as far as possible and in accordance with their legal systems, that the provisions of the Protocol should be applied as appropriate.

The Environmental Protocol designates Antarctica as a natural reserve devoted to peace and science, and applies to both governmental and nongovernmental activities in the Antarctic Treaty Area. The Protocol seeks to ensure that human activities, including tourism, do not have adverse impacts on the Antarctic environment, nor on its scientific and aesthetic values.

The Protocol states, as a matter of principle, that all activities are to be planned and conducted on the basis of information sufficient to evaluate their possible impact on the Antarctic environment and its associated ecosystems, and on the value of Antarctica for the conduct of scientific research. Organizers should be aware that the Environmental Protocol requires that "activities shall be modified, suspended or canceled if they result in or threaten to result in impacts upon the Antarctic environment or dependent or associated ecosystems."

Those responsible for organizing and conducting tourism and non-governmental activities must comply fully with national laws and regulations which implement the Antarctic Treaty system, as well as other national laws and regulations implementing international agreements on environmental protection, pollution and safety that relate to the Antarctic Treaty Area. They should also abide by the requirements imposed on organizers and operators under the Protocol on Environmental Protection and its Annexes, insofar as they have not yet been implemented in national law.

Key Obligations on Organizers and Operators

1) Provide prior notification of, and reports on, their activities to the competent authorities of the appropriate Party or Parties.

2) Conduct an assessment of the potential environmental impacts of their planned activities.

3) Provide for effective response to environmental emergencies, especially with regard to marine pollution.

4) Ensure self-sufficiency and safe operations.

5) Respect scientific research and the Antarctic environment, including restrictions regarding protected areas, and the protection of flora and fauna.

6) Prevent the disposal and discharge of prohibited waste.

Procedures to Be Followed by Organizers and Operators

A) When planning to go to the Antarctic—Organizers and operators should:

1) Notify the competent national authorities of the appropriate Party or Parties of details of their planned activities with sufficient time to enable the Party(ies) to comply with their information exchange obligations under Article VII(5) of the Antarctic Treaty. The information to be provided is listed in Attachment A [see page 147].

2) Conduct an environmental assessment in accordance with such procedures as may have been established in national law to give effect to Annex I of the Protocol, including, if appropriate, how potential impacts will be monitored.

3) Obtain timely permission from the national authorities responsible for any stations they propose to visit.

4) Provide information to assist in the preparation of: contingency response plans in accordance with Article 15 of the Protocol; waste management plans in accordance with Annex III of the Protocol; and marine pollution contingency plans in accordance with Annex IV of the Protocol.

5) Ensure that expedition leaders and passengers are aware of the location and special regimes which apply to Specially Protected Areas and Sites of Special Scientific Interest (and on entry into force of the Protocol, Antarctic Specially Protected Areas and Antarctic Specially Managed Areas) and of Historic Sites and Monuments and, in particular, relevant management plans.

6) Obtain a permit, where required by national law, from the competent national authority of the appropriate Party or Parties, should they have a reason to enter such areas, or a monitoring site (CEMP Site) designated under CCAMLR.

7) Ensure that activities are fully self-sufficient and do not require assistance from Parties unless arrangements for it have been agreed in advance.

8) Ensure that they employ experienced and trained personnel, including a sufficient number of guides.

9) Arrange to use equipment, vehicles, vessels, and aircraft appropriate to Antarctic operations.

10) Be fully conversant with applicable communications, navigation, air traffic control and emergency procedures.

11) Obtain the best available maps and hydrographic charts, recognizing that many areas are not fully or accurately surveyed.

12) Consider the question of insurance (subject to requirements of national law).

13) Design and conduct information and education programs to ensure that all personnel and visitors are aware of relevant provisions of the Antarctic Treaty system.

14) Provide visitors with a copy of the *Guidance for Visitors to the Antarctic.*

B) When in the Antarctic Treaty Area—Organizers and operators should:

1) Comply with all requirements of the Antarctic Treaty system, and relevant national laws, and ensure that visitors are aware of requirements that are relevant to them.

2) Reconfirm arrangements to visit stations 24–72 hours before their arrival and ensure that visitors are aware of any conditions or restrictions established by the station.

3) Ensure that visitors are supervised by a sufficient number of guides who have adequate experience and training in Antarctic conditions and knowledge of the Antarctic Treaty system requirements.

4) Monitor environmental impacts of their activities, if appropriate, and advise the competent national authorities of the appropriate Party or Parties of any adverse or cumulative impacts resulting from an activity, but which were not foreseen by their environmental impact assessment.

5) Operate ships, yachts, small boats, aircraft, Hovercraft, and all other means of transport safely and according to appropriate procedures, including those set out in the Antarctic Flight Information Manual (AFIM).

6) Dispose of waste materials in accordance with Annex III and IV of the Protocol. These annexes prohibit, among other things, the discharge of plastics, oil and noxious substances into the Antarctic Treaty Area; regulate the discharge of sewage and food waste; and require the removal of most wastes from the area.

7) Co-operate fully with observers designated by Consultative Parties to conduct inspections of stations, ships, aircraft and equipment under Article VII of the Antarctic Treaty, and those to be designated under Article 14 of the Environmental Protocol.

8) Co-operate in monitoring programs undertaken in accordance with Article 3(2)(d) of the Protocol.

9) Maintain a careful and complete record of their activities conducted.

C) On completion of the activities. Within three months of the end of the activity, organizers and operators should report on the conduct of it to the appropriate national authority in accordance with national laws and procedures. Reports should include the name, details and state of registration of each vessel or aircraft used and the name of their captain or commander; actual itinerary; the number of visitors engaged in the activity; places, dates and purposes of landings and the number of visitors landed on each occasion; any meteorological observations made, including those made as part of the World Meteorological Organization (WMO) Voluntary Observing Ships Scheme; any significant changes in activities and their impacts from those predicted before the visit was conducted; and action taken in case of emergency.

D) Antarctic Treaty System Documents and Information. Most Antarctic Treaty Parties can provide, through their national contact points, copies of relevant provisions of the Antarctic Treaty system and information about national laws and procedures, including:

- The Antarctic Treaty (1959)
- Convention on the Conservation of Antarctic Marine Living Resources (1980)
- Protocol on Environmental Protection to the Antarctic Treaty (1991)
- Recommendations and other measures adopted under the Antarctic Treaty
- Final Reports of Consultative Meetings
- Handbook of the Antarctic Treaty System (1994)
- Handbook of the Antarctic Treaty System (in Spanish, 1991)

Attachment A, Information to Be Provided in Advance Notice—Organizers should provide the following information to the appropriate national authorities in the format requested:

1. Name, nationality, and contact details of the organizer;
2. Where relevant, registered name and national registration and type of any vessel or aircraft to be used (including name of the captain or commander, call-sign, radio frequency, INMARSAT number);
3. Intended itinerary, including the date of departure and places to be visited in the Antarctic Treaty Area;
4. Activities to be undertaken and purpose;
5. Number and qualifications of crew and accompanying guides and expedition staff;
6. Estimated number of visitors to be carried;
7. Carrying capacity of vessel;
8. Intended use of vessel;
9. Intended use and type of aircraft;
10. Number and type of other vessels, including small boats, to be used in the Antarctic Treaty Area;
11. Information about insurance coverage;
12. Details of equipment to be used, including for safety purposes, and arrangements for self-sufficiency;
13. And other matters required by national laws.

International Association of Antarctic Tour Operators (IAATO) Documents

OBJECTIVES

The International Association of Antarctic Tour Operators was founded by seven private tour operators in 1991 to create a set of commonly agreed guidelines and to better operate responsibly within the Antarctic Treaty System. IAATO is dedicated to appropriate, safe and environmentally sound private-sector travel to the Antarctic.

- To represent Antarctic tour operators and others organizing and conducting travel to the Antarctic to the Antarctic Treaty Parties, the international conservation community and the public at large.
- To advocate, promote and practice safe and environmentally responsible travel to the Antarctic.
- To circulate, promote and follow the *Guidance for Visitors to the Antarctic* and *Guidance for Those Organizing and Conducting Tourism and Non-governmental Activities in the Antarctic,* as adopted by the Antarctic Treaty System (Recommendation XVIII-1).
- To operate within the parameters of the Antarctic Treaty System, including the Antarctic Treaty and the Protocol on the Environment and Annexes, along with MARPOL, SOLAS and similar international and national laws and agreements.
- To foster continued cooperation among its members and to monitor IAATO programs, including the pattern and frequency of visits to specific sites within the Antarctic. And to coordinate itineraries so that no more than 100 people are ashore at any one time in any one place.
- To provide a forum for the international, private-sector travel industry to share expertise and opinions and to uphold the highest standards among members.
- To enhance public awareness and concern for the conservation of the Antarctic environment and its associated ecosystems and to better inform the media, governments and environmental organizations about private-sector travel to these regions.
- To create a corps of ambassadors for the continued protection of Antarctica by offering the opportunity to experience the continent first hand.
- To support science in Antarctica through cooperation with national Antarctic programs, including logistical support and research.
- To foster cooperation between private-sector travel and the international scientific community in the Antarctic.
- To ensure that the best qualified staff and field personnel are employed by IAATO members through continued training and education. And to encourage and develop international acceptance of evaluation, certification and accreditation programs for Antarctic personnel.

CONTRIBUTIONS TO SCIENCE AND RESEARCH

IAATO member companies provide logistic and scientific support to national Antarctic programs and Antarctic organizations. The following describes the 1994–95 highlights in this effort.

IAATO member vessels and aircraft transported a total of over 100 scientists and support personnel to remote field camps and permanent stations throughout Antarctica.

IAATO members supported the Humpback Whale Catalog by contributing fluke photos to Allied Whale, College of the Atlantic, Bar Harbor, Maine.

In a cooperative venture with the Polish Academy of Sciences, passengers and staff aboard the *Ioffe* helped to clear Henryk Arctowski Base of 35 tons of abandoned equipment and hazardous oil products, which was retrograded to Warsaw.

The icebreaker *Kapitan Khlebnikov* convoyed the French resupply vessel *L'Astrolabe* through heavy ice into Dumont d'Urville Station.

Tour operators and travelers continued their tradition of direct financial contributions to organizations active in Antarctica, contributing a total of over $27,000 to the South Georgia Whaling Museum, Falkland Islands Conservation, Antarctic Project, New Zealand Antarctic Heritage Trust, Whale Assist and other organizations.

IATTO MEMBERSHIP, MAY 1997

Office of the Secretariat

111 East 14 Street
Suite 110
New York, NY 10003 USA
Darrel Schoeling
Tel: 212-460-8715
Fax: 212-529-8684
E-mail: IAATO@aol.com

Spokesperson

235 Camden, Suite 32
Rockland, ME 04841 USA
John Splettstoesser
Tel/Fax: 207-594-7594

MEMBERS

Abercrombie and Kent Explorer Shipping Corporation

1520 Kensington Road
Oak Brook, IL 60521 USA
Victoria Underwood
Tel: 630-954-2944
Fax: 630-572-1833

Adventure Network International

Canon House
27 London End
Beaconsfield, Bucks
HP9 2HN United Kingdom
Anne Kershaw
Tel: 44-1494-671808
Fax: 44-1494-671725
E-mail: 106256.1300@
compuserve.com

Aurora Expeditions

Level 1, 37 George Street
The Rocks
Sydney NSW Australia 2000
Greg Mortimer
Tel: 61-2-9252-1033
Fax: 61-2-9252-1373
E-mail: Auroraex@world.net

Hepag-Lloyd Cruiseship Management GmbH

Ballindamm 25
20020 Hamburg
Germany
Bärbel Krämer
Tel: 49-40-3001-4600
Fax: 49-40-3001-4601
E-mail: baerbel_kraemer@
hanseaticcruises.cc
mail.co

Marine Expeditions

30 Hazelton Avenue
Toronto, Ontario
M5R 2E1 Canada
Patrick Shaw
Tel: 416-964-9069
Fax: 416-964-2366

Mountain Travel - Sobek

6420 Fairmount Avenue
El Cerrito, CA 94530 USA
Alicia Zablocki
Tel: 510-527-8105
Fax: 510-525-7710
E-mail: info@MtSobek.com
Web site: http://www.
MtSobek.com

Quark Expeditions

980 Post Road
Darien, CT 06820 USA
Denise Landau
Tel: 203-656-0499
Fax: 203-655-6623
E-mail: 76255.3266@
compuserve.com
Web site: http://www.
quark-expeditions.com

Society Expeditions

2001 Western Avenue
Suite 710
Seattle, WA 98121 USA
John Tillotson
Tel: 206-728-9400
Fax: 206-728-2301

Southern Heritage Expeditions

P.O. Box 20-219
Christchurch
New Zealand
Rodney Russ
Tel: 64-03-359-7711
Fax: 64-03-359-3311
E-mail: hertexp@ibm.net

Travel Dynamics

132 East 70 Street
New York, NY 10021 USA
Jim Smith
Tel: 212-517-7555
Fax: 212-517-0077
E-mail: info@travdyn.com

WildWings

International House
Bank Road, Bristol
BS15 2LX Avon
United Kingdom
John Brodie-Good
Tel: 44-117-9848040
Fax: 44-117-9674444

Zegrahm Expeditions

1414 Dexter Avenue
Suite 327
Seattle, WA 98109 USA
Werner Zehnder
Tel: 206-285-4000
Fax: 206-285-5037
E-mail: zoe@zeco.com
Web site: http://www.zeco.co

ASSOCIATE MEMBERS

Hapag Lloyd Tours GmbH

Schwachhauser
Heerstrasse, 30a
28209 Bremen
Germany
Isolde Susset
Tel: 49-421-34-86-131
Fax: 49-421-34-86-132

JES/Japan Euro-Asia Service

9-3 Rokubancho
Chiyoda-ku, Tokyo 102 Japan
Matsui Sadaaki
Tel: 81-3-3221-9121
Fax: 81-3-3221-9120

Latour Chile

Fidel Oteizza 1933
Providencia, Santiago Chile
Mike Gallegos
Tel: 56-2-225-2883
Fax: 56-2-225-2545

Lifelong Learning

101 Columbia
Suite 150
Aliso Viejo, CA 92658 USA
J. William Diebenow
Tel: 714-362-2900
Fax: 714-362-2075
E-mail: Illxpro@aol.com

Natural Habitat Adventures

2945 Center Green Court
Boulder, CO 80301 USA
Sean Jones
Tel: 303-449-3711
Fax: 303-449-3712
E-mail: nat@nathab.com
Web site: http://www.nathab.com

Oceanic Adventures

Two Jays, Kemple End
Stonyhurst, Lancashire
BB7 9QY United Kingdom
Mark Beaman
Tel: 44-1254-826116
Fax: 44-1254-826780
E-mail: ocean@birdquest.co.uk

Overseas Adventure Travel

625 Mt. Auburn Street
Cambridge, MA 02138 USA
Robin Price
Tel: 617-876-0533
Fax: 617-876-0455

Park East Tours

1841 Broadway
New York, NY 10023 USA
Eric Gordon
Tel: 212-765-4870
Fax: 212-265-8952

Plancius - Oceanwide

Rapenburgerstraat 109
1011 VL Amsterdam
The Netherlands
J. de Korte
Tel: 31-20-4221411
Fax: 31-20-4222126

Playguide Tours

Mandai Bldg
4-4 Kojimachi
Chiyoda-ku, Tokyo 102 Japan
Tenshin Kobayashi
Tel: 81-3-3288-0911
Fax: 81-3-3288-3391

Radisson Seven Seas Cruises

600 Corporate Drive
Suite 410
Ft. Lauderdale, FL 33334 USA
Paul Goodwin
Tel: 954-776-6123
Fax: 954-776-2283
E-mail: pgoodwin@radisson.com

Lives Lost in Polar Explorations

The following is a complete and accurate list of the deaths among members of the parties of polar travelers as it appears in A. W. Greely and J. Martin Miller's *Discovery of the North Pole,* pages 405-406. J.T. Moss, 1909.

Year		*Lost*	*Cause of Death*
1553	Sir Hugh Willoughby	62	cold and starvation
1554	Richard Cancellor	8	cold and starvation
1578	Sir Martin Frobisher	40	cold, starvation, drowning
1585	Capt. Davis	14	cold
1594	Barents	35	starvation, drowning, scurvy
1606	John Knight	3	cold
1607	Henry Hudson	10	cold, scurvy
1612	Sir Thomas Button	14	cold
1619	Jens Munk	62	cold, starvation, scurvy, drowning
1631	Thomas James	14	cold
1633	Isle of Jan Mayen settlers	7	cold, starvation
1634	Isle of Jan Mayen settlers	7	cold, starvation
1648	Deshneff	70	starvation, drowning, cold
1710	James Knight	50	starvation, drowning, cold
1728	Bering	10	cold, drowning
1735	Pronchistcheff	2	cold
1735	Lassinius	53	scurvy, starvation, cold
1739	Charlton Laptier	12	cold, starvation
1742	Bering	31	starvation, cold, scurvy
1773	Lord Mulgrave	8	cold and starvation
1776	Capt. Cook	4	drowning
1818	Parry, first voyage	1	cold
1819	Franklin, first voyage	2	accident
1821	Parry, second voyage	7	cold
1825	Franklin, second voyage	4	cold
1829	John Ross	4	cold and starvation
1838	Pease and Simpson	5	cold
1845	Franklin, third voyage	135	starvation, scurvy, exposure
1848	J. C. Ross, search expedition	1	unknown

Year	*Explorer*	*Lost*	*Cause of Death*
1849	North Star expedition	5	cold, starvation
1849	Plover and Herald	3	cold, starvation
1853	Rae	6	cold, starvation
1853	Kane expedition	3	accident, cold
1860	Isaac Hayes	1	cold
1860	Hall, first voyage	2	cold
1864	Hall, second voyage	3	cold
1870	Hall, last voyage	2	cold and starvation
1872	Pegetthoff	2	cold
1872	B. Leigh Smith	2	cold
1875	English Expedition	4	cold
1878	Jeanette (De Long)	23	starvation, cold, scurvy
1881	Greely	20	starvation
1896	Andree (balloon)	3	unknown
1900	Abruzzi	2	cold
1908	Cook	none	none
1909	Peary	1	drowning
	Total	757	

Editor's Note: All of these polar deaths were in the Arctic.

Aid to International Medicine (AIM) Conference: A Medical Standard for Expedition Travel and Tourism in the Polar Environment

ANNOUNCEMENT OF CONFERENCE

Over the past forty years, five members of our Board of Directors have served in medical positions at clinics, polar stations, or on a variety of ships in the Arctic and Antarctic. We are well aware of the limited availability of responding to medical emergencies in this harsh and challenging environment. The purpose of this conference is to share experiences and offer suggestions so that a set of guidelines may be prepared to improve the safety and health of travelers in polar regions. We realize the need for preventive medicine, shipboard safety, safety in using Zodiac-type watercraft, helicopters, and on the ice itself. We are also deeply concerned about how to address large disasters, and evacuation of casualties and those with life-threatening illness to more traditional care. We appreciate that small cruise ships and ice breakers cannot be medical centers, nor be fully equipped with proper small hospitals. However, they can be modestly equipped for most emergencies.

There has never been a conference solely devoted to these special concerns. We anticipate providing constructive suggestions for improving medical care in the remoteness of the polar regions. This is our goal.

Attendance will be limited to thirty participants and observers. As of this date, a diverse and experienced group of twenty-four experts have registered for the conference.

Individuals or organizations unable to attend are invited to submit written material for consideration at the conference, and for our post-conference publication.

Jack D. Lange, M.D., founder, past president, and chief editor of the world-renowned Lange Medical Publications will attend the conference. A professional staff associate will accompany him to assist in preparing the materials, presentations, and discussions for publication. This publication will be circulated for the benefit of all polar travelers.

Additional attendance is anticipated with representation from many of the following:

AEA International Worldwide Emergency Assistance and Maritime Health Services, Inc.
American College of Emergency Physicians—Cruise Section
British Antarctic Survey
Cambridge University College of Medicine
The Explorers Club
International Association of Antarctic Tour Operators (IAATO)
National Science Foundation—Office of Polar Programs
New Zealand Antarctic Program
Royal Geographical Society
Scott Polar Research Institute

October 27, 28, 29, 1995
Scott Polar Research Institute (SPRI)
University of Cambridge
Cambridge, United Kingdom

The conference will be held at SPRI through the courtesy of

Director, Dr. John Heap, C.M.G.
Honorary Chairman, Dr. Bernard Stonehouse, Senior Associate, S.P.R.I.
Chairman, John M. Levinson, M.D., President, AIM
Steering Committee, Errol Ger, M.D. and John M. Levinson, M.D.

Advance registration is required. Interested individuals should return the registration questionnaire to the chairman, John M. Levinson, M.D., as soon as possible.

- There will be no charge for registration.
- There will be no charge for attending conference.
- There will be a $45.00 (US) charge for the banquet on October 27.

Attendees will come from the following backgrounds:

- Physicians and other medical personnel experienced in shipboard medicine, polar medicine, expedition medicine, and emergency medicine.
- Individuals with special interest and knowledge in safety and communications in the polar environment.

AIM does not have funding to assist participants. However, as a 501-C organization, donations to us are one-hundred-percent deductible in the U.S.A., and may be used to defray costs of attendance.

AIM is underwriting the entire cost of the conference. Donations are most welcome and a full disclosure of all funding for the conference will be given. Our only "special interest" is improving safety and medical care in the remoteness of the polar regions.

PROGRAM

Friday, October 27
Safety, Communications, and Disasters
Physicians, Medicines and Equipment

1000 Final registration and coffee

1030 Welcome from:
Dr. John Heap, C.M.G., Director, SPRI and Dr. Bernard Stonehouse, Senior Associate, SPRI, Honorary Chairman of Conference

1045 John M. Levinson, M.D., F.A.C.O.G., Past President of The Explorers Club, Founder and President of AIM, Inc., and Conference Chairman, will introduce Errol Ger, M.D., F.R.C.S., Co-Chairman of the Steering Committee, and initiate conference.

1050 "ANARE Health Care 1947-95: Lessons for Antarctic Tourism" by Dr. Desmond J. Lugg, Head of Polar Medicine, Australian Antarctic Division and Chairman of the Human Biology and Medicine Working Group of the Scientific Committee on Antarctic Research.

1130 "Multiple Severe Injuries Sustained by Tourists on an Icebreaker in the Chukchi Sea," an account by the ship's surgeon, Richard N. Moersch, M.D., F.A.C.S., a cardiothoracic surgeon who has served on many expeditions as well as ship's surgeon in the Arctic.

1150 "Ship's Surgeon, Medical Inventory, Equipment, Surgical Supplies and Medical Records" by John M. Levinson, M.D., former medical director and ship's surgeon in the tropics and the Arctic and Antarctic.

1210 "Physician Recruiting and Medical Equipment on Board Vessels" by Claude Bachelard, M.D., Le Médecin Chef, polar expedition doctor, and medical officer at Terres Australes et Antarctiques Français since 1981, will present additional input on the subject.

1230 Lunch break on your own

1400 "Safety Equipment and Requirements on Ships, Helicopters, and Zodiac-Type Craft" by John Splettstoesser, a geologist and polar consultant who has done research and exploration in the Antarctic and is a highly respected lecturer and expedition leader, having served for many decades on tour ships. Lecture to be presented by John M. Levinson, M.D.

1430 "Communication Network for Medical Emergencies in the Polar Area and Triage for Disasters" by David Rootes of the agency Poles Apart, who is well-qualified to discuss this subject by virtue of his extensive background working at Antarctic bases, in the Arctic, and at sea. He has special expertise in environmental studies. He will be assisted in this presentation by a physician experienced in the subject matter.

1500 "Criteria to Be Accepted as a Passenger and Professional Liability" by Norman C. Headly, M.D., who practices general medicine and has worked as ship's surgeon on some thirty cruises on seven different ships.

1530 Tea

1600 "How a Passenger Views It All" by Ruth Ann Ger, wife of a ship's surgeon, who sustained a major trauma in the Antarctic.

1615 "Overview of Medical Care within the British Antarctic Survey, Medical Training of Medical and Nonmedical Personnel, and Communications and Medical Care." These topics will be presented by Dr. Alan H. Milne, Editor of the British Antarctic Survey Medical Handbook *(KURAFID)*. This is a valuable addition, as probably no one is better qualified to speak on these subjects.

1700 Discussions on the day's topics.

1800 Adjournment for the day.

The Polar Banquet
Friday, October 27, 1995
University Arms
Cocktails in Fenners Bar at 1930
Banquet in private dining room at 2030
A traditional English dinner will be served
Speaker: Mr. R. K. Headland, Archivist, SPRI
Subject: Historical Anecdotes about Medicine at the Ends of the Earth
$45.00 (US) per person, cash bar
Guests are welcome.

Saturday, October 28
Practical Medicine in Polar Areas
Medical experts will provide a basic and very brief synopsis of caring for major medical problems under the severe limitations imposed by the polar environment.

0900 "Scurvy, a Historical Perspective" by Errol Ger, M.D., F.R.C.S., an experienced Antarctic ship's surgeon, who will discuss what was until recent years the most serious medical problem in polar travel.

0920 "Snowblindness and a Differential Diagnosis of Acute Eye Disorders" by Davis G. Durham, M.D., F.A.C.S., an ophthalmologist with extensive experience in developing countries, who will discuss his experience with the Alaskan Eskimo and related eye problems.

0940 "Hypothermia and Cold Injuries: Relevance to Polar Tourism" by Peter Sullivan, Medical Research Officer, Australian Antarctic Division. Lecture to be presented by Dr. D. J. Lugg.

1000 Coffee

1030 "The Acute Abdomen at Sea, G.U. And Gyn Emergencies" by Carolyn Annerud, M.D., F.A.C.E.P., a well-qualified emergency physician with worldwide ship's surgeon experience including Arctic and Antarctic service.

1050 "Seasickness and Other Intestinal Disorders" by Kenneth R. Haslam, M.D., an anesthesiologist with experience as a ship's surgeon in the Arctic and Antarctic.

1110 "Major Trauma and Burns" by Theodore B. Strange, M.D., F.A.C.S., who served as a ship's surgeon in the Arctic and Antarctic. In World War II he saw extensive service as a U.S. Navy medical officer on destroyers and as a flight surgeon on an aircraft carrier in the Pacific.

1130 "Orthopedics." This topic will be shared by two experienced orthopedic surgeons, Dr. Strange and Dr. Ger, who has special expertise in hand surgery and has lectured and taught this specialty in many countries.

1150 "Pulmonary, E.N.T., and Dental" by Lennart Fagraeus, M.D., Ph.D., Chairman of Anesthesiology, Medical Center of Delaware. Dr. Fagraeus received his Ph.D. for work on high altitude and diving physiology. He is an experienced ship's surgeon, having worked many cruises in Asia and, more recently, to the North Pole.

1210 "Cardiology" by Richard N. Moersch, M.D., F.A.C.S., a cardiothoracic surgeon who is well experienced in basic cardiology for a very limited medical environment.

1230 Tour of SPRI facilities and library by Mr. R. K. Headland, Archivist, SPRI
The remainder of the day and evening are free. Conference secretary can assist with other suggested activities.

Sunday, October 29

Preparation of Information for Publications

0900 Discussions

1000 Coffee

1030 Final summation

1300 End of conference

AIM, Inc., has underwritten the cost of this conference. We are pleased that so many of you have taken the time and expense to travel so many thousands of miles to participate. We are particularly pleased that Mr. Mike McDowell, president of Super Nova Expeditions, Ltd., and Quark Expeditions, Inc., has contributed U.S.$1,000 to help fund the conference. His support of our goal for the polar regions is deeply appreciated.

AIM, Inc., was incorporated on January 18, 1965, "for the purpose of extending help through areas where one or more of the Board have personally served and documented a need." In these thirty plus years, we have placed over $7,700,000 of medical books, equipment, food, medicines, and relief to needy areas throughout the world. No cost figures have been assigned to the many thousands of hours of gratis medical expertise, service, and teaching that has been given, and all medical expeditions are self-funded. We know of no other philanthropic agency that operates as simplistically and with lower administrative expenses. We are a nonprofit 501-C corporation in the United States.

APPENDIX E

American College of Emergency Physicians Guidelines of Care for Cruise Ship Medical Facilities

Medical care on cruise ships would be enhanced by utilizing cruise ships with the following:

1. A ship medical center with medical staff (physicians and registered nurses), examination and treatment areas, and an inpatient medical holding unit adequate for the size of the ship.

Necessary

- 0.10 m^2 of space per infirmary/passenger and crew unit
- Access to wheelchairs/stretchers
- Inpatient beds
  - 1 ward bed/500 passengers and crew or better
  - 1 ICU bed/ship
  - Dimensions (minimum): 2 bedrooms (16 × 13 feet [5 × 4 meters]) and 1 bedroom (10 × 13 feet [3 × 4 meters])
- Examination/stabilization room: 1 room/ship (minimum 13 × 13 feet [4 × 4 meters])

Recommended / Suggested

- Isolation room or ability to disembark quickly (ideally negative pressure, respiratory appropriate)
- ICU beds: 2/ship
- Handicap toilet with shower

Optional

- Emergency dental capabilities

2. Experienced medical staff:

Necessary

- Competent skill level in basic life support, advanced cardiac life support, intubation skills and prior experience in cardiac care
- Current medical licensure in state, province, or country
- Intravenous line placement
- Social skills
  - Team player within ship's hierarchy or command organization
  - Communicate effectively with passengers
  - Meet appearance/dress code expectations of ship's officers
- 24-hour availability

Recommended / Suggested

- Board certification in emergency medicine, family practice, or internal medicine
- General practice experience, plus emergency/critical care experience
- 2 to 3 years of clinical experience
- Advanced trauma life support skill (i.e., chest tube placement)
- Minor surgical skills (i.e., suturing, I & D abscesses, etc.)

Optional

- Surgical skills in appropriate setting
- Certification or skills in advanced pediatric life support

3. When the majority of passengers are U.S. or Canadian citizens and the ship is sailing from U.S. or Canadian ports, a medical staff fluent in English and familiar with the U.S. or Canadian medical systems and medications.

Necessary

Fluency in language spoken by majority of passengers and crew

Well-organized and legible standardized documentation of all care in medical record system similar to land-based facilities and ED records

Recommended / Suggested

"Official language" of cruise line, what passengers expect, translation available

Familiarity with cultural background of majority of officers, crew, and passengers

Typed or legibly recorded documentation of medical records in "official language"

Optional

4. Emergency medical equipment, medications, and procedures:

Necessary

Equipment

- Airway equipment: bag valve mask (1), pocket mask, ET tubes (all sizes), stylet, lubricant, vasoconstrictor, suction equipment (portable)
- Cardiac monitor (1)
- Defibrillator (portable)
- Electrocardiograph
- Wheelchair which is portable throughout the ship
- Stairchair or gurney
- Pediatric supplies in younger passenger settings*
- Refrigerator/freezer
- Extrication device
- Long board, C-collar immobilization capability
- Trauma cart supplies (chest tube equipment, suction, pleuro-vac, etc.)
- Maintenance/replacement program for all equipment

Medications

- Comparable supplies for an emergency department code cart (advanced cardiac life support drugs, sufficient quantities to run two complex codes)

Procedures

- Orientation program for all equipment
- Code team trained and updated regularly
- Mock codes at required intervals with evaluation/review of performance

Disaster plan

Recommended / Suggested

2nd cardiac monitor (back-up)

2nd defibrillator (back-up)

Volume pumps

Ventilator

Pulse oximeter

External pacer capability (suitable to ship)*

Oxygen (portable, in sufficient quantity until able to disembark patient)

Optional

Oxygen concentrator (suitable to ship)*

** The specific medical needs of a cruise ship are dependent on variables such as patient mix (age, illness), number of patient visits, itinerary, etc. These factors will modify a ship's formulary, space requirements, equipment, and staffing requirements.*

5. Basic laboratory capabilities, with consideration of an X-ray unit on larger ships:

Necessary	*Recommended / Suggested*	*Optional*
Hemoglobin/hematocrit, urinalysis, pregnancy tests, glucose (all with quality control program)	X-ray unit recommendation for ships with 1,000 crew/passengers or if transfer 12 hours away X-ray education/maintenance program Capability to perform CXR, extremities, c-spine, abdomen, and pelvis films required if X ray provided Microscope and manual for microscope and lab procedures required if provided Universal crew blood donor list for life-threatening hemorrhage (transfusion kit, procedure, and disclaimer required if provided) Drug/ETOH test kits (protocol required if provided)	Electrolytes (i.e., potassium, glucose, blood urea nitrogen, creatinine)* Blood gases* Cardiac enzymes (CPK-MB, SGOT, LDH)* Coags (PT, PTT)*

6. A passenger information program regarding on-board health and safety:

Necessary	*Recommended / Suggested*	*Optional*
Physical disabilities and passenger requirements (i.e., wheelchair, equipment for hearing or vision impaired)	Preassessment of passengers' medical needs	Move to meet/exceed physical disabilities act requirements/standards

7. A crew screening, health, hygiene, and safety program:

Necessary	*Recommended / Suggested*	*Optional*
An effective screening program for: TB: TB skin tests (i.e., PPD), annual CXR in highly endemic countries Hepatitis B: Initial serology screen (HBsAgn) Syphilis: Initial serology screen (RPR or VDRL)	Initiate/update childhood vaccinations as indicated Clear, comprehensive screening program for all crew with similar action plans Procedure/protocol to screen ill or high-risk crew members with communicable diseases (i.e., syphilis, hepatitis, AIDS) Crew safety program (include universal precautions when indicated, hazardous waste disposal, alcohol and drug education)	

** The specific medical needs of a cruise ship are dependent on variables such as patient mix (age, illness), number of patient visits, itinerary, etc. These factors will modify a ship's formulary, space requirements, equipment, and staffing requirements.*

Medical Statements and Forms

IAATO MEDICAL EMERGENCY EVACUATION PLAN FOR THE ANTARCTIC PENINSULA PROVIDED BY ADVENTURE NETWORK INTERNATIONAL

In the event of serious accident or life-threatening situation requiring medical attention beyond the ship's medical capabilities/facilities, the following procedure should be implemented.

Assessment

Consider the alternatives. A decision is made onboard that the best option for the critically sick or injured individual is emergency evacuation. This decision, by the shipboard physician and patient or family, is made in concert with the expedition leader and captain of the vessel.

Initial action

Prior to contacting the Adventure Network International 24-hour emergency station in Punta Arenas, please ensure the following information is available:

1. Name of the staff member on board who will coordinate the situation.

2. Current position, route, and speed of the vessel.

3. Current weather and recent forecasts available.

4. Information on any other vessels in the local area, and the contact details.

5. Name and precise details of the injured/sick person and his or her condition, with a complete medical evaluation by the ship's physician in writing. Include the time of the incident, abstract from the ship's log, chronology of intervention, and any medical history. Provide the name of the patient's consulting physician at home and emergency contact information for the patient.

6. How many other persons will accompany the injured party from the vessel and the approximately weight and volume of their luggage?

7. What medical facilities/anticipated treatment will be required at the destination, and any drugs needed for the patient or to restock the vessel.

8. The anticipated final destination of the injured/sick person.

Secondary action

1. Contact the 24-hour emergency number and be prepared to provide the above information—and anything else that may be relevant to the situation.

2. The emergency station will contact all known means of evacuation and research the availability of aircraft, cost, and best available option for the passenger and vessel.

3. The emergency station will advise the contact person aboard the vessel and await a decision regarding the injured party.

4. Once a decision is made for action, the emergency station will contact the transportation company and arrange for evacuation at a specified time and place. A suitable landing site will be agreed upon and a suggested time, pending weather conditions. Details of how the passenger will be moved will be given to the emergency station.

5. Medical facilities at the destination will be alerted and an ambulance or other requested form of transport will be at the airport upon arrival of the patient.

6. The emergency station will advise the cruise company's home office or 24-hour contact of the situation and provide the patient's emergency contact information.

7. Two copies of a detailed medical report completed by the attending ship's physician must be transferred with the patient for the attention of the emergency station. A copy will be given to the doctor at the destination.

8. Advise the emergency station of any anticipated additional forms or paperwork that may be required by a medical insurance company.

9. Advise the emergency station of any vessels, stations, or organizations you have contacted regarding the situation.

10. The vessel will maintain regular contact with the emergency station until the passenger is uplifted from the agreed point and a schedule established with the ship's captain for the preferred means of communication (telephone, fax, or radio).

Final action

1. Once the uplift of the passenger is completed, the vessel will be informed of the arrival of the aircraft and passenger at the destination.

2. From this point, the emergency station will coordinate directly with the cruise company's home office regarding the ongoing condition of the passenger, providing regular updates.
3. The emergency station will remain in regular contact with the passenger until the situation is normalized or responsibility is transferred to another party.
4. A full report will be submitted by the emergency station to the cruise company regarding the pickup and services of the station, including an invoice for expenses incurred.

IAATO MEDICAL INFORMATION STATEMENT

All Antarctic travelers with IAATO, both land and shipborne, are currently asked by individual tour operators to provide thorough medical disclosure and, in most cases, to sign a statement of general health. In addition, Antarctic travelers have been required or have been strongly encouraged to also provide a letter from their personal physician.

Recognizing a general concern on the part of Antarctic Treaty Parties and National Programs about the overall health of Antarctic travelers and acknowledging that tourist activities must be self-sufficient, IAATO basically adopted the following medical information form at its annual meeting in July 1996. Certain modification may necessarily be made by requirements of privacy rules between physician and patient in different countries as well as differences due to customs and laws in some nations. This form would be used by all IAATO members who operate ships in the Antarctic. The form standardizes health information that has been routinely gathered by experienced Antarctic tour operators for decades and will be especially useful for new members.

Furthermore, IAATO endorses the Personal and Medical Information Form used by Adventure Network International, the only land-based private operator in the Antarctic.

IAATO GENERAL MEDICAL INFORMATION FORM FOR ANTARCTIC EXPEDITION CRUISING

All travelers must complete every section of this form

No sophisticated medical facilities are available in the Antarctic. Although each vessel carries a qualified physician and a limited infirmary with basic medications and equipment, we ask that you complete this *confidential* medical report so our shipboard physician is fully aware of your medical condition and needs—and can better care for you aboard.

This expedition is intended for persons in reasonably good health. Passengers who are not fit for long trips for any reason, including disability, heart or other health condition, are advised not to join the tour, which would entail an unreasonable risk to your health and to the enjoyment of all passengers aboard. Should any such condition become apparent, we reserve the right to decline to accept or retain you or any other passenger at any time during the trip.

Please return this completed form with registration, including Part III, Medical Advisor's Opinion. It must be received by time of final payment. This is part of our obligation for self-sufficiency under the terms of the Antarctic Treaty System. In addition, you are advised to carry your own regular medications, which may not be available aboard. Passengers are further advised that medical evacuation, if available, is expensive, and that we strongly recommend that you have medical insurance that will reimburse you for this cost.

Part I: Health Statement

I attest that I am in good general health, and capable of performing normal activities on this expedition. I further attest that I am capable of caring for myself during the expedition, and that I will not impede the progress of the expedition or the enjoyment of others aboard. I understand that this expedition will take me far from the nearest medical facility and that all expedition members must be self-sufficient. With that understanding, I certify that I have not been recently treated for, nor am I aware of, any physical or other condition or disability that would create a hazard to myself or other members of the expedition.

Name:________________________ Date:____________

Signature:________________________________

Expedition:________________________ Departure Date:____________

Part II: Medical Information

Name:______________________________ Blood Type:__________

Date of Birth:__________________ Height:__________ Weight:__________

Evaluate your general health: Fair ___ Good ___ Excellent ______

Evaluate your physical condition/stamina: Fair ___ Good ___ Excellent ______

Have you taken out medical insurance? Yes ___ No ___

1. Do you have any medical illnesses, disabilities, or infirmities that have required the regular care of a doctor?
2. List all medications that you are taking at this time and the dosages.
3. Have you been hospitalized or had surgery in the last five years? If so, when and for what?
4. Do you have any heart or respiratory problems? Are you a diabetic? Please elaborate.
5. Do you have any dietary restrictions, food or drug allergies? If so, what are they?
6. Do you have any physical or mental limitations, handicaps or a prosthesis? Are you pregnant? Do you have difficulty in walking or use crutches, a cane or a wheelchair?
7. Name and phone number to be used in case of emergency. Relationship.

Part III: Medical Advisor's Opinion

Please give this form along with your itinerary to your personal physician.

Dear Doctor,

Our traveler is planning an expedition cruise to the Antarctic, where sophisticated medical facilities are unavailable. Each vessel carries a physician and a small infirmary. While not strenuous, travelers who participate on excursions must negotiate a steep gangway, get in and out of landing boats with assistance, and be capable of walking a short distance over uneven and slippery terrain ashore. Please feel free to call us if you have any questions.

We would like to be sure that each of our passengers is in adequate medical condition for the voyage and that our shipboard physician is fully alerted to any potential health problems. We would appreciate your evaluation of:

1. His/Her overall physical condition.
2. His/Her ability to participate in this expedition and excursions.
3. Please elaborate on any medical conditions that you feel our shipboard physician should be aware of.

Thank you for your help.

Doctor's name:______________________________ Date:______________

Doctor's Signature:__________________________ Telephone:__________

City, State, Country:________________________ Fax:______________

ADVENTURE NETWORK INTERNATIONAL
PERSONAL AND MEDICAL INFORMATION FORM
ANTARCTIC EXPEDITIONS AND PROGRAMS

NOTE: All applicants must complete every section of this form:

Part I: Personal Information

Applicant's Name:______________________________________

Program/Expedition:____________________________________

Code: ______________________ Dates: ______________________

Address: ______________________

Phone (day): ______________________ (evening): ______________________

Occupation: ______________________

Passport #: ______________________

Issue Date: ______________________ Expires: ______________________

Citizenship: ______________________

Place of Birth: ______________________ Date: ______________________

Height: ________ Weight: ________ Sex: ____ Age: ________

Evaluate your health: Fair ____ Good ____ Excellent ________

Evaluate your physical condition/stamina: Fair ____ Good ____ Excellent ________

Any special dietary requirements? ______________________

Name and phone number to be used in case of an emergency: ______________________

Relationship: ______________________

Part II: Medical Information

1. Do you have any medical illnesses which have required the regular care of a doctor?
2. Have you been hospitalized in the past 5 years? If so, for what?
3. Do you take any medication(s) regularly? Please list them.
4. Do you have any food or drug allergies? If so, please explain which ones and what effects.
5. Do you have any physical limitations or handicaps?
6. Date of last tetanus inoculation ____________ (Must be within the last 10 years to be valid. This is an international requirement for the journey between your home and Antarctica.)
7. For climbers and/or South Pole clients: Have you ever had altitude-related sickness (HAPE or HACE)?
8. Have you ever had frostbite? Details please:
9. Have you ever had surgery that might be relevant to your expedition? Details please:
10. Blood type: ________

Part III: Medical Advisor's Opinion

Please pass this form, together with your expedition itinerary to your medical advisors requesting their guidance, and return this signed form to us. This information will be passed to ANI's medical officer for review.

Dear Doctor:

Our client is planning to go on an expedition to the interior of Antarctica. This will involve them experiencing extended flying in an unpressurized aircraft. They will also be participating in the activities described in our brochure.

We would like to be sure that our client is in adequate medical condition to gain the full enjoyment of the expedition. ANI's medical officer will be given your notes in order to confirm the client's acceptability.

We would be obliged for your opinion on:

1. His/Her overall physical condition.
2. His/Her ability to participate in this expedition.
3. Any medical condition that you feel might require monitoring by our staff.

We thank you for your cooperation.

Yours sincerely,

Adventure Network International Inc.

Doctor's Signature:________________________________ Date:______________________________

Doctor's Name:____

City:____ Phone Number:________________________

Adventure Network International • U.S. Sales Agent: Quark Expeditions, Inc.
980 Post Road, Darien, CT 06820 USA • Telephone: (203) 655-4848 Fax: (203) 656-2423

Sources of Information on Polar Medicine

The following sources can be consulted for lists and quantities of medicines, surgical supplies, and instruments for polar voyages.

Auerbach, Paul S. *Wilderness Medicine,* 3d ed. St. Louis, Mo.: Mosby, 1995.

Banyan STAT Kits, Banyan International Corp., 2118 E. Interstate 20, P.O. Box 1779, Abilene, TX 79604-1779.

Chinook Medical Gear, Inc., 725 Chambers Ave #12, P.O. Box 3300, Eagle, CO 81631-3300 (Telephone: 1-800-766-1365).

Forgey, William W. *Wilderness Medical Society Practice Guidelines for Wilderness Emergency Care.* Merrillville, Ind.: ICS Books, 1995.

Hill, C.D. "Holland America Line Ship Medical Dept. Physician Orientation Manual." Seattle, Wash.: Holland America Line Westours, Inc., 1994.

Hill. C.D. "Windstar Cruises Ship Medical Dept. Physician Orientation Manual." Seattle, Wash: Holland America Line Westours, Inc., 1994.

International Medical Guide for Ships, including the *Ship's Medical Chest,* 2d ed. Geneva: World Health Organization, 1994.

Juel-Jenson, Bent. *Expedition Medicine,* 5th ed. London: The Expedition Advisory Centre, Royal Geographical Society, 1994.

Milne, A.H. *KURAFID,* 4th ed. Cambridge: British Antarctic Survey, 1995.

"Ship's Medical Chest Foreign Trade Ltd., Seattle, Wash.

"The Ship's Medical Chest and Medical Aid at Sea." HEW Publication No(HSA) 78-2024. Washington D.C.: U.S. Government Printing Office, 1978.

The following two individuals and their organizations are good sources of information on field experience in remote environments:

Anne Kershaw
Adventure Network, International
Canon House
27 London End
Beaconsfield, Bucks HP9 2HN
United Kingdom

Robert Ryan
Public Relations Manager
Royal Flying Doctor Service
P.O. Box 385
Norwood SA 506
Australia
Phone: 08-363-1877
Fax: 08-363-1843

Sources of Worldwide Medical Assistance

Services needed to practice reasonable medicine at sea include the following:

- 24-hour physician consultation to ships at sea.
- Multilingual communication/rescue coordinators to assist physicians in case logistics and communications.
- Expert state-of-the-art communication systems.
- Inventory and certification of pharmaceuticals and medical supplies.
- Training courses enhancing expedition staff ability to safely provide medical care at sea. Some courses are U.S. Coast Guard approved.
- Mariners' medical network which will negotiate preferred rates for patients and their care on emergency basis.
- Air ambulance service.
- Repatriation and medical escort.
- Legal assistance.
- Medical referrals.

Sources of some or all of the above include the following:

- AEA International, Worldwide Emergency Assistance, 4050 Columbia Seafirst Center, 701 Fifth Avenue, Seattle, WA 98104-7016, Tel: 206-340-6000, Fax: 206-340-6006, Telex: 206-683-8206 NHS EW. In 1995, AEA International acquired Maritime Health Services, making them the largest provider of maritime medical services in the world. This company and Medical Advisory Systems (see below) offer worldwide expertise and have had experience with ships and bases in the polar world.
- Medical Advisory Systems, Inc., 8050 Southern Maryland Blvd., Owings, MD 20736, Tel: 410-257-9504, Fax: 410-257-2704, Telex: 410-750-5017. Medical Advisory Systems, Inc., (MAS) provides medical advice, managed medical supply programs, and occupational health services to vessels operating around the world. Their physician staff can be reached for consultation twenty-four hours a day, seven days a week.
- The book *Wilderness Medicine* (see reference section) concerning management of wilderness and environmental emergencies is an excellent resource.
- The Hopkins Access Line (1-800-765-5447), a medical service from Johns Hopkins University Hospital of Baltimore, Maryland, offers a twenty-four-hour access to Hopkins' Specialty Medical Services from over 750 full-time clinical faculty members. This service can be used to make a referral, transfer a patient, get updated information, etc. Similar arrangements can be made with other major medical centers.
- Videotel Marine International, Ltd., is a worldwide producer and distributor of training materials located at 84 Newman Street, London W1P 3LD, United Kingdom, Tel: 44 171-299-1800, Fax: 44 171-299-1818. Their "First Aid and Caring for Casualties at Sea" is a video series offering offsite training to crews on ships at sea. This multilingual training film approach could markedly broaden the expertise available for a polar disaster.

Overseas Transport of Controlled Substances

The following article by Carolyn S. Langer, M.D., J.D., M.P.H. is reprinted from The Wilderness Medicine Letter, *fall 1995, and is used by permission.*

I am often asked by physicians traveling overseas if there is some way to avoid writing prescriptions for controlled substances in their own name or in the name of a colleague. The DEA [Drug Enforcement Administration] would consider such prescribing practices to be inappropriate, and many state Boards of Medicine would view this activity very suspiciously.

Instead, you may adopt a procedure that is implemented by most medical organizations conducting relief missions overseas. You may use a copy of your DEA certificate for Schedule 3, 4, or 5 drugs, or DEA Form 222 for Schedule 2 drugs, to purchase these controlled substances directly from a pharmacy or drug distributorship, eliminating the need for a prescription.

You must also request a letter of exemption from the DEA two weeks prior to your departure. Your request for a letter of exemption should include the following information: your name, DEA number, date of travel, name of organization, destination, specific airline reservation from the last departure point in the United States, duration of the trip, quantity and name of the controlled substances, and a statement specifying that no other medical care will be available because you are traveling to a remote area.

Send your request for a letter of exemption to the following address: Mr. Larry Snyder, Chief, International Drug Unit, DEA, Washington, DC 20537.

After the DEA approves your request for an exemption, they will notify the country of import.

Please note that you will not be allowed to bring these drugs back into the United States because importing controlled substances requires a prescription. Many medical organizations simply donate their unused medications to local clinics.

This procedure should not present any major hassles to physicians, and should also provide comfort in that you will no longer need to place prescriptions in your own name.

References

CHAPTER 1

Asimov, Isaac. *The Ends of the Earth.* New York: Waybright and Talley, 1975.
Bruemmer, Fred. *Arctic World.* Toronto, Canada: Key Porter Books, 1985.
Capricorn Press. *Antarctica.* Sydney, Australia: Reader's Digest, 1990.
Erngaard, Erik. *Greenland Then and Now.* Copenhagen, Denmark: Lademann, 1972.
Headland, Robert K. *Concise List of Arctic and Antarctic Chronology and Related Historical Events.* Cambridge: Cambridge University Press, 1992.
Holland, Clive. *Arctic Exploration and Development c. 500 B.C. to 1915.* New York and London: Garland Publishing, 1994.
Kirwan, L. P. *A History of Polar Exploration.* New York: W. W. Norton & Company, 1960.
Maxtone-Graham, John. *Safe Return Doubtful.* New York: Charles Scribner's Sons, 1988.
Prielou, E. C. *A Naturalist's Guide to the Arctic.* Chichester, England: John Wiley and Sons, 1995.
Sitwell, Nigel, and Richie, Tom. *Antarctic Primer.* Darien, Conn.: Quark Expedition, 1994.
Stonehouse, B. *North Pole South Pole: A Guide to the Ecology and Resources of the Arctic and Antarctic.* London: Priors, 1990.
Walton, D. W. H. *Antarctic Science.* Cambridge: Cambridge University Press, 1987.

CHAPTER 2

Hall, Colin Michael, and Johnston, Margaret E. *Polar Tourism.* Chichester, England: John Wiley and Sons, 1995.
Headland, Robert K. *Chronological List of Antarctic Expeditions and Related Historical Events.* Cambridge: Cambridge University Press, 1989.
———. "Historical Development of Antarctic Tourism." *Annals of Tourism Research* 21 (2) 1994: 269–80.
Holland, Clive. *Arctic Exploration and Development c. 500 B.C. to 1915.* New York and London: Garland Publishing, 1994.
Kennedy, Nadene G. Letter to John Levinson, April 17, 1996.
Lindblad, Lars-Eric. *Passport to Anywhere.* New York: Times Books, 1983.
Maxtone-Graham, John. *Safe Return Doubtful.* New York: Charles Scribner's Sons, 1988.
May, John. *The Greenpeace Book of Antarctica.* New York: Doubleday, 1988.
Schoeling, Darrel. Letter to John Levinson, 1996.
Smith, Valene L. "A Sustainable Antarctic: Science and Tourism." *Annals of Tourism Research* 21 (2) 1994: 221.

CHAPTER 3

Auerbach, Paul S. *Wilderness Medicine,* 3d ed. St. Louis, Mo.: Mosby, 1995.
Burroughs Wellcome & Co. *The Romance of Exploration and Emergency First Aid from Stanley to Byrd.* London: Burroughs Wellcome & Co., 1934.
Capricorn Press. *Antarctica.* Sydney, Australia: Reader's Digest, 1990.
Carpenter, Kenneth J. *The History of Scurvy and Vitamin C.* Cambridge: Cambridge University Press, 1986.
Cook, Frederick A. "Medical Observations Among the Esquimaux." *Journal of Gynecology and Obstetrics* 4 (1894): 282–86.
Drygalski, Erich. *The Southern Ice-Continent.* Cambridgeshire, England: Bluntisham Books, 1989.
Greely, Gen. A. W. *Discovery of the North Pole.* J. T. Moss, 1909.
———. *Three Years of Arctic Service.* New York: Charles Scribner's Sons, 1886.
Hall, Colin Michael, and Johnson, Margaret E. *Polar Tourism.* Chichester, England: John Wiley and Sons, 1995.
Hall, S. *The Fourth World: The Heritage of the Arctic and Its Destruction.* New York: Vintage Books, 1988.
Hawkesworth, John. *Cook's Voyages.* Vol. 1. London: Strahan and Cadell, 1773.
Headland, Robert K. *Chronological List of Antarctic Expeditions and Related Historical Events.* Cambridge: Cambridge University Press, 1989.
Illingworth, F. *North of the Circle.* New York: Philosophical Library, 1951.
Maxtone-Graham, John. *Safe Return Doubtful.* New York: Charles Scribner's Sons, 1988.
May, John. *The Greenpeace Book of Antarctica.* New York: Doubleday, 1988.
McNeill, William H. *Plagues and People.* New York: Anchor Books, 1977.
Millar, W. "Smoking Prevalence in the Canadian Arctic." *Arctic Med Res* 49 (2)(1990): 23.
Parry, William E. *Journal of a Voyage for the Discovery of a North-West Passage.* London: John Murray, 1821.
Phipps, Constance John. *A Voyage towards the North Pole.* London: W. Bowyer and J. Nichols, 1774.
Scott, Robert F. *The Voyage of the* Discovery. New York: Charles Scribner's Sons, 1905.
Sheldon, Bart. Letter to John Levinson from the leader of the American expedition to Baffin Island, August 12, 1996.
Snow, W. Parker. *Voyage of the* Prince Albert *in Search of Sir John Franklin.* London: Longman, Brown, Green and Longmans, 1851.
Taylor, Nathaniel W. *Life on a Whaler.* New Hartford, Conn.: The New London County Historical Society, 1929.
Wilton, P. " 'TB Voyages' into High Arctic Gave MDs a Look at a Culture in Transition." *Con Med Assoc J* 148 (9)(1993): 1608.

CHAPTER 4

Acero, J. M., and Aguirre, C. A. "A Monitoring Research Plan for Tourism in Antarctica. " *Annals of Tourism Research* 21 (2) (1994): 295–302.

AGHS (Australian Government Health Service). "Medical Standards for the Australian National Antarctic Research Expeditions (ANARE)." In *Australian Government Health Service Handbook.* Canberra: Department of Health, Housing and Community Services, 1992.

Aviation Week and Space Technology, December 16–23, 1991: 20.

Aviation Week and Space Technology, January 6, 1992: 19.

Ayton, J. M. "Polar Hands: Spontaneous Skin Fissures Closed with Cyanoacrylate (Histoacryl Blue) Tissue Adhesive in Antarctica." *Arctic Medical Research* 52 (1993): 127–30.

Boyer, P. "Heard Island's Special Qualities Recognised in Draft Management Plan." *ANARE News,* Autumn 1995: 35.

Budd, G. M. "A Polio-like Illness in Antarctica." *Med J Aust* 1 (1962): 483–86.

Butler, R. *The Trials of Antarctica.* Kingston, Tasmania, Australia: Australian Antarctic Division, May 1995.

Cherry-Garrard, Apsley. *The Worst Journey in the World: Antarctic 1910–1913.* London: Constable and Company, 1922.

Deakin, G. "Cardiovascular Research in Antarctica." M.D. dissertation, Monash University, Victoria, Australia, 1991.

DELM (Department of Environment and Land Management). *Guidelines for Tourist Operations at Macquarie Island Nature Reserve 1995/96.* Tasmania: Department of Environment and Land Management, 1995.

Enzenbacher, D. J. "Antarctic Tourism: An Overview of 1992/93 Season Activity, Recent Developments, and Emerging Issues." *Polar Record* 30 (173) (1994): 105–16.

Enzenbacher, D. J. "The Regulation of Antarctic Tourism." In Hall, C. M., and Johnston, M. E., eds. *Polar Tourism.* Chichester, England: John Wiley and Sons, 1995, 179–215.

Fletcher, L. D. "Dental Observations at Australian Antarctic Stations." *Aust Dental J* 28 (1983): 281–85.

Goodwin, M. P. *Letter from the Antarctic.* SPRI file ref. no. (*7): 796.51.7, Scott Polar Research Institute, Cambridge, 1966.

Gormly, P. J. *ANARE First Aid Manual.* 5th ed. Kingston, Tasmania: Australian Antarctic Division, 1992.

Hall, C. M., and Johnston, M. E., eds. *Polar Tourism.* Chichester, England: John Wiley and Sons, 1995.

Headland, R. K. "Historical Development of Antarctic Tourism." *Annals of Tourism Research* 21 (2) 1994: 269–80.

Headland, R. K., and Keage, P. L. "Antarctic Tourist Day-Flights." *Polar Record* 31 (178) (1995): 347.

HRSCERA (House of Representatives Standing Committee on Environment, Recreation and the Arts). *Tourism in Antarctica.* Canberra: AGPS, 1989.

Jones, S. E. "Medical Report, Western Base (Queen Mary Land)." In Mawson, D. *The Home of the Blizzard,* vol. 2, app. V. London: Heinemann, 1915.

King, H. "Epidemiology in Antarctica?" *J. Epidemiol Comm Hlth* 40 (1986): 351–56.

———. "A New Health Register for Australian National Antarctic Research Expeditions." *Polar Record* 23 (1987): 719–20.

Lugg, D. J. "Antarctic Epidemiology: A Survey of ANARE Stations 1947–1972." In Edholm, O. G., and Gunderson, E. K. E., eds. *Polar Human Biology.* London: Heinemann, 1973.

———. "Facsimile Transmission from Antarctica as an Aid to Diagnosis and Treatment." *Med J Aust* 1 (1974): 472–74.

———."Appendicitis in Polar Regions." Diploma in polar studies thesis, University of Cambridge, 1979.

———. "Medical Recruitment for the Australian National Antarctic Research Expeditions (ANARE)." In Fortuine R., ed. *Circumpolar Health 84.* Seattle: University of Washington Press, 1985.

———. "Current International Human Factors Research in Antarctica." In Harrison, A. A., Clearwater, Y. A., and McKay, C., eds. *From Antarctica to Outer Space: Life in Isolation and Confinement.* New York: Springer-Verlag, 1991.

———. *Antarctica: Australia's Remote Medical Practice.* Hobart, Tasmania, Australia: Antarctic Division, Dept. of Environment, Sport, and Territories, 1993.

———. "Antarctica as a Space Laboratory." In Hempel, G., ed. *Antarctic Science: Global Concerns.* Berlin: Springer-Verlag, 1994.

Lugg, D. J., and Gormly, P. J. "Antarctica—Lessons for Australian Outdoor Sports and Recreation." In *Proc. 17th Annual Scientific Conference.* Hobart: Australian Sports Medicine Federation, 1980.

Lugg, D. J., Gormly, P. J., and King, H. "SCAR Accident Survey: Australian Results 1977–1985." *Polar Record* 23 (1987): 720–25.

Macklin, A. H. "Medical Appendix V." In Wild, F. *Shackleton's Last Voyage: The Story of the* Quest. London: Cassell, 1923.

Mawson, Sir Douglas. *The Home of the Blizzard.* Philadelphia: J. B. Lippincott Co., 1914.

Maxtone-Graham, John. *Safe Return Doubtful.* New York: Charles Scribner's Sons, 1988.

McLean, A. L. "Medical Report: Main Base (Adélie Land)." In Mawson, D. *The Home of the Blizzard,* vol. 2, app. V. London: Heinemann, 1915.

"A Medical Standard for Expedition Travel and Tourism in the Polar Environment." Proceedings presented at Scott Polar Research Institute, Cambridge, England, October 29–31, 1995.

Milne, A. H., and Siderfin, C. D. *KURAFID, British Antarctic Survey Medical Handbook,* 4th ed. Cambridge, England: 1995.

Muller, H. K., Lugg, D. J., and Quinn, D. "Cell Mediated Immunity in Antarctic Personnel: 1984–1992." *Immunol & Cell Biol* 73 (1995): 316–20.

Pardoe, R. "A Ruptured Intracranial Aneurysm in Antarctica." *Med J Aust* 1 (1965): 344–50.

Perrin R. "Australian Observer on *Kapitan Khlebnikov.*" *ANARE News* 75 (Autumn 1995): 36.

Pitson, G., Lugg, D. J., and Roy, C. "Effect of Seasonal Ultra Violet Radiation Fluctuations on Vitamin D Homeostasis in Antarctic Expeditioners." *Eur J Appl Physiol.* In press.

Podkolinski, M. T., and Semmens, K. "Intestinal Haemorrhage in Antarctica: A Multinational Rescue Operation." *Med J Aust* 2 (1979): 275–77.

Priddy, R. E. "An 'Acute Abdomen' in Antarctica: The Problems of Diagnosis and Management." *Med J Aust* 143 (1985): 108–11.

Reich, R. J. "Tourism in the Antarctic: Its Present Impact and Future Development." Diploma in polar studies thesis, University of Cambridge, 1979.

———. "The Development of Antarctic Tourism." *Polar Record* 20 (126) (1980): 203–14.

Rivolier, J., et al., eds. *Man in the Antarctic—The Scientific Work of the International Biomedical Expedition to the Antarctic (IBEA).* London: Taylor and Francis, 1988.

Roy, C. R., et al. "Effects of Ozone Depletion on the Ultraviolet Radiation Environment at the Australian Stations in Antarctica." In Penhale, P., and Weiler, C. S., eds. *Ultraviolet Radiation in Antarctica: Measurements and Biological Effects.* Washington, D.C.: American Geophysical Union, 1994.

"SCAR (Scientific Committee on Antarctic Research) Report of Meeting of Working Group on Human Biology and Medicine, Paris, 15–17 July 1977." *Polar Record* 19 (118) (1978): 85–103.

Smith, V. L., and Splettstoesser, J., eds. "Antarctic Tourism." *Annals of Tourism Research* 21 (2) (1994): 231–44.

Splettstoesser, J., and Folks, M. C. "Environmental Guidelines for Tourism in Antarctica." *Annals of Tourism Research* 21 (2) (1994): 231–44.

Stonehouse, B. "IAATO: An Association of Antarctic Tour Operators." *Polar Record* 28 (167) (1992): 322–24.

Stonehouse, B., and Crosbie, K. "Tourist Impacts and Management in the Antarctic Peninsular Area." In Hall, C. M., and Johnston, M. E., eds. *Polar Tourism.* Chichester, England: John Wiley and Sons, 1995.

Sullivan, P. G. "Accidental Hypothermia and Frost-bite in Antarctica." *Med J Aust* 146 (1987): 155.

Sullivan, P., and Lugg, D. J. "Telemedicine between Australia and Antarctica: 1911–1995." SAE Technical Paper 951616, presented at the 25th International Conference on Environmental Systems, San Diego, California, July 1995.

Sullivan, P. G., and Vrana, A. "Trial of In-Water Oxygen Recompression Therapy in Antarctica." *South Pacific Underwater Med Soc J,* 22 (1) (1992): 46–51.

Sullivan, P., et al. "The Australian National Antarctic Research Expeditions Health Register: Three Years of Operation." In Postl, B., et al., eds. *Circumpolar Health 90.* Winnipeg: University of Manitoba Press, 1991.

Taylor, D. "Modification of the Type of Dietary Fat at an Antarctic Station: Impact on Cardio-vascular Risk Factors." M.D. thesis, University of Melbourne, 1991.

"U.S. Icebreaker Story." *USA Today,* June 14, 1996.

Williams, D. L. "Health, Hormonal and Stress-Related Studies on ANARE." *ANARE Res Notes* 66 (1989).

Williams, D. L, et al. "Cell Mediated Immunity in Healthy Adults in Antarctica and the Sub-Antarctic." *J Clin & Lab Immunol* 20 (1986): 43–49.

CHAPTER 5

Aid for International Medicine (AIM). *Antarctic Safety Questionnaire.* Rockland, Del.: AIM, Antarctic summer season, 1993–94.

———. *Notes and Observations on Congressional Meetings, Meetings with NSF, and Background of the SPRI Conference.* Rockland, Del.: AIM, 1991–96.

American College of Emergency Physicians. "Guidelines of Care for Cruise Ship Medical Facilities." In *Cruise Ship and Maritime Medicine*. Dallas, Tex.: September 1995.

"American Researcher Dies in Antarctic." *The News Journal,* Wilmington, Del., May 2, 1997.

"Assessing Ships' Medical Care." *New York Times,* February 4, 1996.

"Cruise Ship and Maritime Medicine." *American College of Emergency Physicians Newsletter* 3 (2) (March 1996).

"Cruise Ships' Medical Care." *Condé Nast Traveler* (December 1994): 37–45.

International Association of Antarctic Tour Operators (IAATO). Bylaws. New York: IAATO, 1991.

International Association of Antarctic Tour Operators. *Guidance for Those Organizing and Conducting Tourism and Non-Governmental Activities in Antarctica.* New York: IAATO, 1994.

International Association of Antarctic Tour Operators Office of the Secretariat. *News.* New York: IAATO, November 1995.

"Is There a Doctor Onboard?" *Condé Nast Traveler* (September 1995): 48.

McCasland, Truman L. *The Ship's Medicine Chest and Medical Aid at Sea.* Washington, D.C.: Government Printing Office, 1978.

Steger, Will. Letter to John Levinson. February 12, 1992.

Sullivan, Cornelius W. Letter to John Levinson, September 25, 1995.

CHAPTER 6

Germain, David. "Alaska Cruise Fire Injures 76." Wilmington, Del., *Sunday News Journal,* July 28, 1996.

Meurn, Robert J. *Survival Guide for the Mariner.* Centreville, Md.: Cornell Maritime Press, 1993.

Miller, Lisa, "A Widow Takes on FAA After Helicopter Tour Crash." *The Wall Street Journal,* August 9, 1996.

Safety Issues and Concerns—Ross Sea Tourist Operations, NSF/COMNAP meeting with IAATO, Arlington, Va., July 13, 1995.

Sexton, Ray L. "Never Been a Ship's Doctor? See What You've Missed." *Medical Economics* (September 30, 1974).

Smith, Dick. *SOLAS Around the World.* Perry Hills, Australia: Australian Geographic Pty., 1992.

CHAPTER 7

Adventure Network International. *IAATO Medical Emergency Contingency Plan.* Arlington, Va., 1996.

Clarke, Wendy Mitman. "Vendee Toll Overshadows Outcome." *Soundings,* March 1997.

Farnsworth, Clyde H. "Australia Rescues Sailors, But Is Wincing at the Costs." *New York Times International,* January 11, 1997.

Lee, Robert Mason. *Death and Deliverance: The True Story of an Airplane Crash at the North Pole.* Golden, Col.: Fulcrum Publishing, 1993.

Sisson, William. "Who Pays?" *Soundings,* February 1977.

U.S. Antarctic Program Safety Review Panel. *Safety in Antarctica.* Arlington, Va.: National Science Foundation, 1988.

CHAPTER 8

Aagesen, G. Personal communication to John Levinson on position of ship's surgeon 1981–82.

Levinson, John M. *Orientation for the Ship's Surgeon for Quark Expeditions.* Rockland, Del., 1993.

Nilsson, H., Powell, C., and Dodd, M. *Instructions for the Ship's Doctor.* New York: Lindblad Travel, 1980.

Quinn, James, et al. "A Randomized Trial Comparing Octylcyanoacrylate Tissue Adhesive and Sutures in the Management of Lacerations." *JAMA,* 277 (19): 1527–30.

Snow, W. P. *Voyage of the* Prince Albert *in Search of Sir John Franklin.* London: Spottiswoodes and Shaw, 1851.

CHAPTER 9

Burr, R. E. "Trench Foot." *J Wild Med.* 4 (1993): 348.
Danzl, D. F., et al.: "Multicenter Hypothermia Survey." *Ann Emerg Med* 16 (9)(1987):1042.
Doyle, F., Zehner, W. J., and Terndrup, T. E. "The Effect of Ambient Temperature Extremes on Tympanic and Oral Temperatures." *Amer J Emerg Med* 10 (4)(1992): 285.
Freund, B. J., O'Brien, C., and Young, A. J. "Alcohol Ingestion and Temperature Regulation during Cold Exposure." *J Wild Med* 5 (1994):88.
Granberg, P. O. "Management of Local Cold Injuries and Accidental Hypothermia under Field Conditions." (Session IV, pp. 227–37). In *Working and Survival in the Cold,* Proc. First International Cold Symposium. Reinertsen, R.E., Brubank, A. O., Påsche, A., eds. Sintef Unimed, 1991.
Granberg, P. O., et al., eds. "Cold Physiology and Cold Injuries." Proc of Nordic Conference on Cold. *Arctic Med Res* 50 (Suppl. 6) (1991).
"Guidelines for Cardiopulmonary Resuscitation and Emergency Cardiac Care." *JAMA,* 268 (16) (1992): 2171.
Herbert, Wally. *Polar Deserts.* London: Collins Publishers, Franklin Watts, 1991.
Hypothermia and Cold Weather Injuries Seminar, Princeton University Outdoor Action Program. World Wide Web address: http://www.princeton.edu/~rcurtis/hypocold.html.
Kirkpatrick, C. T. "Thermal Physiology." In *Aviation Medicine,* 2d ed. Ernsting, J., and King, P., eds. Newton, Mass.: Butterworth, 1988, 235–46.
Lloyd, E. L. *Hypothermia and Cold Stress.* Croom Helm, 1986.
———. "Airway Rewarming in the Treatment of Accidental Hypothermia: A Review. " *J Wild Med* 1 (1990): 65–78.
Mills, W. J. "Field Care of the Hypothermic Patient." *Int J Sports Med.* 13 (S) (1992): 199.
Osczevski, R. J. "The Basis of Windchill." *Arctic* 48 (4) (1995): 372–82.
Paton, B. C. "Accidental Hypothermia." *Pharmocol Ther* 22 (1983): 331.
Rees, W. G. "A New Wind-Chill Nomogram." *Polar Record* 29 (1993): 170, 229.
Smith, D. J., Robson, M. C., and Heggers, J. P. "Frostbite and Other Cold-induced Injuries." In *Management of Wilderness and Environmental Emergencies,* 2d ed. Auerbach, P. S., and Geehr, E. C., eds. St. Louis, Mo.: C.V. Mosby, 1989, 101–18.
Steinman, A. M., and Kublis, P. *Survival at Sea: The Effects of Protective Clothing and Survivor Location on Core and Skin Temperature.* USCG Report CG-D-26-86. Washington, D.C.: National Technical Information Service, 1986.
Sterba, J. A. "Thermal Problems: Prevention and Treatment." In *The Physiology and Medicine of Diving,* 4th ed. Bennett, P. B., and Elliott, D. H., eds. Philadelphia: W. B. Saunders, 1993, 301–41.
Sullivan, P. G. "Accidental Hypothermia and Frost-bite in Antarctica." *Med J Aust* 146 (1987): 155.
Ward, M. P., Milledge, J. S., and West, J. B., eds. In *High Altitude Medicine and Physiology,* 2d ed. New York: Chapman and Hall Medical, 1995, 440–509.
Weinberg, A. D. "Hypothermia." *Ann Emerg Med* 22 (2) (1993): 370.

CHAPTER 10

Berkow, Robert, et al., eds. *Merck Manual,* 16th ed. Rahway, N.J.: Merck Research Laboratories, 1992.
Blackbourne, L. H. *Surgical Recall.* Baltimore, Md.: Williams and Wilkins, 1994.
Eastman, P. F. *Advanced First Aid Afloat,* 4th ed. Centreville, Md.: Cornell Maritime Press, 1995.
Fritz, Thygeson, Durham. "Phlyctenular Keratoconjunctivitis among Alaskan Natives." *Journal of Ophthalmology* (1949).
Gormly, P. J. *ANARE First Aid Manual.* 5th ed. Kingston, Tasmania: Australian Antarctic Division, 1992.
Green, David. *Operative Hand Surgery,* vols. 1 and 2. New York: Churchill Livingstone, 1993.
Hacker, Neville. *Essentials of Obstetrics and Gynecology,* 2nd ed. Philadelphia: W. B. Saunders, 1992.
Kasser Steffansson, V. *Arctic Manual.* New York: MacMillan and Company, 1994.
Milne, A. H., and Siderfin, C. D. *KURAFID, British Antarctic Survey Medical Handbook,* 4th ed. Cambridge, England, 1995.
Orthopaedic Knowledge Update. Rosemont, Ill.: American Academy of Orthopaedic Surgeons, 1996.
The Ship's Medicine Chest and Medical Aid at Sea. Washington, D.C.: U.S. Department of Health, Education and Welfare, 1978.

CHAPTER 14

Auerbach, Paul S. *Wilderness Medicine,* 3d ed. St. Louis, Mo.: Mosby, 1995.
Collis, Robert. "Is There a Doctor on Board? Medical Problems in the Air." *International Herald Tribune,* August 2, 1996.
"Despite the Cost, Travel Insurance Has Advantages." *The New York Times,* November 26, 1995.
"The Healthy Traveler." *Los Angeles Times,* February 11, 1996.
Levy, Doug. "Adding Health Tips to Travel Itinerary." *USA Today,* November 6, 1995.
"Management of Ventricular Fibrillation in Commercial Airlines." *Traveling Healthy,* September/October 1995.
Morris, H. H. "Traveler's Amnesia." *JAMA,* August 21, 1987.
Ryan, T. M. "Trims in the Supply of Medical Personnel in the Russian Federation." *JAMA,* July 24–31, 1996.

About the Editors and Contributors

Kathryn S. Andersen, Ph.D.
President of National Chrysanthemum Society
Horticulturist
Wilmington, Delaware, U.S.A.

Carolyn Annerud, M.D., F.A.C.E.P.
Emergency physician
Former Medical Director of Critical Air Medicine
Ship's surgeon
Coronado, California, U.S.A.

Claude Bachelard, M.D.
Le Médecin Chef of T.A.A.F. Health Department
Polar Expedition Doctor
T.A.A.F./I.F.R.T.P.
Paris, France

Sheldon Bart
Writer/historian
Explorer
Leader, American expedition to Baffin Island 1996
Jersey City, New Jersey, U.S.A.

Carmen Becker and Robert N. Becker, M.D.H., Ph.D.
"The Most Traveled Couple in the World" *The Guinness Book of Records,* 1997 Edition
Travel consultants
Pompano Beach, Florida, U.S.A.

Robert Burton
Arcturus Expeditions, Ltd.
Arctic and Antarctic experience
Huntingdon, Cambridge, United Kingdom

Davis G. Durham, M.D., F.A.C.S.
Ophthalmologist, Past Director of Ophthalmology, Project H.O.P.E.
Senior Vice President, AIM, Inc.
Wilmington, Delaware, U.S.A.

Lennart Fagraeus, M.D., Ph.D.
Chairman of Anesthesiology, Medical Center of Delaware
Ship's surgeon
Expert in high altitude and submarine physiology

Errol Ger, M.D., M.B.Ch.B., F.R.C.S., Edinburgh
Orthopedic surgeon/hand surgeon
Vice President, AIM, Inc.
Ship's surgeon
Centerville, Delaware, U.S.A.

Ruth Ann Ger, B.Soc.Sc.
Medical administrator
Centerville, Delaware, U.S.A.

Kenneth R. Haslam, M.D.
Anesthesiologist
Medical researcher
Ship's surgeon
Chestertown, Maryland, U.S.A.

Robert K. Headland, F.R.G.S.
Historical geographer of the polar regions
Archivist and Curator for the Scott Polar Research Institute
University of Cambridge
Cambridge, United Kingdom

Norman C. Headley, M.D., F.A.C.E.P.
General medicine
Ship's surgeon
Cameron Park, California, U.S.A.

Dr. John A. Heap, C.M.G.
Director, Scott Polar Reasearch Institute
Head, Polar Regions Section, Foreign and Commonwealth Office, 1975–92
Diverse experience in Falkland Islands and Antarctica
Scott Polar Research Institute
Cambridge, United Kingdom

Jack D. Lange, M.D., F.A.C.P.
President and Founder, Lange Medical Publications
Professor of Medicine, University of California at San Francisco
Chairman, Advisory Board of Directors, AIM, Inc.
San Francisco, California, U.S.A.

Carolyn S. Langer, M.D., J.D., M.P.H.
Medical-Legal Editor for the *Wilderness Medicine Newsletter*
Instructor in occupational medicine at Harvard School of Public Health
Lecturer on health law at Harvard Educational Resource Center
Major in the Army National Guard, flight surgeon and commander of a mobile army surgical hospital
Boston, Massachusetts, U.S.A.

John M. Levinson, M.D., F.A.C.O.G.
Ship's surgeon, former Medical Director for Quark Expeditions, Inc.
Professor of Obstetrics and Gynecology, Jefferson Medical College
President and Founder, AIM, Inc.
Past President, The Explorers Club
Rockland, Delaware, U.S.A.

Desmond J. Lugg, M.D., Dip. Polar Studies, F.A.C.O.M.
Head of Polar Medicine, Australian Antarctic Division
Chairman, Human Biology and Medicine Working Group of Scientific Committee on Antarctic Research (S.C.A.R.)
Expeditioner and reseacher in Antarctic
Hobart, Tasmania, Australia

Harry Maher, Ph.D.
Safety and Health Officer, Office of Polar Programs, National Science Foundation
Arlington, Virginia, U.S.A.

Alan H. Milne, M.B., Ch.B., M.R.C.G.P.
Senior Medical Advisor and Medical Officer, British Antarctic Survey
Editor, *KURAFID,* British Antarctic Survey Medical Handbook
General medicine
Aberdeen, Scotland, United Kingdom

Richard N. Moersch, M.D., F.A.C.S.
Cardiothoracic surgeon
Ship's surgeon
Expeditioner with worldwide experience
Redlands, California, U.S.A.

David M. Rootes, B.S., M.Phil.
President, Poles Apart
Research Associate, Scott Polar Research Institute
Former Antarctic station master
Cambridge, United Kingdom

Capt. Brian H. Shoemaker, USN (Retired)
Naval Aviator
Secretary, American Polar Society
Publisher of *The Polar Times*
U.S. Commander, Naval Support Force, Antarctica, 1982–85
Commander, Naval Arctic Research Laboratory, Point Barrow, Alaska, 1974–76
Lakeside, Oregon, U.S.A.

E. Newbold Smith, B.S., M.B.A.
Engineer
Recipient of Blue Water Medal from Cruising Club of American for sailing his 43-foot sloop to Svalbard, from the Chesapeake Bay, a 10,500 mile voyage, to within 598 miles of the North Pole—farther north than any pleasure craft had even been.
Veteran Arctic and Antarctic sailor
Maritime author
Villanova, Pennsylvania, U.S.A.

John Splettstoesser, B.S.
Geologist
Extensive field research, Arctic and Antarctic
Over seventy cruises in Arctic and Antarctic as expedition leader and/or lecturer
Polar author
Associate Director, Institute of Polar Studies, Ohio State University, 1967–74
Rockland, Maine, U.S.A.

Bernard Stonehouse, B.Sc., D.Phil.
Head of Polar Ecology and Management, Scott Polar Research Institute
Leader of Project Antarctic Conservation
Extensive field research in Antarctic and Arctic
Author of polar books
Cambridge, United Kingdom

Theodore B. Strange, M.D., F.A.C.S.
Orthopedic surgeon
Ship's surgeon and flight surgeon, U.S. Navy, World War II
Ship's surgeon
Chestertown, Maryland, U.S.A.

Peter G. Sullivan, M.B., B.S.
Medical Research Officer, Australian Antarctic Division
World-class expert in hypothermia and cold injuries
Expeditioner, medical practitioner, and researcher, Antarctic
Hobart, Tazmania, Australia

A. Diederik Van Galen
Senior Vice President, Boyden International
Inveterate traveler
Paris, France

Robert E. Wheeler, M.D., F.A.C.E.P.
Emergency physician
Ship's surgeon
Chairman, ACEP Section of Cruise Ship and Maritime Medicine, 1995–96
Nashua, New Hampshire, U.S.A.

Index

Page numbers in italic refer to illustrations.